CARA
DELEVINGNE

To Lily and Henry

CARA
DELEVINGNE

THE MOST BEAUTIFUL GIRL IN THE WORLD

ABI SMITH

JOHN BLAKE

Published by John Blake Publishing Ltd,
3 Bramber Court, 2 Bramber Road,
London W14 9PB, England

www.johnblakepublishing.co.uk

www.facebook.com/Johnblakepub facebook
twitter.com/johnblakepub twitter

First published in paperback in 2014

ISBN: 978-1-78219-899-4

British Library Cataloguing-in-Publication Data:

A catalogue record for this book is available from the British Library.

Design by www.envydesign.co.uk

Printed in Great Britain by CPI Group (UK) Ltd

3 5 7 9 10 8 6 4 2

Papers used by John Blake Publishing are natural, recyclable products made
from wood grown in sustainable forests. The manufacturing processes
conform to the environmental regulations of the country of origin.

Every attempt has been made to contact the relevant copyright-holders,
but some were unobtainable. We would be grateful if the
appropriate people could contact us.

CONTENTS

ACKNOWLEDGEMENTS   vii

PROLOGUE   ix

CHAPTER 1: WHEN I GROW UP   1

CHAPTER 2: FASHIONING A CAREER   17

CHAPTER 3: FOLLOWING POPPY   23

CHAPTER 4: ALL ABOUT THE BROWS   31

CHAPTER 5: GIRL POWER   43

CHAPTER 6: A MODEL ADVENTURE   53

CHAPTER 7: MAKING MOVES   67

CHAPTER 8: STYLE AND STYLES   73

CHAPTER 9: SECRETS AND LIES   91

CHAPTER 10: DAREDEVIL BRIT   105

CHAPTER 11: HIGH HEELS AND HARD WORK   121

CHAPTER 12: THE ENDLESS WALK   137

CHAPTER 13: PARTYING HARD   153

CHAPTER 14: RITA AND RIRI   171

CHAPTER 15: NEVER WORK WITH ANIMALS   187

CHAPTER 16: HANDLING THE PRESS   205

CHAPTER 17: TURNING 21   217

CHAPTER 18: MOVING ON?   233

CHAPTER 19: ONE OF THE STARS   251

BIBLIOGRAPHY   273

ACKNOWLEDGEMENTS

A big thank you must go those who have helped make this book possible: Chris and Anna at John Blake for giving me the chance; my dearest Katharine for her endless supply of chocolate, stationary, research, late-night Cara updates and Henry-sitting duties; Granny and Grandman for being there (as always) to help me get my head round the challenge; and Chris, my best friend and biggest supporter. And to Grampy – for a work ethic that knows no limit, you have made our house a home and we can't thank you enough.

PROLOGUE

AND THE WINNER IS....

'I'm happy to announce the award for Model of the Year, 2012 is...'

The atmosphere buzzed with excitement in the large ballroom of the prestigious Savoy hotel, London, as renowned German photographer Ellen von Unwerth opened the envelope that would reveal the name of the winner. It was the biggest night in the British fashion world's calendar and the crème de la crème of designers, including Stella McCartney, Valentino, John Rocha, Manolo Blahnik and Julien Macdonald, had gathered for the Oscars of their industry. Alongside them were the exclusive fashionista contingent and the magazines, TV and radio media, plus an A-list heavy guest list: the likes of Princess Beatrice, Dita Von Teese, Prime Minister David Cameron's wife, Samantha, Alexa Chung, Hollywood starlet Salma Hayek, a heavily pregnant Lily Allen and Colin Firth's wife, Livia, all dressed in their glitziest designer garb to celebrate the pinnacle of British fashion on that chilly November evening.

Dressed in his finest suit, Radio 1 DJ Nick 'Grimmy' Grimshaw and glamour puss James Bond actress Gemma Arterton hosted the prestigious event, which saw guests treated to a parade of lovingly prepared cocktails and bubbly as they arrived, while a lavish sit-down meal in the candlelit theatre and entertainment by singer Rita Ora awaited them later in the evening. As the champagne flowed and the celebrities gossiped about the past year of fashion, it was time to get down to business and to find out whom the industry itself had deemed worthy of winning one of its crowns.

As a collective hush went out across the auditorium, von Unwerth dutifully announced the winner and beamed out at the audience as a deafening applause greeted her announcement: 'The winner of the award for Model of the Year, 2012 is... Cara Delevingne!'

There could only really be one winner when it came down to it, though. In a category that was being fought out between male model David Gandy, Jourdan Dunn and Cara, the smart money had been on Delevingne from the moment the nominations had been revealed in September. Caroline Rush, CEO of the British Fashion Council, revealed that Cara had won because she had 'the diversity and originality that we've seen in all the greatest British models.' And the BFC confirmed she'd scooped the gong in recognition of her contribution to the international fashion scene over the previous year. They praised 'Cara's unique sense of style and flair in front of the camera', adding, 'Walking an impressive 31 shows in September after being described as the star face of autumn/winter 2013 by British *Vogue*, she has a unique sense of style and flair in front of the cameras.'

As she took to the stage to collect her award, the quirky youngster gave Ellen a big hug before addressing a crowd that would have probably given any normal 20-year-old severe stage fright. Not Cara, a self-confessed 'show-off' and someone who had craved and welcomed attention from a young age. 'This is madness!' she said as she stood in front of the microphone dressed all in Burberry – a lime-green metallic shift dress and silver python wedges – in a nod to the fashion label that had catapulted her career into the big-time, back in 2010. 'I can't begin to explain what a shock it is to be standing in front of you all right now. It's unbelievable,' she gushed. 'Even to be nominated was such a shock, thank you so much.'

The joy on Cara's face said it all. Confidently standing clutching her award, all eyes were on her as she spoke of her heartfelt gratitude, making sure she thanked everyone involved in her career but unable to resist a little cheeky humour, too.

'A very clever man told me that a good speech should be under 60 seconds, so don't worry, I'm going to keep it short,' she giggled. 'A big thank you to everyone I've worked with since the beginning. It means so much to me that you've been supporting me, believing in my potential and for hiring my crazy self!'

As the applause died down and the champagne flowed, Cara – with the addition of her shiny new accessory – had time to catch up with her peers. However, it wasn't going to be a late night for the in-demand youngster because the next morning she had an early flight to Miami for yet another job.

'It's nice to go and have a good dance with friends, everyone in there I haven't seen in a long time and they're like family, so it'll be fun,' she told the assembled media, who all wanted to know how she felt about winning and how she'd be celebrating. 'I'm speechless. It's only just starting to sink in,' she told one journalist. 'When they say your name it's like one of those *Zoolander* moments when you think they've said the wrong name. It's out of this world!'

And it wasn't just the media who wanted to pass on their congratulations to the star: there were tweets coming in by the bucket load from her loyal 'Delevingners'– her name for her Twitter fans – and others in the fashion industry. Fellow model Laura Bailey tweeted: 'Model of the year... the extraordinary Miss @CaraDelevingne'. Her celebrity pals were also quick to add their congratulations, including 'wifey' Rita Ora, who performed at the event and later tweeted: 'Congratulations to my baby @Caradelevingne for winning supermodel of the year last night. Coz u baaaaad! Lov u'.

But there was one person who didn't manage to celebrate with Cara until three days after the event: her big sister Poppy. The older sibling admitted she was upset that she hadn't been there to share the glory with her sis and wasn't able to pass on her congratulations until a few days later. 'I was gutted I wasn't there to see her little face and give her a squeeze. I tried to call her to say congratulations but I was unable to get hold of her for about three days!' she revealed later in an interview.

So how had Cara, who had only started modelling professionally three years earlier, managed to pick up such an accolade and become such a mega-star? With more than a million followers on Twitter – not to mention the growing number of parody Twitter accounts set up by her fans (there are 10 at the time of writing) – and her Instagram page, which sees upwards of two million of her followers receive daily images of her pulling silly faces, she is one of the world's most talked-about supermodels. In 2013, there were, on average, 115 daily news stories about her: she received 1.4 million mentions in the first part of the year, with 21,031 news stories in total at the end of August.

Being a famous supermodel is something of a rarity, given that the cycle of celebrity these days is filled with the likes of short-lived reality stars from short-running reality shows. Cara has done what her most famous predecessors – Kate Moss, Claudia Schiffer and Naomi Campbell – all did, back in the early 1990s: she has put supermodels back on the map when fame-seeking reality stars were threatening to take over. With a furiously strong work ethic, Cara doesn't have a singular personality trait that fuels the public's love for her. She is more of a complex character with a number of endearing features. Her tomboyish-ness, her love of fast food, her deliciously uncouth eyebrows, her wacky nature, her quirky Twitter posts – 'Stop trying to define who you are and just be' – are all worth mentioning, and when combined it is her naturalness, her 'one of us' persona, that makes us love her. Her complete unfabulousness, if you like – she gorges on McDonald's and suffers from psoriasis, she gets drunk and embarrasses herself falling over, she spends time with her family and parties with mega-stars. OK, so the last bit is unlikely to happen to us mere mortals, but the essence of Cara is the same. She's cool, she works hard and she enjoys life. So, how has a youngster with the vital statistics:

height 5ft 9in, bust 31A, waist 24in, hips 34in, dress size UK 6 (EUR 34), shoe size UK 6 (EUR 39) become the global icon we just can't get enough of?

CHAPTER 1

WHEN I GROW UP

'When I grow up, I want to be a dentist.
Or a superhero. Or both.'

It was a warm summer's day on 12 August 1992 when Cara Jocelyn Delevingne made her first appearance in the world. Born in London to 33-year-old society sweetheart Pandora and her property developer husband, Charles, 43, Cara was the third child for the couple and the third daughter, making their family unit complete. Cara's two elder sisters, Chloe, 9 and Poppy, 7, loved the new addition to the family, and being slightly older, took on very protective, mothering roles with their blue-eyed, blonde-haired baby sister. 'I spent a lot of my childhood helping to bring up Cara,' Poppy revealed. 'She's like a daughter in many ways. I had an insane fascination; I would dress her up, put make-up on her and teach her every song and dance. She became my little doll.'

However, Poppy later admitted that initially she'd had her nose put out of joint by Cara's arrival: 'I quite enjoyed being the youngest daughter and was horrified when this little creature arrived at the house wrapped up like a potato.'

Having two older siblings also meant that Cara didn't have to share the limelight with any other baby and as the youngest in a grown-up family soon became the centre of attention. Both parents adored her, with her father taking a particularly doting role, building a relationship that would grow stronger over the years as Cara made her way in the modelling world. As a testament to the close relationship they share, in 2012 Cara posted on Twitter an old picture of herself when she was around seven years old, giving her father a cuddle on holiday. Simply captioned: 'Love you dad x', the photo reveals the closeness that father and daughter shared, and even though he was an older parent in some respects, there was never any question of Cara being forgotten or sidelined. 'She could get away with anything because she was so cute as a baby – so delicious,' revealed a family friend.

Born under the zodiac sign of Leo, whose characteristics include the desire to 'be a star', Cara showed early signs of adopting the traits of her star sign, especially a Leo's life pursuit of 'leading the way with energy'. Energetic indeed, Cara was a natural at larking about, dressing up, pulling faces and frolicking as the camera snapped away, characteristics she has kept as her modelling and acting careers blossom. But it wasn't just posing for family snaps that she enjoyed: the carefree youngster was brimming with imagination and loved to show off to her family and friends. She was energetic in every sense of the word, with boundless enthusiasm for acting and performing to any-one who would watch: 'When I was younger, I loved to entertain. I used to make up dance routines, do little plays. I love to perform, basically.'

Cara grew up with her family in West London's Belgravia, one of the capital's most prestigious neighbourhoods, in a Grade II-listed house. Noted for its expansive residential properties, the Delevingne family lived happily in their multimillion-pound mansion before moving to the equally prestigious borough of Chelsea when Charles sold the family home for a reported £10.5 million. It was a successful sale at a time when the property market was looking bleak and down to Charles's skill as a property developer. 'He knows what he's doing when it comes to the housing market, he's very astute,' remarked a fellow resident.

Charles married Cara's mother, Pandora, on 18 June 1983, a year before Chloe was born. Pandora was only 24 years old when she wed; she was known in her youth as an 'It' girl of the 1980s, fun to be around, jaw-droppingly gorgeous, with an effortless ease and with a high social-standing – much like Cara now. Charles fell for his wife at a time when he was considered a good catch too: a well-educated, well-brought-up chap, who has often been described as 'dashingly dishy'.

The marriage was approved by both sets of parents, and brought together an impressive set of ancestors. Charles's grandfather was a politician, 1st Viscount Greenwood, while his aunt Doris – Cara's great-aunt – was a friend of former Prime Minister Winston Churchill.

But it is Cara's grandmother, the Honourable Angela Margo Delevingne, who married Charles's father, Edward Dudley Delevingne, in 1937, who is the most well-known older relative – that is to Cara's avid followers on Instagram.

She helped celebrate her grandmother's 101st birthday last year by posting photos on the website: along with several present-day photos of her giving her elderly relative a cuddle and birthday presents, she also uploaded several vintage shots of her grandmother when she was a young girl, just slightly older than Cara is now. The striking photos show a beautiful young Margo staring into camera – and at first glance you might be forgiven for thinking it was Cara. The thickset eyebrows, for which Cara has become renowned, bear a striking resemblance to Margo's own brows and Cara herself tweeted the similarities, at the same time paying homage to her beloved grandmother: 'Happy 101st birthday to the most inspirational woman in the world!! My granny Gaga #lookatthosebrows'.

In another snap showing Cara giving her grandmother a cuddle, Cara proudly tweets: 'My granny is a legend, she knows exactly how to make me smile! #happybirthdaygaga#101'.

While growing up, Cara spent a lot of time at her grandmother's house because it had the most beautiful gardens, and for an outdoor-loving youngster it was the perfect place for her imagination to run riot.

'I am happy in the English countryside,' she revealed during her Mulberry campaign, years later. 'There is so much freedom and energy. Every time I used to visit my granny in the countryside it was a magical time. She had the most beautiful gardens as she was a keen gardener and had amazing flowers. And being a kid and being in your own world and running around with your imagination, I could have been out there for days.'

But it is not just her father's family who are part of

society's elite; her mother's relatives also offer a notable lineage. Pandora's father is the former English Heritage chairman Sir Jocelyn Stevens (Cara takes her middle name from him), who founded the first British pirate radio station, Radio Caroline, in the 1960s. He married Cara's grandmother, Janie Sheffield, who was a lady-in-waiting to the Queen's sister, Princess Margaret, in 1956. These links with the royal family show to a certain extent the privileged background from which Cara and her family are descended, prompting some observers to comment that she has an effortless ease when dealing with certain social situations because of her aristocratic upbringing.

'I suspect Cara is not particularly fazed by social situations because she comes from a very social family,' says British *Vogue* editor Alexandra Shulman. 'She's part of a big family, she's used to mixing with all age groups. I'm sure that's what gives her some of her confidence and some of her spirit.'

Sir Jocelyn was reportedly a good drinking buddy of Princess Margaret and made the Delevingne family's first real connection with the British royal family. After breaking up with his wife Janie in 1979, he reportedly flew 130 friends out to an upmarket Swiss ski resort to help him celebrate his 50th birthday. With a grandfather who likes to party in style, it is perhaps not that surprising that Cara also enjoys letting her hair down on occasion – partying with Kate Moss at her book launch being just one example. 'She stayed and enjoyed the party long after the hostess [Moss] had left for the night,' revealed a fellow party-guest. 'And why not? She was obviously having a good time!'

A prestigious ancestry, coupled with growing up in a

wealthy suburb of London, meant that Cara was rubbing shoulders with the rich and famous from a young age. Holidays were also spent in various glamorous locations around Europe, including the South of France, where the family rent a house every summer.

'All members of the family, including branches of Pandora's, the girls' boyfriends and close friends, come along. It's all very raucous and jolly,' confirmed a family friend.

Holidaying abroad extensively as a youngster prompted a love of travel and visiting different locations, something Cara now cites as a dream of hers: 'I'm in love with travelling, I want to visit India, Argentina, Jamaica... everywhere! I love the sun, and the seaside,' she confided in a magazine article.

With her family's connection with the royal family going back a generation, it perhaps wasn't too surprising that the links remained – mostly thanks to Pandora, who went to school with the Duchess of York, Sarah 'Fergie' Ferguson. Cara and her sisters, therefore, enjoyed lots of 'play time' with Sarah's daughters, the Princesses Beatrice and Eugenie.

'Fergie went to school with my mother and they're great chums,' revealed Poppy in an interview in 2008. 'We are good friends with Bea and Eugenie and we've been on holiday together lots of times to Spain and Greece, and we always have a fabulous time. Fergie is as every bit as fun as you might expect, so full of life and with a great sense of humour and very down-to-earth. So are the girls. I feel very protective towards Bea and Eugenie, who are so good natured, because everything they do is scrutinised in the press.'

Christmas and New Year's Eve parties were spent rubbing

shoulders with aristocrats and A-listers such as West End musical supremo Andrew Lloyd Webber and his family, Fergie and her daughters and legendary British actress and glamour puss, Joan Collins. In fact, Joan was such a close family friend that she was asked to be Cara's godmother. Chloe, Poppy and Cara also call themselves the 'Dynasty sisters', a reference to Joan, who was of course a star of the Hollywood series.

Life in a high-society family occasionally described by the media as 'country aristocrats' didn't come without its problems, however, and Cara and her sisters had to deal with Pandora's long-time drug addiction. She became hooked on heroin from a young age and readily admits her 'crippling addiction' to the drug meant she wasn't always the perfect parent to her three daughters.

'Sometimes they had to live with me being too ill to mother them, which has been agony for me,' she admitted, while it is thought that Pandora rather jokingly named her second daughter Poppy to remind her of her struggles with the drug. 'I am sure she named [me Poppy] partly for a laugh,' said Poppy in an interview, but there is no mistaking the serious effect Pandora's addiction had on the whole family.

'I watched her struggling with addiction, in and out of rehab, desperately striving to overcome it,' claimed Chloe. 'My mother is the bravest human being I've ever come across.'

Being the youngest sibling, Cara may not have seen or understood when her mother was at her worst, and had the advantage of watching and learning from her older sisters. In an interview with *Harper's Bazaar*, Poppy talked about the time when she and Chloe, then both teenagers, were sat down by their parents for a frank discussion about Pandora's battle. 'The best thing that could have come out of her own dark times is her honesty,' she revealed. But however much the couple tried to protect their daughters – Pandora moved out of the family home and stayed with gambling club owner and family friend John Aspinall so that her children didn't have to experience her daily struggle at close quarters – the threat of her losing out to her addiction was always there.

However, it was the devotion of her father, Sir Jocelyn, in the early stages of her battle with the drug that Pandora cites as her saviour: 'He once hauled me out of the overdose ward in New York and put me into a loony bin in Switzerland and sat there, wherever I was, holding my hand and saying, "Blood is thicker than water".'

Poppy also admitted that she, Chloe and Cara have all been cautioned to look for warning signs of an addictive personality after research revealed it can be hereditary. 'We were warned to look for characteristics in our behaviour, which luckily none of us have encountered,' confirmed Poppy. 'But if I ever have a problem, not only with substance abuse, I know I can go to her [Pandora]. That sort of thing can tear a family apart, but my dad kept it all together. We have a huge extended family and everyone pulled together to fight it and we've come out on the other side stronger and better and more compassionate people. If I ever won an Oscar I'd be so gushing and emotional about them [her parents], I'd make Gwyneth Paltrow look like a tough cookie by comparison.'

The relationship that all three sisters share with their

mother is closer than ever, with Cara on several occasions being reminded that she still needs Pandora's advice and support even if she is on the other side of the world: 'Mum phonecall makes everything better #lovemymum,' she tweeted before her 21st birthday.

With a family nickname of 'monster', given to her by her grandmother, it might seem probable that Cara would develop spoilt younger sister syndrome. But far from being selfish and precocious, it was simple attention – in any form – that she loved: 'I used to make up dance routines, do little plays. I love to perform.'

Still, like any child, sometimes her attention-seeking ways got her in trouble too. 'My earliest memory is getting naked in the supermarket and my mum chasing me round,' she chuckled in a recent video interview. 'The thing I remember most is being butt-naked. I hated clothes. I hated pink things and general girlyness. I loved sport and was a tomboy.'

So how did the 'performer' get into modelling? It might not have seemed such a bolt from the blue that the energetic tomboy entered the fashion world if you took one look at the environment she grew up in. With Pandora working on fashion magazine *Tatler* for a spell and then as a personal shopper for prestigious department store Selfridges, fashion and style were part of the family's everyday life. With an eye for getting the look right on many high-profile ladies – and more recently, being credited for helping dress Catherine, Duchess of Cambridge, on some of her official royal engagements – a sense of style was something that would have subconsciously infiltrated the youngster.

'I loved playing dress-up with my mum's weird 80s clothes, with zips and shoulder pads. And I liked normal dress-up clothes too that I wore everyday. Like Spiderman, Buzz Lightyear, Action Man...' she revealed to *i-D* online. 'When I was five, I remember I wanted to be Action Man, Spiderman or a taxi driver.'

Shunning princess dress-up clothes, Cara wasn't a girly-girl by any stretch of the imagination – she told Net-a-Porter TV that she had really short hair when she was younger because she was such a tomboy, although she hated being mistaken for a boy. And in an interview at the beginning of 2012, she admitted her tomboy tendencies when she was younger raised a few eyebrows: 'The first time I was a bridesmaid, to my auntie, I refused to go down the aisle without my football shorts underneath my dress.'

And it seems things haven't changed much nowadays either as she still loves nothing better than relaxing by having a kick-about with her old pals. 'If I go home and it's the summertime and I'm with all my friends and we're sitting in the park and someone's playing football, I'm totally there,' she said. 'I find that fun, to be playing with the boys in the mud and that kind of stuff. I'm still a tomboy. I obviously dress it up slightly more but when I'm just me, it is all about trainers and flats.'

Close pal and housemate Georgia May Jagger, herself a model and daughter of Rolling Stones' singer Mick Jagger, thinks Cara is the least glamorous person she's ever met. 'Cara's a massive tomboy... And not very fabulous at all! I mean, obviously she is, but I see her in a completely different way,' Georgia told a journalist after Cara won Model of the Year in 2012. 'I know her as she really is, which is funny and wearing, oh, some kind of jumpsuit. And making weird faces. She doesn't care about looking pretty.'

Cara admitted to *Vogue* that she was an energetic youngster: 'Even as a child I remember sleeping was never good for me. I don't seem to get tired; I just get more manic. There's always so much going on in my head.' She always wanted to explore and do things her older sisters were doing. Pandora certainly had her hands full with her youngest daughter. But being such an active child also meant she got to try her hand at lots of different sports, although tennis and surfing were her favourites. She also enjoyed long-distance running and ran for the county of Hampshire when she was just 10 years old. 'Nobody could ever believe that this tiny little blonde thing could get anywhere but I loved it,' she revealed in the same interview.

As well as being a child who was on the go constantly, Cara was also a sensitive soul, and when she was just five years old, she had her heart broken. 'His name was Robert, he broke my heart,' she revealed. 'I can still remember that moment.'

Cara also loved animals from a young age and like many young girls enjoyed horses and horse riding. Growing up in the family home, she was surrounded by pets: 'I had lots of dogs and cats when we lived in a big house.' Her love of animals is something that remains and she showed what a caring and considerate friend she can be when she threw a wake for her flatmate Georgia's dog in August 2012.

'Georgia was devastated when Poppy, her beloved English sheepdog, died, so Cara threw her a mini wake to cheer her up,' reported *The Sun*. 'She got out loads of photos of Poppy and they raised a glass to her in doggy heaven. They ended up getting silly and drunk and having fun, toasting Poppy.'

Pandora and Charles decided that all three Delevingne girls should be educated at the prestigious London day school, Francis Holland School for girls in Sloane Square. For a little girl with bright blonde hair and bundles of energy, it was a place where Cara thrived, even though she might not have been the most well-behaved youngster. In one school snap she is shown sticking her tongue out and holding up her middle finger, swearing at the camera. Even though she would have only been five or six at the time, Cara herself, who re-posted the pic on Instagram's 'flash-back Friday', commented that she was, 'Causing trouble from a young age.'

With all that energy (she says that her trademark trait is her hyperactivity), it might not be much of a surprise to learn that growing up she was a little mischievous, seeking out any opportunity to play up to an adoring crowd – performing to an audience of any kind was something she loved. At eight years old she got her wish to become the centre of attention in extraordinary fashion after she decided to sit alongside Andrew Lloyd Webber when he was playing the piano at a party. And rather than being embarrassed by the episode, it is a tale that the supermodel loves to retell.

'It's one of the best stories I've heard about me,' she recalled with a devilish grin in an interview with *Rush* magazine. 'When I was about eight years old I was at a New Year's Eve party with my family and lots of our friends and Andrew Lloyd Webber was there too. Everyone encouraged him to play his new melody on the piano so he agreed and started playing and everyone was stunned into silence because it was so beautiful. And apparently I went and sat next to him at the piano and started smashing the piano keys. I ruined Andrew Lloyd Webber's beautiful piano recital.'

While that might have made her infamous within the family circle, Cara's first brush with international fame came two years later when she was just 10 years old and was hand-picked to model for a feature on Irish milliner Philip Treacy's hats in Italian *Vogue*. The shots, taken in 2003 by US photographer Bruce Weber, show a wide-eyed Cara wearing a large Treacy creation, sitting alongside model Lady Eloise Anson. And according to the designer, he knew she was destined for a life in front of the lens: 'I think she is going to be as big as Kate Moss. If not bigger,' he stated. 'Cara probably doesn't remember but she was gorgeous then. I think that was the first time she was featured in print.'

It might have been the first time but it was certainly not the last for the cute tomboy, although her official 'break' into the world of catwalk modelling wasn't to come until years later. That early brush with fame, however, didn't stop her from enjoying a normal childhood, although the money she earned from the shoot was certainly exciting for the youngster.

'I'd saved £700 by the age of 10,' Cara told the *Daily Mirror*. 'I thought, "What the hell am I hoarding this for?" So I bought a drum kit. When I was younger I liked money, the feel of it. I would sit with my dad and count his coins and be, like, YEAH.'

But it was getting attention in any shape or form that Cara strived for and in an online interview she recalls that when she was younger, the only thing she wanted to be when she grew up was a dentist or a superhero: 'I always wanted to be a superhero so I could save people and be the centre of attention. I also had this weird passion for dentistry and loved looking inside my mouth. Weird.'

Popular TV shows of the 1990s like *Saved by the Bell*, which starred 2013's *Celebrity Big Brother* contestant Dustin Diamond, *Sabrina, the Teenage Witch*, *The Magic Roundabout* and *Dexter's Laboratory* were some of Cara's favourite programmes and she also enjoyed nothing more than running around with her friends playing Hide and Seek or Stuck in the Mud or games like Twister and Monopoly. The posters she chose to put up on her bedroom wall – being a wannabe musician and self-confessed tomboy, there could only be a couple of choices that reflected both sides of her personality – were of the Spice Girls and Chelsea FC.

During the 1990s pop group the Spice Girls were one of the biggest girl-bands of the time. For an impressionable youngster like Cara, the Spices – Melanie Chisholm (Sporty), Victoria Beckham (Posh), Melanie Brown (Scary), Emma Bunton (Baby) and Geri Halliwell (Ginger Spice, who would later become a good friend of the Delevingne family and attend Cara's older sister Chloe's wedding) – showed that it was cool to have 'girl power', and that shouting, pouting, pulling silly faces and larking around in front of the camera and fans meant you were normal, fun and kooky. When their hit single 'Wannabe' went to number one in more than 30 countries, Cara was just eight years old and became caught up in the excitement of the band that was sweeping the country.

In a weird twist of fate, Cara, who idolised the girl group as a youngster – her favourite cult band is the Spice Girls, her favourite cult movie *Spice World* – would be given the opportunity to star as Posh Spice over a decade later when the Spice Girl musical *Viva Forever!* came to London's West End.

When she turned 12 years old, Cara was adamant that she wanted to be a star, but while modelling might have been fun two years earlier, she had other ambitions – including a desire that stemmed from watching the Disney Channel. She asked her parents for a particularly unusual birthday present. 'When I was 12, I wanted to be a Disney Channel star! I wanted to be Hannah Montana but they said no,' recalls Cara.

When she had just hit her teens, Cara's biggest hobby was music, in particular drumming and writing her own songs. She recalls that her love of playing the drums came about due to her need to put out there the 'noises' in her head: 'I first started tapping out rhythm and noises in my head. And then I decided to articulate these things through an instrument and the drums were my choice. I've been playing ever since.'

At just 13 years old she formed a band called The Clementines with her school friend Marika Hackman. 'Cara sang and I played the drums,' revealed Marika in an interview with American magazine *Nylon*. 'We never wrote anything good but who knows? Maybe now we can do a reunion tour?!'

While nothing might have come from her time in the band, it didn't extinguish Cara's love of music, rather it ignited her passion even more as the years passed. She bought a drum kit with her first modelling pay cheque and recently stated that the last thing she does before going to bed is to listen to some music and play the drums – 'to relax'.

As the Delevingne sisters continued with their studies at Francis Holland, they became a topic of conversation – if only between their classmates – for being three good-looking girls.

'They were head-turningly skinny,' revealed an old school friend. 'At Francis Holland we all wore grey kilted skirts, which were rolled up to the waist. They had so little on their hips and rears – and of course it showed off their super-long legs. They made sure to leave before sixth form; this is crucial if you want to expand your social circle.'

Cara had a strong network of friends around her at the private school and while she enjoyed her school days, thanks to the friendships she formed ('I still hang out with my old school friends, they are the people that keep me sane and grounded. I owe them my life!'), she didn't sail through her studies without a hitch. During her GCSE years, she became withdrawn and quiet, finding the exams in her chosen subjects difficult: 'I found exams impossible, my brain works too quickly for me to be able to write it down fast enough. I had a hard time in my GCSE year; I had a bit of depression, which people find weird because I am a happy person.'

For Cara, whose friends describe her as the life and soul of the party, it was particularly hard to face those who would constantly tell her to 'cheer up'. 'When I was upset I would never tell anyone. I hid it, even to myself, and you can't keep all that inside,' she admitted in 2013.

CHAPTER 2

FASHIONING
A CAREER

'My mum was into fashion and so were my
two sisters. I never understood it.'

On 7 September 2007, Cara's eldest sister Chloe wed her childhood sweetheart, nightclub entrepreneur boyfriend Louis Buckworth, at St Paul's Church in Knightsbridge. It was a suitably glamorous occasion, with a congregation full of famous faces, with the Duchess of York, daughters Beatrice and Eugenie in pretty floral dresses, Joan Collins and Geri Halliwell among the guests. Geri was enjoying a brief comeback with the group, as on 28 June that year at a press conference at the O2 in London, the Spice Girls had announced they would be reuniting as a band and laid out their plans to embark on a world tour. It was the ideal opportunity for 15-year-old Cara to meet one of her idols, and Geri was very encouraging when she discovered that the youngster was interested in a musical career, chatting to her extensively about the music industry and giving plenty of invaluable information about how to make contacts. Dressed in a floaty knee-length white gown with gold detail, Cara didn't make up one of the eight young flower girls, but both she and Poppy, 21 at the time, made sure they were on hand to support their sister in any way they could.

'They are very close as sisters and you could see how emotional they all were on the day. They all looked beautiful, and although it would be wrong to hint that the younger sisters eclipsed the bride on the day, you could see all eyes on Poppy and Cara, as well as Chloe,' revealed a fellow wedding guest in an interview with *Hello!* magazine, which featured the wedding.

After the Italian *Vogue* photo shoot, it would have been fairly easy for Cara to continue her life in front of the camera. But the headstrong youngster had other ideas about what she wanted to do, and while her sister Poppy was making her mark in the modelling world, she certainly didn't want to follow in her shadow.

'After the Bruce Weber shoot, I didn't think about it,' she revealed. 'I wanted to be either a musician or an actress. My mum was into fashion and so were my two sisters. I was never as into it as much but there would always be magazines around the house and I would stare at them and be like, "What is this?" I never understood it, fashion was a very alien thing to me.'

That didn't stop her enjoying the things normal teenage girls like, though, including make-up and hair styles. According to her sister Poppy: 'We all used to go bonkers for GHDs [hair straighteners]. I had a pair and vaguely remember being a complete show-off about them. We were also mad about coloured hair extensions. I had pink and purple for some time, so did Cara. We looked like those My Little Pony toys!'

Although at that stage in her life Cara might not have had any designs to work in the modelling industry, there was one person who had spotted her potential long before the rest of the world. Sarah Doukas, managing director of Storm Model agency, is renowned for her ability to 'scout' potential new talent and bring them to the attention of the modelling world. Back in 1987, five years before Cara was born, Doukas founded the model agency from her home with the aim of launching new faces – people she had discovered herself – to a worldwide audience. She literally 'stormed' the fashion industry, and made her agency the first one in the UK to book and promote models directly with international fashion houses. A year after she launched the business, she made her most famous discovery to date – that of a young Kate Moss. As she waited for a flight back to London from New York at JFK international airport, Doukas spotted a 14-year-old Kate in the queue in front of her. Instantly captivated, she didn't get a chance to speak to the teenager on the flight back to the UK, having been placed in a window seat, so it was up to her business partner and brother, Simon Chambers, to make contact. He reported back to Sarah that the young girl from Croydon was called Kate Moss and yes, she was rather interested in modelling. Now a global superstar, catwalk model, fashion icon and brand – with a clothing line at Topshop, a fragrance range with Coty, a handbag line with luxury retailer Longchamp, and, according to *Forbes* in 2013, second on the top-earning models list with an estimated annual income of £9.2 million – Kate Moss is one of Storm's biggest success stories.

But even though her 'scouting' of Cara wasn't so fleeting or coincidental as that of Moss, the potential of Cara's career to match or even eclipse the supermodel's hadn't gone unnoticed. 'Both have got phenomenal personalities, which not all models have,' Doukas remarked when asked if Cara could be the new Kate at the beginning of London Fashion Week in September 2012.

Sarah Doukas was a long-term family friend of the Delevingnes, as her daughter, Genevieve, had been a close friend of Cara's at school. But it was Poppy who Sarah first signed to Storm after deciding she had the potential to make it in the modelling world and, due to Cara's young age, giving her time to mature.

'I went to school with Sarah's daughter,' Cara told an interviewer. 'I've been best friends with Gen since I was five. Sarah saw me when she came to our school and Gen introduced us. She spotted my sister Poppy first and then waited for me. I had never thought about modelling before, it just happened.'

Cara left Francis Holland after her GCSEs and she and Poppy went to the elite, independent Bedales School instead of Stowes sixth-form college in Buckingham, attended by their elder sister Chloe. Renowned for its liberal ethos and fashionable students as well as its hefty fees (currently around £10,000 per term), the list of Bedalians who attended the Hampshire school includes several well-known names, among them singer Lily Allen, TV presenter Kirstie Allsopp, model Sophie Dahl and Oscar-winning actor Daniel Day-Lewis.

For a creative, energetic Cara, the school was the perfect choice when it came to nurturing her love of all things theatrical – music, acting and performing in general. And the relaxed ethos was also a bonus for the youngster.

'The good thing is you get a lot of freedom. You sleep with the boys. Well, in the same house, but not the same floor. You get to go out to dinner and you can drink with an 18-year-old,' she explained at the time.

Studying psychology, dance and theatre studies at AS level, Cara found dance the most challenging subject because it was made up of 50 per cent theory. But she was a popular student and made lots of friends, including Sting's musician daughter Coco Sumner and Jazzy de Lisser, stepdaughter of the Marquess of Bute. Cara would enjoy regular parties with her new friends: 'Jazzy's brother had an amazing party in their castle in Scotland recently.'

In 2008, a year before Cara officially signed to Storm, Poppy was the star of the Delevingne family when it came to modelling. At 5ft 11in she is the tallest of the Delevingne sisters and in February that year she was hailed as 'Britain's Claudia Schiffer'. With a distinctive look that is often described as 'quirky English Rose', Poppy's career went from strength to strength and she became the face of Anya Hindmarch, Laura Ashley, Made in Heaven jeans and Bamford. She also starred in campaigns for Agent Provocateur, Diesel, Chanel, Mango, Jigsaw and Louis Vuitton and in February 2008 was the talk of London Fashion Week after walking in the Julien Macdonald show. A typical socialite, she was often 'papped' at various red-carpet events alongside her good pal actress Sienna Miller and never far from a high-society party, alongside Princess

Beatrice or Dasha Zhukova (Roman Abramovich's Russian model girlfriend), that would fill the pages of *Hello!* magazine. But her modelling career would never reach the dizzy heights that Cara is currently enjoying, quite possibly because of her decision to move to New York in 2008 to pursue an acting career.

'I know it seems a little crazy but I've always wanted to act,' she explained in an interview in April that year. Making *Tatler*'s Ten Most Eligible Girls, Poppy revealed that she would be staying at the Duchess of York's apartment in the Big Apple while she tried her hand at acting. 'I may now be based in New York but rest assured, I haven't gone for good,' she insisted. 'I fell into modelling and stayed because it was great fun but it's time to leave my comfort zone and use my brain a bit more.'

CHAPTER 3

FOLLOWING POPPY

'Poppy was a model and I never liked to do
the same things my sisters did...'

It was while studying for her A-levels at Bedales in 2009 when she was 17 years old that life changed dramatically for Cara. Desperate to be involved in any sort of acting role, she took on the part of Martha in a school production of Edward Albee's *Who's Afraid Of Virginia Woolf?* 'I like tough characters, I don't want a part to be easy,' she told the *Evening Standard* magazine in 2009.

After enjoying her time on stage, she wanted to feed her acting obsession and the same year got wind that Tim Burton was making a big-screen production of *Alice in Wonderland* with Johnny Depp and decided to send in an audition tape. It was a brave (some might say over-ambitious) move for the youngster but then she had never lacked aspiration and, in true Cara style, made an audition tape that was sure to get her noticed. Kooky as ever, her video made a big impression and she made it through to the final stages of casting for the lead role of Alice in the adaptation of the Lewis Carroll story, even going to Tim Burton's house in London for an interview.

'My interpretation of Alice was a little crazy. I overplayed it – the way a young girl would overplay all her emotions. I sent my tape off and then I was at a wedding and this woman came over to me. She said, "You don't know me but I know exactly who you are."' The woman in question, it transpired, was Lili Zanuck, who is married to Richard Zanuck, the producer of the film. 'She told me she loved my tape, and I went to Tim Burton's house and met with him,' Cara revealed in an interview with *W Magazine*.

The experience of meeting the legendary director was the first time Cara's confidence might have slipped and she readily admits to how nervous she was about the occasion: 'I was so scared. It [his house] was all maroon inside, filled with all this odd stuff from *The Nightmare Before Christmas* and his amazing paintings. He's a crazy man.'

Even though Cara was disappointed when she didn't get the part, she had no regrets about the experience and she understood that they were looking for a very specific Alice-type. 'I didn't get the part but that experience lit a fire in me,' she explained. 'They wanted an Alice with a deep sadness in her eyes; maybe I just wasn't sad enough.'

While the role of Alice eventually went to Australian actress Mia Wasikowska, Cara refused to let her dream of acting die. If anything, it made the youngster more determined than ever to focus on her biggest dream: 'To do a film with Meryl Streep. And I would have loved the Meryl Streep role in *The Devil Wears Prada*. My dream acting role would have always been Alice in *Alice in Wonderland*.'

While she lost out on the lead, there was a little light at the end of the rabbit hole when photographer George Bamford asked her to play Alice in his Wonderland-themed photo shoot.

The year 2009 might not have looked too promising on the acting front, but this was the year when Cara officially signed to Storm Model agency. Nevertheless, while she had seen the success that Poppy was currently enjoying as a model, she wasn't convinced that she wanted to follow in her sister's footsteps.

'Poppy was a model and I never liked to do the same things my sisters did,' she explained. 'Acting is what I've wanted to do my whole life. The way modelling took off, I just didn't expect it. It was lucky that I had connections but at the time modelling wasn't even a ripple in my mind.'

Even Pandora knew that her youngest daughter wasn't going to be satisfied with a career in modelling when she harboured such a desire to be an actress. 'She wants to be an actress, she likes playing villains and mobsters,' she told the *London Evening Standard*. 'Not mobsters,' corrected Cara, 'I like tough characters. I don't want a part to be easy.'

However, Storm's Sarah Doukas had other ideas for the teenager and was convinced she could make a name for herself in the modelling world because of her personality as much as her looks. 'I've know her since she was four years old and she was hilariously funny even then,' she confirmed. 'The Cara I know is cute, sexy, and more than a little unpredictable, but she's also very hard-working, unpretentious, gracious and generous – and she has great empathy with the women of her generation.'

So it was at the end of August in 2009 that 5ft 9in Cara (slightly shorter than the typical catwalk model), officially became a model. And right from the word go, she was determined to set herself apart from the other girls in the industry with a stand-out look. 'In the beginning I was thinking, "How do I set myself apart from other girls?"' she confessed. 'So many girls were taller, skinnier and prettier. And I'm not a girly girl at all. As a teenager I kept thinking, "I'm so short, I have no boobs, what do I do?" I didn't get boobs until I was around 18!'

But confidence is something that Cara has never been short of, and in the end she decided that modelling could help channel her inner performer. 'Maybe that's why I've been noticed,' she mused a year later. 'I treat the camera like a person – I gaze into it. Photos are a flat thing and you need to put life into them.'

Twenty-three-year-old Poppy was especially happy at her younger sister's new foray into the fashion industry and told *Vogue.com*, 'I couldn't be more excited about having my little sister at Storm with me. We're so close and she's completely stunning. I know Storm will look after her brilliantly. Also, I get to keep a close eye on her at all times, as big sisters like to do.'

In her usual style, Cara joked that she only agreed to sign to earn herself some money: 'I became a model because I needed the money! No, because it's a great job and I meet some amazing people. And then for the money, but it's not the only reason.'

One of her first photo shoots was for the bi-annual *LOVE* magazine in the autumn of 2009, in which she poses in a half-page solo shot, sharing the page with a 19-year-old fashion writer, Julia Frakes. Wearing a polka-dot shirt-dress by McQueen and a stripy sweater by Paul Smith, her hair is piled messily high on her head in a loose quiff – which covers one of her eyes and, of course, one of those trademark eyebrows. Pouting slightly while staring directly into the camera, in the accompanying caption Cara is described as a 'drama student and model'. Katie Grand, editor-in-chief of *LOVE*, has been hugely influential on the young model's career and a few years later she would work with Cara again, this time putting her on the front cover of the magazine alongside Kate Moss, as well as using her for regular *LOVE* features and advertisements.

'She's amazing, bright and gorgeous,' explained Katie, when asked to pinpoint why she thought Cara was so successful. 'Her energy is infectious and most of all, she is fun.'

Family friend and make-up artist Charlotte Tilbury, who later worked with Cara on a *Vogue* photo shoot, believes that Cara's personality goes a long way towards explaining her popularity – among designers/photographers and fellow models, too.

'She's the kind of girl that you just want to hang out with. She's witty, intelligent and there's never a dull moment with her. Her face is strikingly beautiful, with those dark eyebrows, defined features and piercing blue eyes. She reminds me of Jean Shrimpton [the iconic British model of the 1960s who is considered to be one of the world's first supermodels], but has great range as a model: she can go from classic beauty to quirky, from commercial to conceptual, with ease.'

While most girls her age would have been solely focused

on a modelling career once signed by a top agency, Cara still had a strong desire to do something musically and it was towards the end of 2009 that her dream came true – in part.

Geri Halliwell, whom she knew first as a fan and then as a friend at her sister Chloe's wedding, introduced her to the legendary producer and man behind the Spice Girls' phenomenal success, Simon Fuller. Cara flirted with popstardom (although she once revealed she is a 'world-class beat boxer – you should hear the noises I can make with my mouth') by recording an album with Simon, and was subsequently offered a record deal. For the model who had always dreamed of getting into music, this was an incredible opportunity.

Even though nothing seemed to come of her sessions in the recording studio, it quenched her musical thirst for a time and, after talking it through with her family and friends, she decided to focus on her modelling career. This was to prove a wise move and in December that year, *The Ones2Watch* online magazine listed Cara as the face of fall/winter 2009, with four accompanying headshots. In an explanation as to why she is listed on the website, the caption reads: 'With the air of an *enfant terrible*, Cara is not to be upstaged by big sister Poppy. This incredible girl was first featured in print at the age of eight when she posed with Philip Treacy's pet pug for a Bruce Weber/Italian *Vogue* editorial. Since joining Storm this year, Cara has been photographed by Andrea Carter-Bowman and Daniel Jackson for *LOVE* magazine. Now studying acting and just back from performing in a production of *Who's Afraid Of Virginia Woolf?*, Cara is becoming a name to remember.'

On 22 December, *Vogue.co.uk* listed Cara as number one

in their 'Model Faces To Watch For 2010' list, with an accompanying short bio on the youngster. In it, Cara cites Marc Jacobs as her favourite designer and AllSaints as her favourite High Street designer. She also says that the best thing about the job is how 'interesting' it is and that she studies for her A-levels in her spare time. It is a somewhat muted, even flat interview by the Cara we know to be overly excitable and keen to list her musical aspirations and love of acting. This was the first glimpse of a more timid Cara as she started out in the fashion industry, perhaps under the heavy influence of the bosses at Storm, who were keen to promote their new signing.

The next big decision to face was whether to continue her education at Bedales as she was due to sit her A-levels the following year but with more and more photo shoot bookings coming in, Cara and her family decided that she should leave her studies to concentrate on modelling. It was a big decision for Cara, but one that was wholly supported by her parents and siblings.

'Cara didn't want to make the decision on her own, she wanted to talk everything over with her parents and Poppy, who of course was a living example of how tough it could be to make a name for yourself in the modelling industry,' revealed a family friend. 'But it was thought at the time that Cara had so much ambition to make it as a model – which would in turn lead to other opportunities – it would be wise to put her A-levels on hold.'

So she did. And in 2010, the big names in the business started to pay attention to the youngster...

CHAPTER 4

ALL ABOUT
THE BROWS

'I'm terrible at runways. I just can't walk in
high heels but I've been practising with my sister Poppy.'

The beginning of 2010 held a great deal of expectation for Cara. Leaving higher education behind to pursue a career being photographed was a gamble, but with the support of her family and friends it was to be a gamble without any drastic consequences, should it all go horribly wrong. As a friend of Pandora's said: 'Her mum wasn't exactly going to shun her if nothing came of the modelling. Besides, most of her school friends had taken early gap-years, so if nothing else, this could be Cara's.'

It was inevitable that the media would pick up on two siblings – especially two glamorous, leggy blonde sisters – making their way in the modelling world. At first it was just the fashion journals, the likes of *Vogue*, *Harper's Bazaar* and the fashionista blogs, which featured articles on Poppy and Cara. Then as interest grew, the *Telegraph*, the *Independent* and the *Daily Mail* featured extensive articles on the girls and the family, revealing their aristocratic background and a who's who. 'Model Sisters: Poppy and Cara Delevingne,' ran the *Saturday Telegraph*'s fashion spread, with the sell: 'The Delevingne sisters, Poppy and Cara are regular fixtures on the fashion circuit – but who exactly are they?'

Poppy, who was still the most well-known of the siblings in the industry, encouraged Cara to attend more social engagements too, and brought her along to the *Remember Me* premiere on 17 March in London's Leicester Square. Looking a little bewildered at the red-carpet event, Cara posed with Poppy as the awaiting press snapped away, with one or two needing clarification from the PR team as to who was with model Poppy. Smiling coyly, with her hair scraped back, minimal make-up and a leather mini-dress with a sweetheart neckline, Cara was getting her first taste of the paparazzi, something she would be dealing with to a much greater degree in the years to come. For the time being, however, the paps weren't that interested in the newcomer.

In August, Cara attended the celebrity-heavy V music festival in Staffordshire, where she was invited into the MAC VIP make-up tent to have a 'festival make-over'. Make-up artist Sadie Hunt paid tribute to the very 'natural' beauty that Cara was and revealed what 'look' worked best for the teenager: 'I kept Cara's look quite natural, she doesn't need a great deal of product to make her look stunning.'

Dressed very casually in a retro black T-shirt by TruffleShuffle and skinny jeans, fresh-faced Cara, who was described on the festival's website as Poppy's sister, had recently celebrated her 18th birthday and took the opportunity to let her hair down. Smiling sweetly for the cameras – she hadn't quite built up the confidence for those wacky poses and gurning expressions she now likes to pull – Cara spent time hanging out backstage at the music festival weekend, rubbing shoulders with a more mixed bag of celebrities, including Alexa Chung, Pixie Lott, Hollywood actress Drew Barrymore, Eliza Doolittle, Gemma Arterton, Jameela Jamil, Princess Beatrice, actors Billie Piper and Laurence Fox (also Piper's husband) and fellow model David Gandy among others.

Storm management also made sure that Cara was seen at the right social engagements, never any trivial red-carpet invite but events that would give her the right image. Poppy continued to accompany her to such parties, including the launch of Justine Picardie's new book, *Coco Chanel: The Legend and the Life*, at Claridge's in September.

Cara was also able to mix a little business with pleasure when she starred in Bryan Ferry's music video for 'You Can Dance', a track from his album *Olympia* that was released in October 2010. Dancing sexily in front of the stage on which Ferry sings, it was a successful mix of posing, dancing and acting for Cara and she would later feature with him on the front cover of *S Moda* magazine in 2012. Ferry had reportedly seen Cara in some photos earlier that year and cast her as one of the leading girls in the video, as well as his 'Shameless' music video, and had used her images on several of his recent tours.

In November 2010, Cara was among the select few invited to preview Mulberry's spring/summer 2011 collection at Morton's in Mayfair, alongside Eliza Doolittle, Edie Campbell, Bonnie Wright and Tali Lennox. And later that month, she was snapped on her own outside Somerset House when she attended their annual Christmas Winter

Wonderland launch and was interviewed about what she was wearing for a 'Street Chic' feature. It was clear that she was slowly becoming more comfortable at these social situations and growing increasingly chatty with the press – her trademark cheekiness was starting to show, too.

'I'm wearing a Reiss jacket over an American Apparel T-shirt and A/wear jeans. I've accessorised with a Topshop scarf, an old hat and Carvela boots,' she revealed. But she was unable to resist a quick mention of what she wanted from Father Christmas, too: 'I would love an iPad for Christmas!' she giggled.

It was towards the end of 2010 that Cara's biggest signing to date came when she was asked to star in the spring/summer 2011 campaign for Burberry. Following in the footsteps of the likes of *Harry Potter* actress Emma Watson, who was the face of the S/S 2010 collection, the fashion giants were looking for young, fresh-faced stars that oozed personality for their collection, and Cara fitted the bill perfectly. Starring alongside British fashion model Jacob Young, she appeared relaxed and suitably sultry as she posed on Brighton beach for the new Burberry Prorsum range. And while it was one of her first big shoots, there was an air of confidence and professionalism about her that fooled those working on the shoot. 'Cara was totally at ease, she didn't look at all overwhelmed by the prospect of working with such a big fashion house,' recalled one observer.

The campaign was shot by the legendary Mario Testino, one of world's most prolific fashion photographers. In a career spanning more than 30 years, he has worked with the biggest names in the modelling business and the showbiz industry and is regularly asked to photograph the British royal family. Among his most notable clients are Britney Spears, Cameron Diaz, Gwyneth Paltrow, Madonna, Kate Moss and Lady Gaga. He was also the photographer chosen by Prince William and Kate Middleton for their official engagement photos. His work has featured in *Vogue*, *Vanity Fair* and *V*, to name but a few high-end glossy publications, and he works not only for the Burberry fashion house, but also for Gucci, Versace, Calvin Klein, Estée Lauder and Dolce & Gabbana.

Working with so many big-name stars and with such prestigious fashion brands, Testino is the man to impress, and on that chilly winter's day on Brighton beach in 2010, Cara did just that. Not only that, a few years later the photographer made the bold claim that she was one of his favourite new models and bore a striking resemblance in terms of style and personality to that of Kate Moss.

'She's fabulous, no? She's great, I work with her on all the Burberry ads,' he said of Cara at the launch of his first US exhibition in 2012. 'She's such fun. She is like the new Kate in a way, if you think of her personality and energy and attitude.'

Cara spoke of the Burberry advertising experience with *Models.com* later that year and described it as a life-changing experience: 'It has changed my life so much. The actual shoot was a nightmare, though; it was so cold in Brighton! It could not have been colder and I'm in spring/summer clothes. But it was great. I was just shoving heat pads into every bit I could. It was amazing working with all of those people and it really started a whole new thing for me, I haven't stopped since.'

She also spoke very highly of Testino, who has since become a lifelong friend. 'Working with Mario is a joy. He's very young spirited, and it's always lovely and a pleasure to spend time talking to him about all different things,' she told *Hollywood Life* magazine. 'He's a firm friend.'

Two years later, when asked what her standout fashion shoot was, she revealed that her first with Burberry, whom she now classes as 'family', was the most memorable.

'I've become friends with everybody who did both campaigns. The shoot was a joy. Looking back, I thought it would be really scary but it actually felt so normal on set. It was the beginning of a chapter for me, a breakout shoot.'

The Burberry spring/summer collection 2011 featured a number of other modelling stars in its campaign, including Tara Ferry, Tali Lennox, Sacha M'Baye and Jourdan Dunn, alongside British musicians Karen Anne and Johnny Flynn, plus British actors Sophie Kennedy-Clark and Matthew Beard. Working with other models boosted Cara's confidence and allowed her to be a little more at ease with the job. Her bubbly, energetic personality crept into the photo shoots and the other models enjoyed watching her lark about, not afraid to act a little goofy. It was little wonder then that Jourdan Dunn wanted to strike up a friendship with Cara. The model was already slightly more established in the business, having been spotted by Storm model agency in her local Primark when she was just 16 years old. By the time she started working with Cara she had already made a big impression on the modelling industry, and in 2008 was the first black model since Naomi Campbell to walk a Prada catwalk in over a decade. Only a few years older than Cara, the two girls shared a similar sense of humour and became firm friends from that point onwards, and although this was the first time the pair had worked together, it wouldn't be the last.

In fact, the next time the 'besties' (as they are now referred to) appeared together was in February the following year at London's 2011 Fashion Week, a bi-annual event that displays the latest upcoming trends for the new season. Organised by the British Fashion Council, it is held twice-yearly in February and September and makes up one of the 'Big Four' fashion weeks (sometimes called Fashion Month), along with those held in New York, Milan and Paris.

This was to be the first time Cara would take to the catwalk and it was a nerve-wracking experience for the teenager, who would be stepping out in the Burberry Prorsum autumn/winter 2011 collection. The British heritage brand had named its collection 'Coats of Many Colours' and the catwalk was set up in a 1,000-seater tent in Kensington Gardens. To make matters even more intense, the show was being simultaneously streamed live to 150 countries, including to a 32m digital screen in Piccadilly Circus, which was a world first. Cara was paralysed with nerves before the show and to make matters worse, during rehearsals she took a tumble on the catwalk because of the skyscraper heels she had to wear. Thankfully, when it was time to showcase the collection, designed by chief creative officer Christopher Bailey, Cara managed to walk down the runway without a hitch. Speaking after the show, she revealed how she had used her love of acting and performing to help her overcome the nerves of strutting her stuff on the catwalk.

'I've always been a real drama queen; I have been my

whole life. I love theatre, I love performing, love playing a part. I use acting every day in modelling. You play a role. On the catwalk, it's not me. I wouldn't have the confidence to do it [walk on a catwalk] but you've just got to snap into it and be like, "I'm a supermodel, I can do it."'

The show began with a film of a snowstorm and Jourdan Dunn opened and closed the proceedings, with Cara sixth in line to hit the catwalk, wearing a lime military-style jacket and matching oversized bag and black-and-white flat cap. Walking out to a soundtrack of Dusty Springfield, Roger Daltrey and Adele, 52 models were used to showcase the collection and the closing walk-out featured them all wearing clear PVC capes over their clothes as a batch of fake-snow fell upon them.

Watching from the front row was a who's who of the fashion industry's elite and showbiz royalty. Prime Minister's wife Samantha Cameron, who had attended three shows previously that day, shared the front row seats with actresses Kate Bosworth and Rachel Bilson, plus Alexa Chung, the Duran Duran boys, Topshop supremo Sir Philip Green and the editors-in-chief of American, French, Italian and British *Vogue*s: Anna Wintour, Emmanuelle Alt, Franca Sozzani and Alexandra Shulman.

If Cara had showed any sign of nerves out on the runway it might have been justified with that collection of stars watching her every step, but thankfully the show went without a hitch and she was a success. Speaking afterwards, though, she couldn't shake off the annoyance of falling over during rehearsal, but she was adamant that practice would make perfect. She also, rather touchingly, realised that her sister Poppy would be the best person to help her improve.

'I hit my knee quite badly,' she confessed. 'I'm terrible at runways, I just can't walk in high heels but I've been practising with my sister Poppy so one day I'll learn.'

It was in an interview two years later, with over 100 catwalk shows under her belt, that Cara reflected on how different she'd been at the beginning of her career and the excitement she felt about working in the industry in those first few months.

'When I started modelling, it was just a job, and I was so excited – everything was so new, so crazy. I didn't overthink anything. I just did it and enjoyed myself along the way,' she told interviewmagazine.com. 'But after a few seasons you get used to it, and there's a lot you actually have to think about, and I don't know, it just makes you much more aware of what you look like and what other people think. It's a bit of a nightmare.'

The year 2011 wouldn't just be the year of her first catwalk show, either – it was to bring about a number of opportunities that would mark Cara out as the model everyone was talking about. Literally the biggest campaign she starred in came from her Burberry spring/summer collection shoot, as she appeared on 40ft billboards in New York's Times Square at the end of April. She is said to have been so chuffed with such a feat that she used the picture as a screensaver on her iPod.

'I can't believe it, it's crazy!' Cara commented at the time, while *Mail* online ran an article suggesting such an accolade was something '*Tatler*-friendly girls in pearls would hawk their country pile to emulate'. The accompanying Femail feature, titled 'They're so socially ambitious, they make the Middletons look shy and retiring... meet the Dynasty sisters', mentions Cara's accomplishments in the modelling world first, an early indication that while her sisters were still of interest in the press, it was 18-year-old Cara who was beginning to take over in the public eye. The article, while a little derogatory when it described Chloe, Poppy and Cara as 'three sisters so socially ambitious even a Middleton might pay homage', also claimed that Poppy would soon find Cara stealing her limelight: 'Cara has always been thought to be the prettiest and it's likely she'll eclipse Poppy,' said a friend of the family in the same article.

Invitations to various social events were beginning to pick up and Cara soon found herself on the list for more and more prestigious gatherings, such as the Vivienne Westwood 'Get a Life' palladium jewellery collection launch in February. In March she was photographed for American *Vogue* for a shoot entitled 'Tech Mate', again for Burberry in a snakeskin biker jacket alongside British model Edie Campbell, and also that month she posed for *Numéro* magazine, in a shoot entitled 'Les Yeux Noirs' (Black Eyes). An altogether different fashion shoot, it featured headshots of Cara wearing bushy fake black eyebrows. In reference to the title, her brows were big and dark, giving her a distinctive monobrow look.

While the eyebrows might have been fake this particular shoot marked the beginning of her natural brows getting attention – from that point onward, they caused quite a stir in the media. Natural, thickset eyebrows are Cara's trademark look and something that sets her apart from dozens of other perfectly plucked girls. The extent of the eyebrow fascination in the world's media has now reached jaw-dropping proportions: at the time of writing, Cara's eyebrows have their own Twitter page (with an impressive 3,300 followers), and Google released a report in 2012 stating that there had been a huge increase in people using their search engine to Google 'Cara Delevingne' and 'fuller eyebrows', while searches for 'eyebrow plucking' and 'tweezers' have fallen dramatically. Beauty expert Nilam Patel, HD Brows founder and known as the 'eyebrow queen', believes that Cara's *au-naturel* brows have caused the sales of tweezers to plummet.

'Everyone is really into that bold-brow thing Cara has been rocking. Once she came onto the scene, it's been much easier to convince clients that this is a great look that can suit everyone. We've seen sales of our growth serum increase in the last year, as well as sales of our brow pencils, which create superfine hair strokes to mimic a fuller brow.'

Cara's signature bushy brow look has been an inspiration that women seek to emulate. The Internet is full of websites offering advice and tutorials on how to 'fake' Cara's bushy brow – including several YouTube videos that explain how to achieve the 'thick and youthful brow of Cara' – and several beauty features have commented on whether everyday women should adopt such a look. The *Daily Mail* ran a full feature on 'Can Real Women Pull Off Cara Delevingne's Eyebrows?' while tabloid and magazine articles have now begun to describe Cara as a: 'bushy-browed beauty', 'wild-browed supermodel' and 'bushy eyed-browed star'.

MAC make-up artist Terry Barber predicted that 2012 would be the year when 'a strong brow look, à la Delevingne' would be in vogue. He was right and the interest in her eyebrows was such that people began asking her what she did to maintain such a look.

'I never really touch my brows, apart from the bit in the middle. I have to, otherwise I'll have a uni-brow,' she admitted. 'But I've never plucked or threaded them. People always ask me what is my secret and I'm like, "You just don't pluck them." It's really straightforward. I mean, I do, obviously, a little because otherwise I'd have a monobrow, but it's just about keeping them wild, keeping them free and woolly.'

As well as having hundreds of fans of her look, various celebrities have also commented on why they love Cara's brows. Lily Collins, actress and daughter of musician Phil Collins, has also been picked up by the media on her less-than-trim brows. 'It's kind of like we [Lily and Cara] got a little brow club going on. She's got this stunning face and she's doing so well, it's amazing,' Collins told reporters when asked what she thought about Cara's look.

Even Poppy has admitted to being envious of her sister's brows, revealing, 'I'd really like to have bigger lips, like Rosie Huntington-Whiteley [English model and actress]. And Gisele's bottom would be ace too. Ooh, and my sister Cara's eyebrows. They really do have a mind of their own.'

But the perils of her job mean that Cara's tomboy look sometimes suffers for her art: 'It's when they [the make-up artists] bleach them, that's what annoys me the most. They are already coarse enough and curly enough. I wake up and they look like my grandmother's!'

CHAPTER 5

GIRL POWER

'They said I looked like Posh Spice. That's really mean...'

In May 2011, Cara attended the Costume Institute Gala in New York and for the young model, the event (more casually known as the Met Ball) was thrilling. Speaking to *Models.com* afterwards about the occasion – during which she shared the red carpet with the likes of Madonna, Beyoncé, Rihanna, Jennifer Lopez, Nicole Richie, Gisele Bündchen and *Twilight* actress Kristen Stewart – Cara couldn't hide her excitement.

'It was unbelievable, the Met was just incredible! I had to stop myself from... my jaw was literally dropping, constantly! I couldn't hold a conversation as you'd be talking, then you'd see a favourite actor walk by. The table I was on was in the middle of everything too; it had like a spotlight on it, not a spotlight but a... you know. Florence and the Machine performed around us and we were there, like cheering on the Brits. It was amazing, there were so many funny stories. I wish I could remember them all but it was all so intense.'

Later that month, Cara and Poppy attended the Trust in Fashion evening, a night of fashion and fundraising for the charity Rainbow Trust, whose carers support families of children with life-threatening or terminal illnesses. Storm Models provide the catwalk models free of charge, and Poppy, Cara and Jourdan Dunn took to the runway to help raise as much money as possible.

That year also saw Cara enjoy a night to remember when she met two of showbiz industry's biggest divas, the late Whitney Houston and Mariah Carey. Houston, a former gospel singer turned pop-powerhouse in the 1990s, who sold over 200 million records worldwide, died in February 2011 at just 48 years old after being found in the bath of her hotel room. Carey, another singing sensation of the 1990s, is well known in the music industry for her diva behaviour, backstage demands and ridiculous riders. For Cara, rubbing shoulders with them both was a moment to remember.

'I was lucky enough to meet Whitney Houston before she died,' gushed Cara to Net-a-porter.com. 'I actually ended up having a moment where me, Whitney and Mariah Carey were cheers-ing without champagne. That was pretty cool.'

She has had other encounters with female musical icons, too. In June 2011, Cara attended the launch of new fashion label Willow at the Riding House Café in London. It was while she was sipping champagne at the event that word got round that Cara had been asked to star in the upcoming Spice Girls' musical, *Viva Forever!*, which was due to hit the West End the following year. For a young girl who had dreams of becoming an actress, it would have seemed like the ideal opportunity to get some experience of acting under her belt. But Storm weren't happy with the direction in which this might lead Cara's career and flatly refused to allow her to entertain the idea. The press were keen to ask about the rumours and in typical style Cara spoke very openly about why she had turned down the role. Poking fun at The Spices and not denying the rumours – or indeed trying to hype them up – she hadn't had the media training that some in the industry had, so when asked if she really had turned down playing the Victoria Beckham character in the musical, her excited eagerness took over.

'Of course, I loved the Spice Girls. I loved Geri and Baby, but who liked Posh Spice? They said I looked like her and I said, "That's not cool, that's really mean." My agent said, "No, you can't, it will be a career killer."'

The interest gained momentum and Cara was asked whether had she been allowed to take on the role, she might have been worried about singing in the musical, which was written by Jennifer Saunders. Of course she was quick to shout down such chatter and made sure everyone knew about her previous studio time with Simon Fuller.

'When I started modelling he took me under his wing and I wrote and recorded two albums of music but at the time I was so young,' she told one journalist.

And it was then that she revealed the true reason why she had not accepted Fuller's offer to make it as a music star: 'They said, "Right, we can make you into this thing and change your name", and I said I wanted to know who I am and be who I am and not who someone wants me to be, and I put that on hold.'

It was a simple and clear message to the press – Cara

wasn't going to do anything she didn't want to do. No matter how much she wanted to start a career in the music industry, she didn't want to be stereotyped into a manufactured 'pop star'. It was also the first time that her personality really made its presence known: here was a supermodel with a talent, a bit of fire in her belly and who wasn't afraid to speak her mind about what she wanted from life. Not only did this make her more noticeable in the fashion world, but the world's media also took note.

'There would be the odd interesting snippet we'd put in the magazine about her initially,' confirmed one of the feature writers of *Star* magazine. 'Then suddenly she wouldn't just be in the fashion pages; we'd pick up on what she was saying on Twitter and suddenly have a lot of stuff to ask her about. She is very opinionated and not afraid to speak her mind, which always makes for a brilliant interview.'

And it wasn't just Cara's comments that were marking her out as magazine and red-top fodder, she was becoming more socially active, which meant she was being spotted by the paps at more events. Of course, it helped that she was also linked to another famous face: Tyrone Wood, son of Rolling Stones' star, Ronnie Wood. The couple got together in 2010 and one of the first snaps of them cosying up together was at the anniversary of the Alice by Temperley collection in London. But the romance was not to last and at Glastonbury the following year, Cara revealed that they had split. It wasn't that much of a surprise to those who knew her, however, as Tyrone was older and her career was just starting out and so being in any relationship was going to be hard. Fiercely independent, Cara was also tired of people considering her to be just a 'spoilt rich girl' who didn't have to work. She had a point to prove and wanted to make a name for herself, without the help of her wealthy family or a wealthy man on her arm.

'I never want to rely on a man,' she told the *Daily Mail*. 'I never want to be just the girlfriend of a rich man. I could have had all that with Tyrone, he is lovely and kind and we had a lot of fun together but I want to be someone in my own right.'

And more importantly for the 18-year-old, they both wanted different things from the relationship. 'I think Tyrone got too serious too quickly, but that's because he's 27. That's not for me. We did have a good time though and I'm still very fond of him. It's not his fault.'

Tyrone Wood wasn't going to be the last high-profile man that Cara would be linked to, though. One Direction's Harry Styles and singer Jake Bugg would also be linked with the star over the coming months, but close friends of Cara insist she is happiest when 'flying solo' and not with a boyfriend.

'She doesn't always "get" boys,' said a pal. 'She's such great fun when she's single, always larking around and making people laugh. Sometimes she feels she has to be a bit more grown-up when she's not flying solo.'

So it was at Glastonbury 2011 when newly-single Cara enjoyed rubbing shoulders with A-listers including Kate Moss, Jessie J and Tinie Tempah, while U2 and Coldplay entertained the festival-goers in Somerset. Still making the pages of the heavyweight fashion journals, in July she again appeared in American *Vogue*. In a spread entitled 'Taking Hold', she was interviewed about what was in the Prada python pochette from *Prada.com* that she carried at the festival. She revealed it held 'Chanel mascara, hairbrush, Trebor mints and my iPod.'

Make-up was to be the direction in which Cara next found herself heading when Burberry announced they wanted the fresh-faced star to front their spring/summer 2012 beauty range, which in turn led to the fashion house using the youngster and pal Jourdan Dunn for their autumn/winter beauty range too. In between Burberry shoots (they also had her fronting their 'Shop The April Showers' collection in the spring), High Street brand H&M wanted edgy, down-to-earth girls to front their H&M Authentic Collection for autumn/winter 2012 and Cara fitted the bill perfectly, posing for photos in pretty denim dresses and more edgy jackets alongside Hungarian model Barbara Palvin. Dominic Jones Jewellery also wanted her to form part of their campaign, and she modelled their new lines of jewellery alongside singer Florence Welch and actor Clara Paget.

In August Cara found time to let her hair down and celebrated her 19th birthday at V Festival, alongside models David Gandy and Daisy Lowe, actors Laurence Fox, Matt Smith and Douglas Booth, singers Ellie Goulding and Pixie Lott and actress Billie Piper. When asked by *Vogue* how to achieve her 'festival look', she replied, 'I'm wearing vintage shorts, a vest from New York and Reebok trainers. My bag is Mulberry and the shades are Burberry. My festival advice is to wear minimal make-up and it's all about packing wisely.'

As well as requests to showcase new collections in advertising campaigns, there were more catwalk shows to star in, and on Monday, 19 September, Cara once again took part in the Burberry Prorsum womenswear spring/summer 2012 collection for London Fashion Week. Having grown in confidence and stature since her first time on the catwalk, it was Cara, not Jourdan Dunn, who opened the show in a tightly-fitting plum trenchcoat.

Sienna Miller, the good friend and flatmate of her sister Poppy, was in the front row, grinning as her pal's sister strutted past, while Poppy herself was spotted whooping and cheering as Cara strutted past. Denise Lewis, Donna Air and Rosie Huntington-Whiteley were also in attendance as Christopher Bailey showcased his latest collection from a transparent marquee in Kensington Gardens. The show was a great success and praise was heaped on the 18-year-old by various stars, all wanting to know more about her.

'She oozes confidence on the catwalk, which is quite rare considering she is still quite a novice on the runway,' commented one fashion editor. And it wasn't just the assembled press who were impressed either.

'There is clearly something about Cara that makes her stand out from the thousands of models who are just clotheshorses – she has that look,' confirmed PR expert Mark Borkowski.

There was a growing interest in Cara as a person too and the editorials featuring the teen increased. *Vogue* featured Cara and Poppy in their Special Edition Best Dressed list, while *Tank* magazine had her taking part in a fun six-double-page spread that involved the youngster dressing up as 'twins' and the use of a short black wig.

She also made her first magazine cover with *Vogue* UK in November. It wasn't the official magazine – rather a supplement *Vogue* in association with H&M – but it was the first time her face had appeared over the letters of the infamous fashion journal. DNA Model Management listed her in their December 'Powerhouse' issue, alongside other models on their books, including Linda Evangelista, Edie Campbell and Atlanta de Cadenet Taylor. Turkey's *Vogue* ran five pages of her pulling various poses, while *Vogue* China followed suit and had her taking part in a snow-themed winter shoot.

W Magazine decided to include Cara and Poppy in their 'Soul Sister' feature, where photographer Max Vadukul captured 23 famous siblings under the tagline: 'As the saying goes, you can fool the world but not your sister'. The pair were dressed in black full-length gowns and bright pink and purple headgear, and in a playful suggestion about Cara stealing her thunder, Poppy has her hands wrapped around her sister's neck.

The invites kept coming thick and fast and Cara found herself in demand to attend a range of events, including the Moët & Chandon Etoile Awards in September, and later the Women of the Year Awards in November, dressed in a shimmery gold Burberry dress. Also that month she attended the *GQ* Style/Carolina Herrera Drinks event and the UGG Australia flagship store launch in London, and in December the Burberry Pre-Fall 2012 party.

There was some time off for the youngster too, which was a blessing as she spoke of her need to rest and wind down – computer games are her relaxation of choice: 'I play *Call of Duty* and I'm not going to lie, I wear a headpiece too! I love nothing better than playing my Xbox. I'm such a boy,' she revealed.

But if she thought 2011 was a busy year, little did she know what was in store for her the following year, when one of the biggest campaigns she would be involved in was announced.

CHAPTER 6

A MODEL ADVENTURE

'They call me "Cara the model". I'm just Cara.'

Christmas was going to come early for Cara when Burberry announced the exciting news that she and British actor Eddie Redmayne would be the stars of Burberry's spring/summer 2012 campaign. It was the first time a couple, rather than a group, would take centre stage for the fashion label's advertising campaign since 2008 when Sam Riley and Rosie Huntington-Whiteley modelled together.

It wasn't the first time Eddie, then 29, had worked for Burberry, having starred in their spring/summer 2008 campaign, and of course Cara was a regular on the Burberry catwalk so putting these two gorgeous people together was a genius ploy by the marketing department. Eddie, who was known in the press as a 'sex symbol' (you can still currently buy 'I love heart Eddie Redmayne' mugs from Amazon), was previously best known for his role in the film, *My Week With Marilyn*, and the BBC adaptation of *Tess of the*

D'Urbervilles with Gemma Arterton. But these adverts were about to propel them both to bigger things.

Talking about the making of the campaign, Eddie said, 'I have worked with Burberry before and it's always a fantastic experience. Christopher [Bailey] wanted something playful from the shoot and so Cara and I had a genius couple of days fooling around. Hopefully the enjoyment we had is reflected in the campaign. I'm a huge fan of Christopher Bailey; he's a brilliant designer and a brilliant man. The fashion world can be a bit intimidating but Christopher remains a kind, grounded gem of a man.'

The photos, taken by Mario Testino, were intimate yet playful, with Cara lying seductively on the floor in a tailored Burberry trench, pulling Eddie's collar towards her as he lies behind her in a suit and matching gentleman's coat. The shots were described as 'sizzling', 'smoking hot' and 'sure to set pulses raising' by *Grazia* magazine, who also commented on the 'hotness of Miss Cara Delevingne'.

Of course Eddie was prepared for the media coverage that would come the following year when the campaign was officially launched having been in the media glare after his work in the TV and film industry – he would later star in the TV adaptation of the book *Birdsong* and the film *Les Misérables*. But for Cara, the sudden, focused media attention would be an eye-opener.

After spending Christmas with her family and a few days' well-earned rest, Cara was about to celebrate the New Year in style when the media picked up on her starring in the Burberry spring/summer 2012 campaign and that she was to be the new 'face' of the fashion label. All of a sudden, celebrity magazines were carrying photos of the pair of them under the headline: 'Eddie and Cara blossom in Burberry', and Cara was being questioned over whether there was any romance with the actor, who was nine years older than her. Eddie was also asked what it was like working with Britain's youngest, hottest model and revealed the experience was 'wonderful', going on to say, 'I've known her [Cara] for a while. She's a really fun, playful girl and it was really relaxed, actually. She is wonderfully energetic – a ridiculously beautiful and very down-to-earth girl. We had a ball working together.'

With such praise from Eddie and the glamorous snaps attracting attention from fashion outlets and newspapers and magazine alike, thanks to the pairing of Cara with a famous British actor, the 18-year-old was in demand. Now she had a title after her name – 'Cara, the face of Burberry' was used to describe her in editorials, and articles the following month revolved around how normal women could emulate her natural, yet beautiful look: 'Cara's secrets: How Cara's Burberry Beauty is achieved' is just one example of the tutorials on YouTube.

In January, she appeared on the front cover of *S Moda* magazine with Bryan Ferry, as previously mentioned, and the same month appeared in *W Magazine* with pal Jourdan Dunn for a 'Best In Class' feature.

At 19 years old, Cara had moved out of the family home and was now living with her sister Poppy in London: 'Our house is a mess, it's covered in so many clothes, you can't see the floor!' And it was Poppy who accompanied her young 'mini-me', as she liked to call her, to the various catwalk shows in Milan, New York, Paris and back to London as the fashion weeks kicked off. Cara found herself more in demand than ever for designers wanting her to showcase their autumn/winter 2012 collections and she herself admitted that this was her first 'proper' season.

'It's my first serious season, I guess,' she told one interviewer who got time to chat with her backstage at Milan. 'People tell you stories about it but you don't realise how much work it is until you properly get into it. I didn't realise how much I'd be doing!'

To say she was doing a lot was an understatement – over the four fashion weeks in four countries, Cara would be walking in more than 20 shows, jetting across the globe to grace the catwalks of the various designers who wanted her to model their designs. It wasn't hard to see why she was in such demand – young, energetic and with a vibrant personality that shone through when she modelled, fashion designers of every calibre were eager to get her to showcase their designs.

Starting out in New York, Cara totted up nine shows for the likes of DKNY, Donna Karan, Thakoon, Rag & Bone – where she wowed spectators with her 'tousled mane' – and finally Jason Wu, later tweeting: 'Thanks @jasonWu for recruiting me to your army'. She also had time to walk for Oscar de la Renta, Marc Jacobs, Carolina Herrera and Tory Burch. The *Telegraph* very quickly picked up on her becoming 'THE' girl of the season when on day two she walked the catwalk in both the Jason Wu exhibition and Rag & Bone.

The following week it was time to head back to Blighty to take part in London Fashion Week (LFW), but this time the only show she would be walking in was Burberry – and being the face of the label, it would have been surprising had she not done so. Poppy was on hand to capture a cute picture of her sister backstage, tweeting: 'star of the show backstage @caradelevingne', while in the front row were a mixture of celebrities eager to see the 19-year-old in action on that chilly February day. Her partner-in-Burberry-crime, Eddie Redmayne, was one, alongside his *Birdsong* co-star, Clémence Poésy, Hollywood actress Kate Bosworth, *The Voice* judge Will.i.am, Holly Valance, Will Young, Samantha Cameron and Anna Wintour. Cara led the finale to rapturous applause, with all the models carrying umbrellas as the transparent tent was showered with fake rain from the outside while confetti rained down inside.

During LFW, Grazia's online magazine, *Grazia Daily*, spotted Poppy at the Henry Holland Show and asked her what she thought of her sister's achievements in the modelling world so far. As proud big sisters go, Poppy was definitely up there with the most gushing of praise.

'When I see her on the catwalk, I feel unbelievably proud. I'm like the embarrassing parent at the nativity play, screaming and whooping and she gets horribly embarrassed. But at the same time, she loves it and I love supporting her. She's only doing Burberry for London but she'll be at Paris and Milan.' When asked whether she gave her younger sister any advice, she admitted that Cara was beyond needing her help at this stage.

'Do I give her any tips? No, not any more, she doesn't need any tips. Maybe a few years ago I did, but definitely not now. We worked together recently, we did a shoot for *W Magazine* and we loved it. We have a good energy together and it was a good balance. It's always good to have some sibling modelling.'

Next stop was Milan, where Cara was scheduled to take part in six shows including Fendi, Trussardi, Moschino, Blumarine, Dsquared and Dolce & Gabbana. When she hit Milan, it was time to be transformed into a Medusa-style goddess with tight plaits running across her forehead for Fendi, and later that day a more futuristic look with brown-smokey eyes and metallic outfits when she hit the runway for Blumarine. Two days later she took to the catwalk for Dolce & Gabbana in a lace and embroidered dress – cheered on in the front row by Oscar-winning actress Dame Helen Mirren – before it was time for a complete change at the Dsquared show when she sported a Bridget Bardot look complete with big blonde beehive, icy-pink pout, baby-pink jacket and cigarette in hand. Speaking after the show she confessed that she had loved working on the Dsquared show: 'I'm surrounded by friends at Dsquared – I love them, it's always great fun.'

And after the show, she was asked by an eager fan how she was enjoying the Milan Fashion Week, to which she replied, 'It's a bit stressful!'

The final stop in the Fashion Week Big Four was Paris and one of the more prominent show weeks. Cara was walking in seven shows and the celebrities were out in force to sit in the front rows of the various fashion labels.

On hand to support his daughter, Sir Paul McCartney was in the audience to watch as the Stella McCartney collection was paraded and Cara walked the catwalk wearing some very bright and false blue eyelashes for the British designer's show. The rest of the week she walked for Nina Ricci, Sonia Rykiel (from where she found time to tweet some backstage fun photos), Cacharel, Paul & Joe,

Kenzo and Chanel. Kanye West, Alicia Keys, Katy Perry and sister Poppy were all in the front row of the Chanel show, which was dressed up with giant crystal props. For a model who is well known for her bushy brows, it seemed somewhat ironic that her eyebrows received special attention for this show – with her hair scraped back flat against her head, Cara's busy brows were bejewelled with green and blue beads and sequins.

It was a look that only certain models could pull off while still looking effortlessly beautiful and Cara was one who could. Working for Chanel was to be another turning point in her flourishing career, with Chanel's head designer and creative director Karl Lagerfield commenting, 'Cara is different. She's full of life, full of pep. I like girls to be wild but at the same time beautifully brought up and funny.'

Vogue fashion bookings editor Rosie Vogel said, 'She's not your typical model in that she's not the standard 5ft 11. But then neither's Kate Moss. But what she lacks in inches, she makes up for in confidence. She's unique – she has a wonderful versatility to her and a great personality, which is crucial. She's really lively and dynamic and still feels very modern.' The brows won approval, too: 'I like that she has those heavy brows – it adds something very different.'

With *Vogue* describing her as their 'crush of the season' and *Grazia Daily* revealing that they had a serious 'girl-crush on supermodel du jour, Cara', the model herself had more down-to-earth concerns about her beauty: 'My skin gets worse during the shows because of all the travelling,' she was heard to tell a journalist backstage during Milan Fashion Week.

But as well as the positive praise that was being heaped on

Cara, there was one designer who didn't feel she was quite right for his fashion label, and he made a rude remark about why he would be banning her from his shows. Marc Jacobs decided that Cara was too short to star in his Louis Vuitton autumn/winter 2012 show and called her a 'dwarf' according to Jacobs' close confidante and *LOVE* editor-in-chief Katie Grand.

'I was trying to get her [Cara] in the show, but it was the show in which everyone was very tall and very long. I remember Marc looking at me and saying, "Why is that dwarf in here?" and me being devastated,' revealed Katie. In the interview Katie goes on to explain that although Cara's modelling card read she was a good 5ft 9in, in the catwalk industry that is quite short.

'I apologised to her afterwards,' confirmed Katie, who also made sure she frequently put her on the cover of her magazine, *LOVE*, because she 'felt bad' about the incident. Jacobs later chose Cara – who hadn't a clue what the designer said about her at the time – to walk in both his eponymous label and Louis Vuitton in the spring/summer 2013 shows, calling her a 'sweetheart' and in the fickle world of fashion, also chose to star her in his 'Protect the Skin You're In' campaign.

But it wasn't just during the shows themselves that all eyes were on Cara. She was now a recognisable face going into and coming out of fashion shows, and her casual, laid-back approach to being photographed made her a big hit with her fans. She stopped, she grinned, she pulled funny faces – here was a model who interacted with fans and photographers and who seemed to enjoy playing up to the cameras. But that was the performance-loving Cara coming out and she was happy to 'act' for the media. Meanwhile the media continued to focus attention on Cara's family and features or interviews about the model gave her background history of being from a well-off family. Sometimes it was just mentioned, other times the media inferred she was nothing more than a 'spoilt rich girl' or a 'snob'. *Daily Mail* journalist Alison Boshoff commented that, 'Apart from her beauty, there is another thing which Delevingne likes to play down: her status as a high-society sweetheart.'

People were starting to take notice of the youngster and to her credit, she was happy to speak to press and fans alike when they stopped her. One eager reporter asked what she loved most about being a model and she described the friends she made and the places she visited – Rio being a particular favourite as she says she loves Brazilians: 'They are so cool, so much fun and they have really good energy about them.'

With a successful 'first' season of fashion weeks behind her, you might forgive Cara for taking a well-earned rest. But she was in demand and as she became more widely recognised, she was becoming something of a regular in the fashion magazines and celebrity columns, too. As the Olympics were coming to London, she took part in the '*Vogue* Fashion Olympics' feature and had to describe what event she would be best at, should she take part. For sporty Cara it was an easy answer, of course: 'I'd run long distance – I used to run for Hampshire county when I was young at school – I did a lot of long-distance running, I was quite good. I'm glad I don't have to compete with Jourdan [Dunn] in the sprint, though. In fact, maybe we should set up our own Burberry Olympics – that would be ace.'

In March, Cara took part in an interview with *i-D* magazine alongside other models who had to describe themselves and reveal what they would do if they were Queen for the day. Cara described herself as: 'hyper, loud, British, eyebrows, drama', and said if she was monarch for 24 hours she would 'make every Friday animal dress-up day and get rid of taxes. Vote for Cara, everyone!'

Editorial work piled up over the next few weeks and Cara was photographed for *Ponystep* magazine in a feature entitled 'By the Seaside', and *Lula* magazine, in a feature called 'Love out of Lust'.

In April 2012, Cara was one of the lucky few celebrities to be invited to take part in a feature for *Harper's Bazaar* entitled 'Dinner with Dolce & Gabbana'. In it, the design duo throw an Italian-style feast for London's It girls and Cara is snapped by fashion photographer Terry Richardson having a raucous evening with the likes of Pixie Geldof, Amber Le Bon, Eliza Doolittle and Tali Lennox. As the red wine flows, the designers egg the girls on to kick up their skirts and get on the tables, and they happily oblige. 'You know it's getting a little naughty when Terry says to tone it down!' laughs Geldof. The party was also joined by Bryan Ferry's sons, Otis, Isaac and Tara, and *X Facto*r judge and Take That star, Gary Barlow, to whom Cara snuggles up in the group shot at the end of the article.

Also that month, Cara starred in a *Grease*-themed shoot for website *Contributing Editor*, in a feature entitled 'Look At Me I'm Cara D'. It was a collection of black-and-white and colour shots and dished up a host of biker chic – in one vintage-style snap she is pictured in a leather biker jacket riding a Triumph with a cascade of blonde curls falling over her biker jacket. The fashion editor of *Contributing Editor*, Karen Clarkson, who styled Cara for the shoot, noted this versatility was the very reason she was so much in demand: 'Cara delivered in spades, showing just how dynamic and versatile she is as a model.'

On 7 May 2012, Cara and her pal Jourdan Dunn were once again invited to the Costume Institute Gala in New York and this time she was ready for her appearance on the red carpet. Both girls decided to make an event of their girly-getting-ready afternoon and teamed up with *Vogue.com* to showcase what they did in order to look red-carpet perfect. Taking snaps of each other in their dressing gowns and while having their make-up done by Burberry Beauty make-up artist Wendy Rowe, they looked like any other girls getting ready for a night out and enjoying every minute of getting glammed up. The only difference with these two was that it wasn't a night down the pub but an evening at one of the most glamorous fashion events of the year. Wearing a black knee-length prom-style dress from Burberry and matching Burberry shoes, handbag and studded gloves, Cara added her own twist by accessorising with a large white and rose-gold flying beetle necklace by her jewellery designer friend Dominic Jones.

'I was very excited and honoured when Cara called me up asking if I could kit her out for the Met Ball,' Jones revealed to *Vogue*. 'As a young designer you don't get many opportunities to get your work worn to such a high-profile event, as the attendees have the whole world to choose from.'

It was a mark of Cara's status in the fashion industry that she was able to showcase young designers and that people would take note. *Elle* magazine listed her and Jourdan on their 'best dressed' list for the event and it was a night to remember for the catwalk queens, who shared the red carpet alongside the likes of Beyoncé, Cameron Diaz, Jessica Alba, Lana Del Rey, Mick Jagger and Brit comic James Corden. Often described as the fashion world's answer to the Oscars, the A-listers were out in force for the gala, which was held at the Metropolitan Museum of Art's Temple of Dendur, a structure from Egypt first exhibited in the museum in 1978. That year, the Met Gala was celebrating the *Schiaparelli and Prada: Impossible Conversations* exhibition hosted by actress Carey Mulligan, American *Vogue*'s Anna Wintour and Miuccia Prada herself. Guests were treated to plates of baby lobster, American caviar and veal Milanese, as well as cookies in the shape of Prada shoes, while the mayor of New York, Michael Bloomberg, took to the podium to announce he was there 'on behalf of all New Yorkers'. Bruno Mars provided the entertainment and it wasn't long before everyone was up on their feet dancing – including Cara, who showed off her samba skills with Mario Testino. She later tweeted pictures of herself smiling away with singer Azealia Banks, looking like they were having a wonderful time.

The following month, Burberry announced that Edie Campbell would be joining Jourdan and Cara to make up a new cast of the Burberry Beauty campaign and Christopher Bailey explained why he had chosen the trio: 'We wanted to create an iconic shot and have worked with three British beauties – Cara, Jourdan and Edie – all of whom embody the natural elegance of Burberry Beauty.'

June also saw Cara feature in *Vogue* magazine in a shoot entitled 'London Pride', which was headed: '*Vogue* has a Capital time with Britain's leading lights'. She was described as a 'Sunny delight model' and the feature also starred pal Jourdan, who modelled alongside Olympic hopeful Louis Smith, plus Douglas Booth, Lara Stone, Rosie Huntington-Whiteley and Pixie Geldof. And it was *Vogue* again, this time the Russian edition, who used her for a futuristic spread the following month. Wearing a black short wig that looked like a modern Cleopatra, Cara pouted her way across a nine-page spread.

Towards the end of June, she attended the Serpentine Summer Party at Kensington Gardens, a showbiz bash that is a perennial staple on the London social calendar and an ideal opportunity for the capital's style icons to show us what to wear for the party season. Cara wore a floor-length black maxi dress to the party, which was also attended by Mischa Barton, Portia Freeman, Holly Valance and Donna Air. The *Telegraph* commented that Cara appeared to be having a 'Morticia Addams moment' in her all-black ensemble, but noted that she 'smouldered in the Chanel gown with classic clutch'.

With the social invitations flooding in, Cara was fast becoming a regular feature on the world's guest lists.

CHAPTER 7

MAKING MOVES

'It was such a dream come true...'

Modelling contracts continued to pour in for Cara, and she was proving a hit, both on the catwalk and in advertising for designers who wanted her to showcase their collections. She was fast becoming a talked-about success, and for most young girls that would be satisfying enough. But for someone who 'loved to perform', modelling itself wasn't ever going to satisfy such an attention-seeking appetite. Her experience auditioning for *Alice in Wonderland* – making it through the casting process to the very end but seeing the lead role go to someone else – had whetted Cara's appetite for more acting work. So it was at the beginning of 2012 that her acting dream finally came true when she was given a part in the costume drama, *Anna Karenina*.

Anna Karenina, a 1877 novel by Leo Tolstoy, was adapted by Tom Stoppard into an epic romantic film depicting the tragedy of the eponymous heroine, a Russian aristocrat and socialite. Keira Knightley was cast in the lead role of Anna, who is married to senior statesman Alexei Karenin but has an affair with the affluent officer Count Vronsky that leads to her ultimate demise. British A-lister Keira, who first found fame in the film *Bend it Like Beckham*, before starring as Elizabeth Swann in Disney's *Pirates Of The Caribbean: The Curse Of The Black Pearl*, Elizabeth Bennet in *Pride & Prejudice*, and in *Atonement,* alongside other A-list Brits Jude Law and Matthew Macfadyen. Heart-throb Jude is most well known for films such as *The Talented Mr Ripley*, *Enemy at the Gates* and *The Holiday* and as playing Dr Watson in the *Sherlock Holmes* movies directed by Guy Ritchie. Norfolk-born Matthew is probably best known in his role as Tom Quinn, head of Section D, in the popular TV show *Spooks* and previously worked alongside Keira Knightley in the 2005 costume drama, *Pride & Prejudice*, when he played Mr Darcy.

The film was being shot in Russia, in theatres used for the indoor sets, and outdoors where temperatures could reach minus 40 degrees. Cara was to play Princess Sorokina, 'the virgin', in the costume drama – the 'pretty little thing' that interests Count Vronsky, played by Aaron Taylor-Johnson. It was a non-speaking part; she was cast for her natural beauty to be the woman that inspires the jealous venom of Anna, who has an affair with Vronsky but is plagued by Cara's innocent virginal beauty. After Anna and Vronsky get together, Anna convinces herself that he is having an affair with Princess Sorokina; she hallucinates that they are making love and laughing about her behind her back and consequently throws herself in front of a train.

Make-up artist Ivana Primorac commented on *Style.com* that Cara was a 'joy' to work with on set. She also described the look she created: 'She is the catalyst for making Anna slightly mad and jealous, so we wanted to make her very beautiful and with a fresh, young look. I used these beautiful Armani blushes, which were key for enhancing the peachiness of her skin, and Chanel Vitalumière Aqua foundation since she had quite a tan at the time of filming and we had to make her look paler and more porcelain-like.' Not surprisingly, there was one part of Cara's face she didn't have to touch: 'She has fantastic eyebrows already so we left those alone and then piled about four kilos of hair on her head!'

At the premiere in London's Leicester Square in September, Cara posed on the red carpet in a shimmering metallic silver Burberry peephole frock, looking every inch the Hollywood actress, even though her part was, of course, relatively minor. She shared the red carpet with the main stars of the flick, Keira Knightley in a gorgeous Chanel gown, Jude in a dapper, buttoned-up three-piece suit, as well as other celebrities like *Sherlock* actor Benedict Cumberbatch and model Laura Bailey.

When questioned on the red carpet about her acting experience, Cara told one interviewer how the prospect of acting in this epic romance had been a little nerve-wracking – even for someone as confident as she: 'I was so excited I couldn't sleep for the first few nights,' she confessed. 'It was such a dream come true to be part of a Joe Wright film. Acting has always been my dream, even more than modelling. It's where I see my future. I tried to channel my experience of modelling but it's actually really different.

When I was being filmed I found myself posing but it's not just about that. I just had to really concentrate on the part and the character.'

But the question that journalists wanted to ask her most was what it was like to work with A-list stars such as Keira Knightley and Jude Law, knowing that Cara wasn't afraid to speak her mind about anything. 'They were so great, we all completely gelled,' she responded. 'After three days when you put a load of actors in one room they just have to create. It was so great, in my first time acting, to get direction from Joe and tips from the others. Keira was so helpful, she was really supportive.'

For Cara, the most nerve-wracking part of the film were the love-making scenes, but Knightley, who is seven years older than the model, gave her some useful advice on those intimate moments: 'Keira was really supportive, she just told me to lose myself in it. Forget about me and be the character, and I really took that on board as I was really nervous about the sex scenes, the intimate ones. But Keira had her own in the film and had done it all before.'

Now that she was getting attention from press and journalists from the film industry, Cara was keen to let it be known that she was serious about acting and was hoping to work with director Joe Wright on other projects. 'I love his films,' she effused. 'I'll have to audition for it, though! Acting is my dream.'

Generally the film was well received by the critics: the *Guardian* described it as 'a bold and creative response to the novel', while *Rolling Stone Magazine* commented, 'The story has been filmed many times, but never with this kind of erotic charge. Knightley is glorious, her eyes blazing with a carnal yearning that can turn vindictive at any perceived slight.' But it was *Now* magazine's Rosie Gizauskas who saw great potential for the youngster and wrote that she had a lot to offer the acting world in an online article entitled 'Is Cara Delevingne Going To Be The UK's Next Big Movie Star?'

She wrote: 'Cara had a bit part in one of my fave films last year and she looked drop-dead gorgeous on screen. But I reckon she should go for more roles. Taking up acting will silence critics who think she is just a pretty face. I think she should take on film roles by the horns and prove to the world that she's got talent as well as looks. Go, Cara, go!'

And of course her sisters and family were also very proud of her first movie role. 'They are pleased that she [Cara] has been able to fulfil a dream she's had since she was a little girl,' confirmed a close family friend. 'Although they're sure it's just the tip of the iceberg when it comes to future movie roles!'

The film was a success and Cara was getting noticed not just for being a model but someone with ambition. And the press couldn't fail to notice that she also enjoyed partying...

CHAPTER 8

STYLE AND STYLES

'I know Harry, he's a good friend of mine.
But suddenly it's like Mrs Harry Styles, die!'

A t the beginning of August 2012, before the month of Fashion Week mayhem commenced, Cara hit the headlines and gossip columns for reasons other than strutting her stuff on the catwalk or acting. She had been spotted leaving the exclusive Olympic Games VIP club at Omega House with Harry Styles, the curly-haired heart-throb from One Direction. The pair jumped into Harry's black Range Rover at 1am and sped away from the waiting paparazzi, eager to get snaps of the two together. A fortnight previously, Harry and Cara had reportedly been spotted sunbathing on the roof of Shoreditch House, an exclusive members-only club in London, and the press were speculating that they had got together earlier that summer when Harry's close friend Nick Grimshaw, Radio 1's breakfast host, had introduced them, and that they had been texting ever since.

Harry makes up one of the five members of the globally

successful British boy band, who first found fame on the reality talent show, *The X Factor*. Alongside his bandmates Niall Horan, Zayn Malik, Liam Payne and Louis Tomlinson, the 19-year-old has enjoyed worldwide success since auditioning for the show in 2010, in which the band came third. The show's head judge and record boss Simon Cowell signed them up to his record label, Syco, and they released their first album, *Up All Night*, in 2011. 'What Makes You Beautiful', their debut single, hit the number-one spot in the UK charts after becoming the most pre-ordered Sony Music Entertainment single in history and they performed the song in front of a worldwide audience at the London 2012 Olympic closing ceremony. Harry is known as the 'heart-throb' of the group, thanks to his infectious smile, flirty nature and boyish looks – his curly locks attract the most attention from his female fans. 'The chicks dig it,' he told his mum, Anne Cox, about his floppy barnet.

Snaps of the two youngsters together caused quite a stir in the media, thanks to Harry's growing fame and Cara's – in relation to Harry's – relative obscurity.

'Cara and Harry get on like a house on fire,' reported the *Daily Mirror*. 'Cara's a tomboy and has a lot of male friends and Harry's a cheeky guy and their personalities clicked right from the get go.'

The tabloids speculated over the relationship and it was discovered that Cara's sister Poppy had previously mentioned taking a liking to Harry during London Fashion Week in February: 'I want to sit on Harry Styles' lap, I have a total crush on him. He walked past me at the Aquascutum show recently and I was salivating. I like his curly hair and he looks like a little cherub.'

The speculation grew and rumours circulated that Poppy had asked him to sing at Cara's 20th birthday party. *The Sun* newspaper reported that the party was to take place in London on 12 August, the same day as the Olympic Closing Ceremony. An unnamed source told the newspaper: 'As Harry and Cara have hit it off, they thought it would be nice to ask him if he'd sing to her. Whether it's a special rendition of "Happy Birthday" or something else is undecided. It all depends if Harry has the guts. Cara's a decent singer herself so she'd appreciate a tuneful serenade.'

But despite all the positive hype that the couple were in a relationship, it wasn't long before Cara was on the receiving end of some pretty harsh abuse from fans of the heart-throb on Twitter. Not one to ignore abuse, Cara decided to repost some of the more negative comments on Twitter and respond to the more envious fans. One wrote: 'sorry to inform you, but you look like a dude :/ #NoHate #TellingTheTruth', to which Cara replied: 'hahaha well it seemed to have worked well for me'. Another fan simply wrote: 'I don't like you sorry', to which Cara retorted: 'fair enough, but you don't really know me and then you apologise after? Funny'.

After a while, Cara decided that it was time to put the rumours to rest once and for all and tweeted: 'please just stop guessing, you don't need to know'. It was a direct plea to Harry's overzealous fans, although later she caused confusion among the Directioners (the name 1D's fans are known by) by tweeting to singer Azealia Banks: '@azealia-banks: I have a crush...crushes are exciting...!!!' It was a teasing comment that did little to dispel the rumours as to whether or not they were dating, nor did her following comment, which was designed to thank those who had sent her supportive tweets: 'I want to say thank you guys to everyone who is sticking up for me and also how much I appreciate the kind words. LOVE YOU GUYS.' Later, she added: 'Everyone just stop hating on each other, LOVE IS IN THE AIR'.

At the end of August, Cara joined Harry and Grimmy for an evening at the Mahiki nightclub in Mayfair after the trio had been to see Rita Ora perform her first headline show at Scala nightclub earlier that night. It was to be a pivotal meeting with the 'Hot Right Now' singer; over the following months their friendship grew and the two became firm friends. Rita, who is only a year older than Cara, is a British singer-songwriter who found fame with her debut album *Ora*, which reached number one in the UK in 2012. The album had two number-one singles, 'R.I.P.' and 'How We Do (Party)', and Albanian-born Rita (her parents moved to the UK when she was a year old) also featured on DJ Fresh's 'Hot Right Now' track, making her the artist with the most number-one singles in the UK singles chart of 2012. Rita and Cara first became pals during the summer when they attended various parties with mutual friend Nick Grimshaw, and Rita later revealed in an interview the following year why they clicked so well: 'We are really similar but come from totally different backgrounds. I found someone who is exactly like me, who isn't really from my world. We just kept seeing each other and naturally started talking more and more, and now we are always together.'

It was a friendship played out heavily in the UK press, mainly because both Rita and Cara used Twitter and Instagram to showcase their various exploits together.

As the international fashion weeks commenced in September, it was back to business for Cara in 2012, as she flew to New York to take part in seven major shows in the Big Apple, kicking off on Friday for Jason Wu wearing bright red lipstick and with slicked-back hair. On Sunday there was a certain laid-back look to the DKNY show that Cara walked in, wearing long denim shorts and a long white shirt that suited her tomboyish personality: 'A brand born and inspired by the city of New York,' read the notes by Donna Karan. The Thakoon show paid homage to Cara's brows, which were greatly emphasised on her and the other models, while the Carolina Herrera show on Monday coincidentally had a similar look for the eyebrows – again, heavily emphasised – and a very grown-up looking Cara walked in a belted trench and swept-back hair.

The Marc Jacobs show, later on Monday, was a hit, with some famous faces all clambering to get a seat in the front row, including *Bridesmaids* actresses Kristen Wiig (with newly-dyed dark hair) and Rose Byrne, Alexa Chung, Amanda and Atlanta de Cadenet, Kelly Osbourne and actress Abbie Cornish. Immediately after the show, *Supermodels-Online* took to Twitter to exclaim: '@Caradelevingne rocked the runway last night for Marc Jacobs #NYFW', while *Vogue.com* tweeted: 'oh @caradelevingne, how we love your brows'. Those barbed 'dwarf' comments were long forgotten as Cara was congratulated by the world's media and Jacobs himself, who described her as 'sensational'. Next up, Cara rocked the catwalk at the Oscar de la Renta show in a neon-pink mini-dress complete with feathery over-skirt, while the Marchesa show was a highlight for New York Fashion Week as it was held in Grand Central Station, Manhattan's major transportation hub. The venue and the show itself attracted the likes of A-listers Kanye West and Kim Kardashian in the front row and Cara took to the runway in a suitably extravagant Grecian-style gown and bejewelled gold leggings and sandals and then a purple drop-waist dress.

Backstage at the Jason Wu show, she was asked why she liked the designer and the show. 'It's all about strong women, the music and the lighting,' she replied. 'It shows women for what we can be. It's a proper show.'

But it wasn't just the fashionistas who wanted to watch Cara, she had a following of fans waiting for her outside the New York shows, fans who wanted to be pictured with her and to video her. One fan (who describes himself as @247papstv) repeatedly told her that she was the 'hardest-working woman around', and even caught up with her when she stopped for a late-night McDonald's after one runway show. She didn't mind – she was happy to pose, pull silly faces and chat to those who had waited out in the cold to see her. 'I fucking love New York!' she proclaimed as she posed for the umpteenth photo while her taxi waited to take her back to her hotel.

Back on home turf, the press hadn't forgotten the stories around the talked-about relationship with a certain One Direction member and continued to try and find out the truth as to whether they were indeed a couple. One journalist stopped her outside the Topshop show and asked her to clarify the rumours, to which Cara replied, 'I'm not going to answer that question. I like to keep my private life private, that's all I'm going to say.'

She took to the catwalk in the Topshop Unique show on

day three of LFW sporting a side-swept fringe and a space-age dress. Jourdan Dunn opened the show, which was watched by Daisy Lowe, Girls Aloud star Nicola Roberts and Pixie Geldof. Afterwards, Cara explained why she loved Topshop: 'I used to come every weekend and spend my pocket money and just come and try and get as much stuff as possible. Topshop is the place where everyone goes for that one thing, like you go to a party and see all the girls in the same top from Topshop.'

Former model Twiggy took her daughter Carly to watch Cara grace the catwalk for Sass & Bide, dressed in a short cutout black dress and heels. Then there were shows like Issa and Preen. For Preen, Cara wore a floaty see-through mid-calf kaftan, while for Issa, her hair was piled high in a beehive and she wore a pretty white and flowery shift dress. For Mary Katrantzou, she modelled a stamp-inspired shirt-dress; by contrast, she was recruited to walk in the Giles by Giles Deacon show in a delicate blue-crystal dress and bright pink lipstick. The show, and its star model, proved a hit with *Vogue*'s Emma Elwick-Bates: 'I loved the fact that as well as the opulent occasion wear, he'd moved forward with it. That crystal dress on Cara looked incredible – dressy but insouciantly cool.'

In the Matthew Williamson show, a designer who had launched his first collection, Electric Angels, with the likes of Kate Moss, Jade Jagger and Helena Christensen back in 1997, Cara wore tailored shorts, a fitted blouse and a dip-dye jacket and had the honour of opening. Watching proudly from the front row was sister Poppy, model Portia Freeman and American 'It' girl, Olivia Palermo.

But having Harry Styles in the front row of the Burberry

show in Kensington Gardens did nothing to dispel the rumours about their relationship. Sitting attentively between Dita Von Teese and Dev Patel, he watched as Cara took to the runway in an over-sized brown jacket and small pair of knickers. Also in the audience were Wimbledon champion Andy Murray and his girlfriend Kim Sears, Olympic gold medal cyclist Victoria Pendleton, Tali Lennox, Olivia Palermo, Lady Victoria Hervey, Anna Wintour and Mario Testino. It was an impressive list of A-listers watching Cara walk, testament to both the designer's influence and the model's ability to attract the stars.

'Harry was smirking every time Cara came along the catwalk,' revealed one onlooker. 'He kept looking away to avoid putting her off, but you could definitely tell there was chemistry there – even from the audience.'

Later, Harry went backstage to meet with Cara and when asked what he thought about her catwalk show, he gushed about how 'amazing' she was: 'She [Cara] was great: she did a great job, she looked amazing! It was a great show. I thought the collection was really amazing – I've always been a big fan of Burberry. The colours are nice and subtle and they aren't too much and it's easy to wear,' he told a reporter before giving a giggling Cara a hug and kiss. He then got the gossip columnist tongues wagging once again when asked about his favourite look on a girl, jokingly saying, 'Burberry. Whatever makes them feel most comfortable.'

Professional as ever, Cara tried to keep the focus on the catwalk rather than her love life and was happy to chat about her Fashion Week essentials: 'Mine include water, eyebrow gel, face wipes and food – and sleep!' she said, before joking that once the four big fashion weeks were over, she was most looking forward to having a well-deserved break: 'I'm looking forward to my bed and sleeping once it's all over!'

But there was to be no break from the catwalk just yet and it was time for Cara to head to Milan to take part in one of her busiest weeks of catwalk shows, which was to include: DSquared2, Anthony Vaccarello, Just Cavalli, Moschino, Dolce & Gabbana, Fendi, Ermanno Scervino, Emilio Pucci and Trussardi. DSquared2 was a particular favourite of Cara's as it was no ordinary runway show: she had to walk onto the catwalk dressed in leather biker cap, chains draped around her neck, wearing a white cotton T-shirt, hot pants and leather-belted sandals, and then haughtily shrug off the attention of some photographers who pretended to hound her on the catwalk.

'I do love it when there is a bit of a role involved in my part at the shows. I love having that bit of direction. I enjoy acting, that's what I've always wanted to do,' she declared.

Front-row celebrities included Jedward, the Irish twins who shot to fame on *The X Factor* for being uniquely wacky, who explained that their Milan Fashion Week debut was down to wanting to watch 'hot girls'!

'Dean and Dan [the designers] invited us to come to the show and we thought we'd come to the women's show because of all the hot girls like Cara. It's a really cool look, it's all rock star crosses and jewellery and all of the high-tops are really high, they're really cool to wear.'

Also walking in Moschino in a monochrome playsuit; Dolce & Gabbana in a colourful ensemble in a show entitled 'Sun, Sea and Love'; Emilio Pucci, in which she starred with pal Jourdan Dunn in a printed shirt-style dress; Ermanno

Scervino, where she wore a pretty lace dress, but it was Just Cavalli that proved a highlight for Cara, who took to the catwalk in a flirty, floaty print dress. She also mentioned that the Trussardi show, in which she wore a straw hat and pulled off a dodgy short fringe, was great fun to do: 'Just Cavalli was amazing to be in and I had a lot of fun at Trussardi as well. We had fringes, wore flats and everyone looked very, very cool: it was amazing. Wearing the flats was weird because everyone always usually puts me in heels because I'm working with a lot of tall girls. I quite like being the short one now. I'm the shortest. Go, shorties!'

And despite her heavy workload in Milan, Cara hadn't lost the ability to have fun and was pictured backstage at the Trussardi show playing up for the cameras by pulling some weird dance moves – in the style of 'Walk Like An Egyptian' crossed with *The Karate Kid* – along with some funny facial expressions.

At the Gabriele Colangelo show she wore a bright orange square dress, while the Ports 1961 fashion house show had her in virginal white shift gown and white plimsolls, and Missoni's show in a blue-futuristic skin-tight top and knickers in powder blue and neon pink lipstick. For Fendi's show, which saw the likes of Hollywood actress Sharon Stone, *Charmed* actress Rose McGowan and Filipino fashion blogger Bryanboy on the front row, Cara wore a large white shift coat with her hair scraped back in a yellow hair band, and at the Iceberg show looked elegant in a short black dress.

With her flight to Paris delayed, Cara – complete with biker boots, black jeans, and still heavily made up from her DSquared2 show – jumped at the chance to watch a show for Cavalli, rather than take part in it and got chatting to the *Telegraph* about her experience that week: 'It's been completely mental, Milan: mental. DSquared2 just now was particularly great. I love the outfits they've given me to wear. Yes, I've enjoyed it so much but it has all been so busy that it's hard to keep my feet on the ground sometimes.'

She went on to say how much she enjoyed acting and loved having a role to play, as in the DSquared2 show: 'I concentrate on being myself on the catwalk now. When I first started, I used to try and do a certain thing that I thought was right, that model thing, but now I just get into it. It's a confidence thing; you have to have a certain confidence not to care that you are on the catwalk. One problem for me is that I was never good with high heels – and I'm still not the best – so it's about not worrying about that, it's about losing yourself and getting into the part and the moment.'

When asked what she was most looking forward to in Paris, the final of the four fashion weeks, she added, 'I'm looking forward to Chanel. It's always amazing. And Stella will be great. I love that show, you always get a great energy from backstage and get inspired by the music. It's all about the music, you really need that.'

So, it was time for Cara to hit the French capital. If she was exhausted, and with such a gruelling schedule you might be forgiven for thinking that surely would be the case, she didn't show it when leaving Milan. Travelling to the final stage of the fashion week tour, though, she was almost unrecognisable when papped coming off the Eurostar in a grey sporty onesie and bright green beanie. But even though she might have felt weary at that point, Cara wasn't ever going to show it. In fact, in an interview the following year when a journalist remarked about her non-stop work schedule during the fashion weeks, Cara revealed that she always hits the catwalk as a professional: 'Even if I'm exhausted, I always try to go into a show with a smile on my face. It's always good to try and bring the energy up. If I'm in a bad mood, people are going to act bad.'

Big sister Poppy accompanied her to the final leg too, sitting front row at the Chanel show as Cara strutted her stuff for the legendary Karl Lagerfeld. Also front of house were Kanye West and Jennifer Lopez as Cara took to the solar-panelled-effect runway in between 13 near-real-size wind turbines in a cute strapless denim number. The Louis Vuitton show was another big landmark in her career and supported again on the front row by Poppy, who watched her sister come down one of four escalators forming the runway. The models travelled down in pairs, in a nod to the styling of the 1960s and 70s, in cute mini-dresses.

British designer Stella McCartney launched her spring/summer 2013 collection in the gilded foyer of the Paris Palais Garnier with the likes of Kate Moss, Hollywood actress Salma Hayek and, of course, her dad, legendary Beatle Sir Paul McCartney, sitting attentively. It wasn't until the following season that Cara would take to the runway for the designer herself, but she was able to catch some of the action from the show, during which she tweeted: '@StellaMcCartney awesome show, so proud to be British!' in support of the designer.

In total, Cara walked a jaw-dropping 53 shows during the spring/summer 2012 fashion weeks, a huge achievement for a veteran supermodel, let alone someone who had only been in the industry a few years. Meanwhile the press was beginning to pick up on the intense following that she was creating and became besotted with her every move – designers wanted her on their advertising campaigns, girls wanted to be her friend, boys wanted to date her and social commentators, including Karen Hyland from *The Sun*, wanted to 'bottle up that fabulous mix of fun and sexy that Miss D oozes from every Burberry-make-up applied pore'.

'Is it just me or is Cara Delevingne everywhere this season?' asked the Twitterverse, prompting bloggers, online fashionistas and magazine columnists to chart her rise to stardom so far.

'What really sets Cara apart from her model compatriots is her personality,' suggested one New York fashion editor. 'It's hard for one lone model to pull the attention of the fashion press by being (seemingly) omnipresent. Yet it seemed like all the fashion crew wanted to talk about was British model and socialite Cara Delevingne. The British press in particular seem besotted with her but we [the American press] were pretty captivated too, and judging by the many street style and backstage photos in which she is pulling some pretty ridiculous faces, Cara is a model who doesn't take being beautiful so seriously.'

It probably helped that during New York Fashion Week Cara posted a picture on Instagram of herself dressed up in a giant hotdog fancy dress costume with the comment: 'Would you like some fries with that?' It received more than 15,000 'likes' and was picked up by the *Telegraph.co.uk*, who listed it as one of their highlights of the week. Fans wanted to be friends with her, girls loved her and while there was plenty of support for the phenomenal success Cara was enjoying, there was also the matter of her personal life that received just as much attention.

The interest in Cara and Harry's blossoming romance continued long after the fashion weeks, with *Look* magazine reporting that he had given her a key to his home. The growing interest meant that Cara continued to receive abuse on Twitter from Harry's so-called fans and things took a serious turn when she found the level of hatred aimed at her reaching frightening proportions: she started receiving death threats from her online followers. Speaking after the supposed romance had died down, Cara admitted she'd found the intensity of abuse aimed at her alarming – especially as the romance wasn't even officially confirmed.

'Harry is a good friend of mine, you know, but the thing is, everyone has been linked to him. Alexa [Chung], Pixie [Geldof], we've all been around him and then, all of a sudden, I get, "Ah, they're going out!" Those crazy fucking . . . sorry, little girls [One Direction fans]! One week I had 40,000 followers and then I had 70,000 on Twitter and suddenly it's like Mrs Harry Styles, die, bitch, die. And it's funny because I've always been quite good at taking criticism because I criticise myself a lot, generally.'

Good natured as ever, Cara joked that she sometimes thinks of a quirky retort to the more light-hearted tweets she gets, but doesn't understand how some of the youngsters can focus such anger at anyone: 'Some of them are quite funny, like sending me pictures of tweezers and saying, "Do you know what these are?" and I'd retweet it and be like, "No, I've never seen them in my life before, what are those for?" I'll give it back. Some of them can be quite creative about it, too. But the "die in a hole" ones? Like, whose nine-year-old daughter are you? That's fucked up.'

The reported romance between Cara and Harry wasn't to last, however. To confuse matters, at the end of September Harry attended the wedding of comedian James Corden to Julia Carey in Somerset and was spotted leaving the evening reception with Australian singer and actress Natalie Imbruglia. He reportedly received a cheer from the assembled guests when he came down for breakfast in the morning. Now the press focus was on Harry and Natalie (for the time being) and Cara was no longer on the scene as his reported girlfriend. Things were to change the following year, but for now the fact that Cara's name wasn't being linked to the ladies' man was a blessing for her management company. In November it was reported by *The Huffington Post* that Cara's modelling agency had been keen for their rising star to distance herself from serial romancer Harry over fears that it was deterring high-end fashion houses booking her to represent them.

'Cara's management think Harry is the wrong image for her. They believe that being linked with Harry could damage her high-end jobs and they want her to stay out of the papers. But if anything, it's just made Harry more keen,' a source told *The Sun*. 'Telling two young people "no" is just going to make them want to meet up even more.'

If her relationship with Harry was no longer getting into the tabloids, her growing friendship with Rita Ora certainly made sure Cara's name was in the gossip columns. The pair tweeted pictures together and were officially snapped by the paparazzi at various parties over the winter months. For an attention seeker like Cara, being in the spotlight with a famous face was fun and something she worked to her advantage. As the cameras began to follow her more and more, she discussed this new level of fame with her housemate, Georgia May Jagger, who confirmed, 'It's crazy with her at the moment. [We talk about her fame] all the time. She's being followed by the paparazzi and it's mad.' Cara moved in with Georgia in February 2013 as Jagger was looking for a pal to rent the spare room in her North London home. 'Cara had the money to pay for her own gaff but preferred to live with Georgia first,' a source told *The Sun*. 'She wanted to have some fun.'

But for the youngster there was to be no let-up: September brought about more advertising campaigns – Burberry, Blumarine (who wanted her to model for their autumn/winter designs), and High Street label Zara – a favourite of Catherine, Duchess of Cambridge – who had Cara act in one of their advertisements, getting dressed and larking about in front of the camera, with the odd pout thrown in for good measure. She was in her element. And in October, Chanel launched their resort 2013 campaign and cast Cara as their star. Dressed in Marie Antoinette crossed with Little Bo Peep-style costumes, she was photographed lounging on a gold-embroidered chaise longue, staring seductively at the camera, and in another shot barely covering her modesty with an arm while fanning herself with a large ostrich feather.

Karl Lagerfeld, who had showcased the Chanel resort collection to the gardens of Versailles the previous season, again with Cara fronting the campaign, was still taken with the French Revolutionary style for 2013 and chose her as she shared his vision perfectly. Newspapers were keen to keep reporting on the model and this was yet another reason to write about her. *Telegraph.co.uk* asked: 'Could Cara Delevingne be the next Keira Knightley?' answering their own question with, 'Model of the moment Cara Delevingne channels a very racy period costume look for the latest Chanel resort campaign, coupled with her set of unmissable eyebrows, desire to act and the fact she's just joined the Chanel payroll – she certainly stands a very good chance [of being the new Keira].'

And since Keira was a hit in the UK and the States, it seemed fairly fitting that Cara too should follow in her footsteps. At the beginning of November 2012, she flew across the pond to take part in the exclusive Victoria's Secret fashion show...

CHAPTER 9

SECRETS AND LIES

'The best advice I've ever been given is try
everything once so you can form your own opinion.'

In 1995, Victoria's Secret, the largest American retailer of glamorous lingerie, started holding an annual fashion show which is broadcast on primetime US TV. Suddenly, lingerie was mainstream entertainment and the shows involved elaborate sexy costumes, glamorous, eye-catching set design and the latest hit music from a host of A-list musicians. The event attracts mainstream celebrities – the likes of actress and TV presenter Tyra Banks and models Miranda Kerr and Alessandra Ambrosio have all strutted with their 'angel wings' – with special performances from top music stars. Each show, one lucky model wears the famous 'Fantasy bra', a diamond-encrusted brassière designed by a renowned jeweller and worth $2.5 million. In 2012 it was Ambrosio who received the honour. In February 1998, the Victoria's Secret Angels had been officially brought in to take part in the show and the most photographed supermodels in the world vie to make it into the 'angel' line-up – names such as Heidi Klum, Gisele Bündchen, Naomi Campbell and Claudia Schiffer – which is officially released before each show.

On 7 November 2012, Cara, Jourdan Dunn and Lily Donaldson formed a British invasion of the ultra-glamorous VS show when they took to the catwalk as the famed lingerie brand's 'angels' in New York. The show, which featured performances from top music stars Rihanna, Justin Bieber and Bruno Mars, had later been broadcast on US Network CBS on 4 December and was watched by more than 13 million viewers. And for the first time in its history, coverage of the annual event aired on UK TV on 22 December on the E! Entertainment channel. Speaking before it was broadcast, Karlie Kloss, one of VS's glamorous models, told of her excitement that the brand was now going to get a worldwide audience.

'I am so excited to share the VS show with all of the Victoria's Secret fans in the UK,' she revealed. 'Last year, I was in London when the show aired and I had to watch it online since it wasn't available on television. I'm happy that all of the UK fans will be able to watch the show.'

Taking part in the catwalk spectacular was a huge accolade for Cara's career – despite the numerous shows she had walked during Fashion Week, this show was to be broadcast and watched by millions of viewers. But while most supermodels would stick to a stricter-than-normal regime before a big show – especially as it would involve flashing a lot of flesh – Cara, being Cara, revealed that she had no plans to starve herself before the big day.

'I've been working every day in different countries so I

haven't really had time [to diet],' she responded when one American journalist asked about her diet in the run-up to the VS show. 'I had McDonald's for lunch the day before the show and pizza for dinner. I need to eat otherwise I feel faint – I get in the worst moods if I don't eat.'

But that's not to say she wasn't taking her role as a Victoria's Secret model seriously. She knew that it was a pivotal point in her career and she admitted in a backstage interview that she had 'never been so excited about anything so much!'

'This is the Olympics for supermodels!' Cara exclaimed. 'I am psyching myself up – actually I am freaking myself out! I am a bundle of nervous, anxious energy. Me and Jourdan [Dunn] are staying at the same hotel and we can't believe it's actually happening. I love that we are representing the Brits! There are lots of Americans and Brazilians but it's nice to be the quirky Brits.'

The process of becoming an 'angel' was a lengthy one, however, and as she sat in her satin pink dressing gown, with her hair being styled and her make-up applied, Cara explained why, despite the excitement of the upcoming show, she was also suffering from a bout of butterflies.

'I'm so nervous! A couple of weeks ago I did a Victoria's Secret shoot that made me officially join the family. I've been wanting to join them for a while, but my schedule's been crazy. I never expected to be chosen as a VS girl, it's so crazy. As a model it's the epitome of the sexy woman and all the girls I've met are all so lovely and so friendly, it's like joining family.'

But joining the family, as she puts it, isn't a simple process, as models have to be 'cast' for the show and attend auditions. It was Cara's laid-back, kooky attitude that impressed the casting panel, and she found herself invited to join.

'Apparently I went in, scratching my shoulder, slouching with a "I don't-really-care" attitude and he [the casting agent] said to me afterwards that he just loved my attitude and liked the fact that I didn't care and wasn't trying to be something I'm not. He liked the funny English girl. It was a bit like being in a talent show. Although he did say that people thought I might be a bit too weird for VS but he loved me anyway. That's true!'

The 2012 show had six themes: the first was the Circus theme, which set the pace of the show – all fun, glamour and glitter. Then it was Dangerous Liaisons, which focused on seduction and flirtation, and Rihanna performed her song, 'Diamonds'. The Grammy-award winning star, whose hits included 'Umbrella', 'Don't Stop the Music', 'Take A Bow' and 'Only Girl (In The World)', took to the stage in a black corseted gown slit to the thigh, long black lace gloves and thigh-high stockings. The next section was Calendar Girls, and Bruno Mars serenaded the 12 models who came out, depicting the 12 months of the year. It was in the fourth instalment that Cara's big moment came: in the section entitled 'Pink is US'. 'We wanted each of our models to be in pink and be different characters of different toys. Pink is cool, pink is hip, pink is us,' explained a show organiser.

Justin Bieber, in white baggy jeans, high-tops and vest, took to the stage for the second time that evening to perform his single 'Beauty And A Beat' as the models came out. As he danced about the stage, jumping on the props and moving across the catwalk, he was visibly distracted when it was Cara's time to come down the runway. She played down the attention from the teenybopper and continued like a professional, playfully sashaying to the end of the catwalk before enthralling the crowd with a cheeky blow of her toy windmill. It was safe to say, she was in her element! Later, Jourdan, who had the honour of closing that section of the performance, strutted past Bieber in a skin-tight white PVC catsuit.

The next section, 'Silver Screen Angels', was the most glamorous part of the evening, featuring luxurious and opulent lingerie, and Bruno Mars came back to perform 'Young Girls'. The closing section, 'Angels in Bloom', depicted each girl as a flower and Rihanna returned to the stage to perform 'Fresh Off The Runway' in a light pink lace robe, pink bra and high-waisted knickers. All the models and performers came out for the finale to rapturous applause, marking it as another successful show for the lingerie brand and for Cara, a fun way to round off a busy catwalk year.

During rehearsals, Cara was backstage on roller skates, trying to practise the art of skating down a runway and stopping to pose at the end. Dressed in a pink candy stripe bra top, matching mini ra-ra skirt and over-the-knee white socks, the idea was to get her to skate seamlessly to the front of the catwalk, little blue windmill in hand. But those who were witness to her skating practice soon decided that this might not end well and so she instead opted for lace-up red-and-white platforms.

'I'm not wearing roller skates; I'm not. I had the rehearsals in skates and it was too hard. I couldn't stop unless I was holding on to something, so it didn't work,' she later explained. 'I wanted Bieber [Justin] to move around the stage so I could hold on to him but that didn't work. Why can't he move around? It's my first show and I'm absolutely terrified as it is. Then I was told that I'm closing the section so it would be a lot of pressure and I'm like, "Shut up!" And then they tell me I'm holding something?! It's only a little windmill, it's fine.'

As well as making a career-long dream come true by starring in the show – and as an added bonus with her pal Jourdan – there was still heat surrounding her on-off romance with Harry Styles after a source told *Heat* magazine that 'Hazza' had sent Cara flowers and a present before she took part in the VS show to wish her luck.

'Harry is smitten with Cara and they are secretly very close,' the source said. 'Harry even thinks she could be "the one" but he's keeping things low-key. His dad has given his approval and thinks Cara is great. He sent her flowers and a present before she hit the catwalk for Victoria's Secret because it was her debut. He texted her all the way through, telling her how gorgeous and wonderful she looked.'

And while rumours circulated that the One Directioner was still keen on Cara, there was speculation from her end that she openly flirted with teen popstar Justin Bieber to make Harry jealous.

'She's still into Harry and joked she wanted to be pictured with Justin to make him jealous,' a source told the *Mail Online*. 'She told friends she was going to go for it with Justin, and she did. She was flirting with him backstage even before the show began.'

And while she was certainly excited about starring in the show with Justin – she tweeted a photo of the pair of them together with the message: 'At the @VictoriaSecret show with @justinbieber! so sweet!' – there was another international artist that Cara was star-struck by: Rihanna. Uncharacteristically, she was a little in awe of the Barbadian recording artist and spoke of her excitement backstage; 'I am in love with Rihanna! I am so excited to be sharing a stage with her. To meet her will be so exciting.'

Not one to let an opportunity pass her by, Cara decided to introduce herself to the global star, and from that point on the friendship between them was born. 'I went up to her and was like, "Maaam, you are so amazing, I love you, you look so hot out there performing. You put us all to shame,"' recalled Cara. It was a gushing greeting from the never-shy youngster, but she didn't let the moment go by without being a little cheeky either.

'I slapped her on the bum!' she reveals. It wasn't the first time the pair had officially met – 'I saw her when she was here [in London] two years ago doing a gig and then she sung at the Victoria's Secret show,' recalls Cara. But it was from that point on that the pair started seeing each other on a regular basis and began to hang out whenever they could. It was friendship which, given the fact they were both global celebrities and much in demand, was to have to fit into two extremely busy schedules.

Cara revealed to *Grazia* magazine that the friendship works well because Rihanna doesn't have that many close female friends that she can trust: 'She is the best, she's such a sweet, down-to-earth girl. She doesn't have that many girlfriends but we have a lot in common. I don't think many girls understand her.'

Later that month, another high-profile pal needed some

attention. It was Rita Ora's 22nd birthday on 26 November and Cara was determined to treat her new BFF to some fun. She Instagrammed a snap of Rita in a gold sparkling dress eating her birthday burger before heading off to enjoy a Big Sean gig in London. Earlier in the day, keen to show off her goofy sense of humour, Cara wore a tiger onesie to party with her pal and Rita copied the look in her own bird-inspired get-up. They took to Twitter to show off their looks, Cara in her famous tiger Japanese kigurumi (a kind of Japanese pyjama) costume in bright yellow, while Rita's blue owl kigurumi costume was a far cry from the glamorous heels and party dress that the birthday girl would normally wear.

Cara had, by that point, already become famous for her tiger onesie after travelling to New York with Jourdan Dunn for the Victoria's Secret Show in it, plus bright blue beanie. Jourdan had tweeted a photo of the tiger-suited Cara posing in front of one of her Burberry portraits while they waited for their flight. But the onesie look wasn't a new one for the 20-year-old: Cara was fast becoming as famous for her laid-back, quirky style away from the catwalk as she was for her glamorous outfits on it. Sometimes described as 'grungy', 'edgy', 'toy-boy-esque' and 'uber hip', her dressed-down style of biker boots, jeans and array of different hoodies was something that fashion commentators and gossip columnists praised. 'Here is a supermodel who is one of us!' shouted the various headlines, while the *Mail Online* praised her ability to be versatile in her fashion. 'Cara is loved for her ability to transform from girl-next-door to fashion vamp,' they concluded, as the model was snapped heading to and from the various shows in her trademark jeans (her favourite item of clothing), scruffy trainers and beanie hat. And it was this element of her 'not-caring' attitude to fashion that made her, as a supermodel who was meant to love all designer labels, so appealing to an army of regular girls.

The growing trend for onesies, and in particular, those with an animal theme, is often blamed on Cara's love of the comfy playsuit – in December that year, retailers saw a 52 per cent increase in sales of the garment, thanks in part to the supermodel's popularisation of them. And of course, it helped that every time she donned another wacky onesie, she wasn't embarrassed to post the pictures on her Twitter feed. Described by the *Mail Online* as 'The Onesie Queen!', the feature raised the question that Cara might start her own all-in-one fashion line after she tweeted a picture of herself in her tiger one with the caption: 'I think I should have my own line of onesies!' to her followers. They of course instantly tweeted back with their encouragement: '@ellastyles yess best idea' and '@freyaalister Yess!!! You should do that. Love you so much Cara'.

By this stage, it would have been difficult for any fashion fan to ignore Cara's penchant for dressing up, and *Grazia* magazine provided a run-down of some of her best fancy-dress moments, citing her 'fun-loving approach to fashion' as 'one big reason she's one of this year's rising stars'. In November, she was photographed in a giant panda onesie in a sleeping pose for *Style.com* and told the publication that she liked to 'wear it round the house'. During the Children in Need appeal that year, Cara took part in the special designer Pudsey Bear auction at Christie's, which saw 19 of the special Pudseys, created by world-renowned fashion designers, auctioned off for the charity. The event raised a whooping £152,000 for Children in Need and Cara took to the stage in her own bear suit – the same giant panda onesie. Having fun on a night that was focused on raising as much money as possible, she brought out the Pudsey designed by Sibling to auction. Giles Deacon's Pudsey, which featured £20,000 worth of Swarovski crystals, rendered the highest bid at £24,000, while the Louis Vuitton bear went for £20,000.

On the other hand, it wasn't just onesies that Cara was fast becoming known for when she wasn't hitting the catwalks. In fact, the wearing of any kind of fancy dress – headgear, wacky glasses and other comical accessories accompanied by silly poses – was another reason why she was getting so much press attention. She played up to it and to the regular paparazzi was becoming known as a 'goofball' – and it doesn't take a fashion degree to see why. At the beginning of October, she posed a pic of herself and pal Azealia Banks on Instagram channelling their inner mermaids when they dressed up for the Mermaid Ball, a massive party thrown by Azealia at the London Aquarium. It followed events held by Azealia in New York and LA, and the girls used it as an excuse to dress up – and why not? *MTVstyle.com* couldn't get enough of the pals in their party costumes and declared: 'Each girl looked awesome, Cara rocking the blonde waves and a blue and green dress, while Azealia worked a sparkly purple number.' Cara took to Twitter before she arrived at the party, exclaiming: 'Feeling very at home in the aquarium with @Azealiabanks getting ready to unleash the inner mermaid! Who's ready?!'

American model pal Karlie Kloss, who is the same age as

Cara and has known her since they worked together at New York Fashion Week and took part in the Victoria's Secret catwalk show, shares a similar sense of humour to Cara, which is why she's happy to goof around on the camera for Instagram, too. Cara tweeted a picture of herself wearing a bunny-rabbit onesie while Karlie got down on one knee in a mock-proposal pose, tweeting: 'So many proposals last night! How could I say no? @karliekloss @ poppydelevingne @cdelevingne Carlie Delkloss!'

As well as goofing around with her model pals, Cara had the chance to act more grown-up in the company of supermodels when she attended Kate Moss's book-launch party on 16 November in London. She rubbed shoulders with some of the biggest names in the fashion and entertainment industry, who attended 50 St James Street, Mayfair for a glamorous party hosted by Marc Jacobs to celebrate the launch of *Kate: The Kate Moss Book*. It was a photographic retrospective designed by Moss herself, who welcomed guests in a sweeping floor-length gold dress. Cara opted for a vintage Adidas bomber jacket and skinny jeans for the event, keeping the look glamorous with dark eye-make-up. At the party she posed alongside model and actress Liberty Ross, which was also attended by Florence Welch, Stella McCartney, Alison Mosshart, Boy George, Noel Gallagher, Davina McCall, Sir Philip Green and Edie Campbell. The likes of Pixie Geldof and her father, Sir Bob, danced until the early hours with Cara, as DJs Queens of Noize and Nick Grimshaw entertained on the decks.

Florence was the first to cut some serious shapes on the dance floor in her floor-length Marc Jacobs dress, and revealed she felt like a 60s film star: 'Cara and Pixie joined in later, giggling away to the beats of their friend Grimmy [Nick Grimshaw].'

Whether it was the luxurious cocktails on offer – guests were treated to 'Kate 76' cocktails, a concoction of Cîroc Vodka and Veuve Clicquot Champagne created especially for the event – or the fact that this was the first time Cara had really let her hair down for a while, the following day the newspapers were full of pictures of the star leaving the party looking somewhat worse for wear. The *Mail Online* showed pictures of a visibly drunk-looking Cara stumbling out of the venue and being helped into a taxi. This was the first time that the model was snapped in vulnerable condition – she was in no fit state to pose and her previously perfectly applied make-up was smudged across her face, a far cry from the normally child-like goofiness that Cara portrayed. *The Sun* made a big deal of the fact that Cara 'actually out-partied party-loving Kate at her own book launch', while *Entertainmentwise.com* reported that even 'rock 'n' roll queen Kate managed to look picture perfect throughout the night'. The pictures also showed Cara with a strange cut-like mark on her neck, which the press immediately picked up on. Again, it was the first time there were pictures of Cara looking less than 'flawless'.

'Cara seemed to make the most of the free bar at the star-studded bash,' reported *Entertainmentonline.com*. 'The model stumbled out of the venue throwing weird dance shapes as worried onlookers gazed at a sore-looking cut on her neck.' The article even reported that she might have got herself into a fight inside the party, saying, 'She looked like she'd been in a scrap as all of her make-up had come off and she was left with dark eye-shadow smeared across her face and her foundation rubbing off to reveal her spotty, blemished skin.'

Thefrontrowview.com simply stated that 'although she started the party looking stunning, as she made her exit she looked dishevelled and drunk.' But Cara wasn't fazed by the attention and fans were quick to jump to her defence: 'so what if @caradelevingne lets her hair down? No biggie, she is young free and single! #calmdowndear' tweeted one of her Delevingners.

November also saw Cara star in the latest issue of *Vogue Italia*, photographed by Ellen von Unwerth (who was, later that month, to present her with the Model of the Year award). It was a raunchy shoot for Cara, showing her topless in over-the-top 80s-style feather boas, sequined skirts and leopard-print skyscraper heels. The shots were risqué but fun, and perfect for Cara under the headline: 'It-list of 2012'.

And she certainly was 'it' when the British Fashion Awards came to London at the end of the month...

CHAPTER 10

DAREDEVIL BRIT

'I have a love-hate relationship with the word "moist".
I don't know why, but I kind of really hate it!'

The British Fashion Awards at the Savoy Hotel on 27 November 2012 would be a night like no other for Cara. With bestie Rita Ora on her arm, the pair strolled down the red carpet together at the event and posed for the cameras – Rita in a tailored white suit and Cara in a metallic Burberry dress, looking every inch a winner before it was announced that she had been voted Model of the Year. Going up against her modelling bestie Jourdan Dunn, who later tweeted a photo of herself, Cara and Rita together, Cara couldn't believe how she had come to collect such a prestigious award – '#still speechless,' she tweeted later while her Twitter feed was awash with congratulations from Delevingners.

After the awards, she received even more attention from the press, who asked her about modelling and being a catwalk sensation. But rather than focus on the runway,

Cara was keen to tell anyone who would listen about her passion for music and acting, and why she had career ambitions that didn't involve being photographed for a living. 'I want to be in the movies, writing movies,' she told the *Telegraph*. 'I'd love to be in a film with Meryl Streep or Martin Scorsese. There are so many things that I want to do, maybe like a possessed child or an evil something… I don't know. I would take any role!'

Newspapers ran features on Cara, who everyone was calling 'model of the moment' (*Daily Mail*), while also picking up on her family in articles entitled 'The Devingne Delevingnes' (*London Evening Standard*).

At the end of November, Cara showed off her playful side when she took part in *LOVE* magazine's video advent calendar, dressed in lots of different sexy, festive outfits, including a red and white striped Santa hat and roller skates – something she perhaps felt more comfortable wearing after her experience in the Victoria's Secret show! She also found time to showcase the autumn/winter 2012–13 collections in Glen Luchford's shoot for the November issue of *Vogue* and had fun with some rather mischievous puppies when she was photographed at a car boot sale on location in Sussex. Not forgetting the amount of parties and awards she hit the red carpet for that month – whenever there was a party, London's latest 'it' girl was invited – and Cara could dress for any occasion. She glammed it up at the London Evening Standard Theatre Awards in a gorgeous, low-cut Burberry gown, but also rocked the more casual look at both the Trapstar X Hitman party at Concrete in Shoreditch, wearing a denim jacket, Hudson jeans, trainers and a Trapstar beanie hat, and at the opening of the Leon

Max store at London's The Lonsdale Club, wearing a leather jacket, leggings and beanie.

In the hectic run-up to Christmas, she still found time to spend with Rita Ora, and the pair continued to showcase their friendship the best way they knew – on Twitter and Instagram. Rita posted a black-and-white snap of herself and Cara lying on the ground, gazing at each other intensely with the caption: 'All I need in this world of sin is me and my girlfriend @caradelevingne # bonnie&clyde #Thelma&louise'.

But there was also time to hang out with her newfound pal, Rihanna, who had jetted over to the UK on Simon Cowell's insistence that she make an appearance for the *The X Factor* final after performing the previous month during the live shows, when she sang 'Diamonds'. On the night when James Arthur took the *X Factor* crown, Rihanna performed two hits, 'Stay' and 'We Found Love'. Presenter Dermot O'Leary asked whether she was enjoying her time in the UK and on the show, to which she replied that she'd 'had a blast' and would come back 'anytime'. Simon Cowell was even rumoured to be in talks about getting her a position on the judging panel after being impressed by her knockout performances.

At the beginning of December, Cara worked for Chanel once again, this time heading to the chilly hills of Scotland to take part in the pre-fall 2013 show. As the snow began to fall, fashionistas, press and Cara's sister Poppy sat with warm coats and cosy blankets – provided by Chanel, of course – on their knees as Cara and the other supers, including Edie Campbell and Stella Tennant, paraded around the courtyard of Linlithgow Palace, birthplace of

Mary Queen of Scots. Designer Karl Lagerfeld chose the setting because he 'liked the emotion of it'. Explaining further, he said, 'This is about the queen of fashion and the Queen of Scotland – who was also French, you know.' Cara, who was styled in a regal-esque beehive, walked out as the chimney-pot fires roared, clad in a tartan overcoat, frilly collar and brooch on one occasion, and a thick woolly sweater and white tights on another. None of the models wore heels; Cara wore flat brown lace-up boots to complement the romantic, yet primitive theme of the show.

Praise from the press – fashion magazines and celebrity weeklies alike – continued to pour in. Cara was a face that readers recognised and liked to read about, even if the accompanying article was only about her pulling a funny face for the camera. *Grazia* magazine placed her at number five in their 'Best Dressed of 2012' and said, 'Cara could pull off the proverbial dustbin bag, her off-duty kooky style, combined with some stellar red carpet looks have earned her serious fashion stripes this year'. Accessories designer of the year Nicholas Kirkwood agreed: 'As much as Cara is a top model, she's also a cool, easy-going girl, with none of those diva antics. I think that's something that is very British.'

It was also very British to show a 'stiff upper lip', which is something Cara found herself doing when she appeared on the front cover of *i-D* magazine with a tarantula on her face. The giant black spider is snapped crawling across her cheek and covering her right eye and while the magazine is renowned for always featuring a celebrity with one of their eyes covered – Kate Moss had a blunt fringe cut over hers, while Karl Lagerfeld graced his with an eye patch – the December issue with Cara was definitely one of their most fearless ideas up to that point. After seeing the cover the UK press decided that brave Cara would have no issue with creepy-crawlies in the Australian jungle – unlike actress Helen Flanagan, who was on primetime TV at the time, struggling to deal with the smallest insect in the hit ITV show, *I'm A Celebrity... Get Me Out of Here!*

The shoot took place at London Zoo and Cara, wearing Sister by Sibling clothes and neon-pink eyeliner, didn't show any fear of the creatures she posed alongside. Her co-stars included a Komodo dragon, which she crouched beside, an owl, with which she embarked on a staring contest, a snake which she held aloft, and a lizard that looked as though it was whispering a secret message in her ear. She also posed alongside a ringtail lemur in a picture that had them both snacking from the same bowl, and in a treat for her Twitter fans, she tweeted this image with the caption: 'I miss this lil dude'.

Her fans were impressed and so were the press, remarking, 'Is there nothing she can't do?!' (*The Examiner*), while one blogger suggested there was only one word to describe the December cover: 'fierce!' The article continued: 'Delevingne is the most daring of the bunch after allowing the potentially deadly creature (with the capacity to render her blind) to sit on her right eye. Cara won't hesitate to be labelled the fashion industry's clown, like when she was asked to wear a hot dog costume, but this latest stunt shows a true daringness.'

She was one of eight stars to take part in the 'wise up' *i-D* issue, which also featured models Lara Stone and Arizona Muse, film-maker and actress Lena Dunham, and creative director of American *Vogue*, Grace Coddington. As well as showing off her 'nothing fazes me' attitude, her goofball personality shone through as she posed in a lion onesie that she'd bought from the London Zoo gift shop. The accompanying article focused on the words of advice that Cara had been given over the years, including: 'Go to sleep, everything will be better in the morning' and 'Have fun and enjoy yourself and keep calm and breathe. Rules are made to be broken'.

On 16 December, the *Telegraph* reported that Romeo Beckham, the middle son of David and Victoria Beckham, had been chosen by Christopher Bailey to star in the new Burberry spring/summer 2013 advertising campaign. Romeo, 10 years old at the time, was a youngster who the press saw as following in his mother's fashion footsteps after *GQ* magazine included him in their Best-dressed Men of the Year list. Former 'Posh' Spice Girl Victoria had a keen eye for fashion after launching her own VB label in 2009. She even had her own show in New York Fashion Week that year, so it was no surprise to many that one of her children – Romeo was her second son between Brooklyn and youngest son Cruz, and then there was toddler daughter Harper – would inherit their mother's love for the fashion industry. And of course hubby David, while an international footballer by trade, was no stranger to being in front of the camera either, modelling for H&M and Adidas and promoting 'Brand Beckham', which includes fragrances, hair products and, of course, clothing.

The campaign, shot by Mario Testino, saw Romeo in a Burberry trench coat larking about, while Burberry models Edie Campbell and Charlie France posed without moving. In other photos for the campaign, Cara had a starring role alongside Becks junior, but it was the youngster who ended up being the joker this time around, pointing and grinning at Cara, who posed in a nude leotard and cropped trench coat. In another image, the pair wear metallic coats, Cara in a purple fitted jacket and Romeo in a lilac one, jumping around the set. Christopher Bailey had nothing but praise for the young Becks when the full campaign was officially launched in April 2013, saying that the 10-year-old was a joy to work with: 'Honestly, he's the sweetest. Romeo loves fashion, completely loves it and he had a real opinion. I've known Victoria and those guys for a long time; they are just lovely, grounded, gentle, well-mannered little kids.'

The chief creator also went on to praise Cara's rise to stardom, an incredible journey from her days shooting in her first Burberry campaign. 'Cara is uber professional,' he declared. 'She enjoys it. She has no airs and graces at all, she is very kind. No matter how high her star is in the sky, if she comes in here she is exactly the same with everyone she has always worked with. I feel very protective of her.'

When asked what she thought about her rise to stardom, Cara revealed that it was her pals in the industry – Jourdan Dunn and Karlie Kloss – who have helped her get where she is today: 'Who is the wind beneath angel wings? All my friends, I have learnt so much from them – Jourdan and Karlie, if it wasn't for them I wouldn't know what I am doing. They are always like, Cara shut up or Cara do this! They tell me what I need to do!'

Later that month, Cara showed herself to be a good pal to Rita Ora when she jetted off to New York to support her pal, who was performing at the Highline Ballroom in Manhattan. Finding a gap in her busy schedule to fly to the States on 17

December, Cara cheered on Rita, who was supported by Iggy Azalea and Havana Brown. The four of them then Instagrammed a picture of themselves after the show enjoying a post-performance party before it was time for Cara to jet back to Blighty to spend Christmas with her family. It was a brief respite for the youngster, but some much-needed time off was in order. Her family insisted she enjoy Christmas with them as normal, and in true Cara style she spent Christmas Day in an animal-print onesie. But as it was a special day, she made sure the rest of her family also joined in the fun and tweeted a picture of her eldest sister Chloe in matching brown animal print onesie, too. Cara might have been tired from working, but she still had fun, and with 2013 set to be one of her busiest years yet, it was a well-deserved break.

'As she's been living out of a suitcase the past few months, being at home with her family at Christmas is just the break Cara needs,' revealed a friend of the family. 'She is only 20 after all. It's quite exhausting for her, not that she'll ever admit it!'

But while she was enjoying time 'just being Cara' with her family, there was one other special person who wanted to wish her a happy Christmas. According to *Nova.com*, Harry Styles, who had been enjoying a much-publicised romance with American singer-songwriter Taylor Swift, was keen to get back in touch with the model and sent a series of texts over Christmas after his relationship with Swift fizzled out.

'Harry's not used to being dumped and he hasn't got Cara out of his system,' confided a family friend. 'He wanted to wish her a happy New Year.' Cara was unfazed by the situation and was her usual friendly self with Harry, wishing him a happy New Year in return.

But Cara didn't have much chance to see in 2013 at a relaxed pace for she was soon hopping on a plane to New York to attend a dinner held by designer Jonathan Saunders in the Big Apple. The meal, on 10 January, was also attended by her pal Karlie Kloss, and Cara wore a striking ultramarine and bronze dress from Saunders' pre-autumn/winter 2013/14 collection – one of the perks of being a model?

But while her love life may have been less than straightforward, there was one person who was firmly in Cara's life in the New Year: best pal Rita Ora. To say that the friendship between them was stronger than ever was like saying Cara liked to sing, or act, or perform. The pair saw in 2013 not just as besties but in true 'wifey' style. Rita altered an image of Cara, taken backstage at Paris Fashion Week in February 2012, when the model was snapped wearing a Dimepiece 'Ain't No Wifey' top. She photoshopped the T-shirt to say 'Rita's Wifey' and tweeted the picture; she also gave her friend a pair of purple Nike trainers as a present for the New Year. Cara was over the moon, snapping herself in the trainers: 'my first pair of Jordans! Thanks Wifey @ritaora' and at the Chanel Show for Couture Fashion Week in Paris, she was thrilled to have BFF Rita watching from the front row, tweeting: 'so happy my wifey came to see me.'

Not only did the girls share a similar sense of humour (and love of onesies), both enjoyed teasing the media with sexy pictures of themselves in intimate poses. On 15 January, Rita treated her fans to a sneaky black-and-white sultry snap of herself and Cara puckering up in a kiss pose, millimetres from locking lips. The photo was taken for an official shoot with the iconic portrait photographer Rankin for a soon-to-be released feature in *The Hunger* magazine, but the 'Hot Right Now' singer couldn't resist sharing the snap of herself and wifey.

'No words... from one bad bitch to another. Thank you RANKIN @caradelevingne more to come hehehe.' Cara then shared another picture on Instagram with the tag: 'love my boo'.

As well as hitting Twitter with snaps of their relationship, the bezzies were pictured together at various events, confirming what Rita described as the pair being totally 'wifeyed up'. So keen was Rita to see her pal at the end of January, she didn't let jet-lag get in her way and just hours after stepping off a flight from Thailand – where she was spending time with the rapper Snoop Lion, formerly known as Snoop Dogg – Rita hit the town for a night out with Cara. The pair were snapped holding hands after leaving the Groucho Club, both looking a little chilly in the fresh New Year's air after spending the evening with Florence Welch, 'Grimmy' and T4 presenter Miquita Oliver.

But it wasn't just her girlfriends that had Cara hitting the gossip columns; since she'd been linked with the One Direction ladies' man her love life was also proving a source of interest. In an interview she did in the New Year issue of *LOVE* magazine, Cara revealed that she would like to be in a relationship but knows she is a 'bad girlfriend'.

'I want to fall in love, I think. I've never [been in love]. Everyone I know has been in love or in relationships now and there's only ever been... There's been people telling me they love me but it freaks me out and I just run, run. I think I'm a bad girlfriend,' she admitted.

Cara poses with her award for Model of the Year at the British Fashion Awards 2012.

© Getty Images

Above: Model sisters: Cara followed older sister Poppy into the industry, despite wanting to become an actress.

Below: Charles Delevingne, Pandora, Cara and Poppy meet Prince Charles at a charity event in July 2013.

© *Getty Images*

Above left: James Cook, Poppy, Pandora, Charles and Cara Delevingne attend 'The Animal Ball' at Lancaster House in July 2013.

Above right: With 'wifey' Rita Ora and godmother Joan Collins at the Glamour Women of the Year Awards in June 2013.

Below: Partying with older sisters Poppy and Chloe at Soho House in March 2011.

© *Getty Images*

Above: With former love interest Jake Bugg – both of them wearing Burberry – in January 2013.

Below: Alison Mosshart, Paloma Faith, Sienna Miller and Cara's rumoured flame Harry Styles watch on as she walks for Burberry during LFW, September 2013.

© *Getty Images*

Above left: Besties: with Ellie Goulding and Rita Ora at the Glamour Women of the Year Awards 2013.

Above right: Alongside old friend Georgia May Jagger and Kelly Osbourne at an event celebrating the September issue of *W* magazine, 2013.

Below: Onstage with Rita Ora at Club DKNY, June 2013.   © *Getty Images*

Above left: At the London premiere of *Anna Karenina* in September 2012.

Above right: With the cast of *Kids in Love* at the Red Bull Music Academy
Sound System in August 2013.

Below: On the set of a DKNY photoshoot in New York in October 2013.

Above: Sharing a joke onstage during the 2012 amfAR's Cinema Against AIDS during the 65th Annual Cannes Film Festival.

Below: Stunning photographers on the red carpet at the 66th Annual Cannes Film Festival in May 2013.

© *Getty Images*

The most
beautiful girl
in the world.
© Alberto Pizzoli/
AFP/Getty Images

Asked what sort of guy would make her ideal boyfriend, Cara revealed that an older man would suit her better: 'The thing with young men is… and it's not just young men, like I've been out with people 28, 29, and they're such fucking arseholes. It makes me think I just need to go out with someone who's 40 to be OK. I literally feel like I'm these boys' mothers.'

She continued to make her point, saying, 'I'm done with boys; they're so annoying. All they care about is their willies. I want to behave more like a boy. I want to be the strong one. People see me as being a crazy bitch but I'm the opposite inside. I just don't think that I trust men. That's the problem. I can appreciate a beautiful-looking man but he's not my type.'

Whether or not this was a direct dig at Harry the press picked up on her comments and still decided that there was hope for Harry and Cara when Styles tweeted: 'Today was the most amazing day I've had so far…In my life ever', on 13 January. The media decided it was because there had been a reconciliation.

'Cara likes Harry a lot but at the moment she's put her career and ambition first, but they're still in touch and Harry wants her back,' a source told Yahoo!

But soon after the *LOVE* interview came out, Cara found herself being linked with another famous face, upcoming musician Jake Bugg. While it was still early days and nothing was officially announced, Cara and Jake, then 18, were spotted on several occasions. At the beginning of February, *The Sun* reported that Cara and 'council estate music sensation Jake Bugg' were dating after they were pictured at a Burberry fashion party. The event, hosted for the young singer-songwriter in central London, was part of 'Acoustic Live' – an idea from Christopher Bailey to promote UK musical talent and up-and-coming British musicians who feature in the Burberry advertising campaigns.

The singer took to the makeshift stage at the brand's flagship Regent Street store and Cara was pictured enjoying the music. Other guests included Pixie Lott, model Oliver Cheshire and actor Harry Treadaway, but it was Cara and Jake who set tongues wagging when they left the party and headed off together in a taxi. If the 'Lightning Bolt' singer hadn't potentially upset Harry by being pictured with Cara, he had definitely upset the One Direction fans with his barbed comments about the band in an interview with *Q* magazine.

'One Direction? The young girls will grow up and forget about 'em. There is only [one direction] they'll be going after that, isn't there? Down. I'm interested in which songs artists will be remembered for in 50 years' time.'

With her romantic life under intense scrutiny (*Grazia* placed her on the front cover with the headline: 'Cara bags Britain's coolest boy!'), lots of work was still to be done and Cara took part in a fun, colourful shoot for the DKNY spring/summer 2013 season, snapped on the streets of New York in various playful poses. Then there was the launch of the Zara spring/summer campaign, plus she starred in the edgy Pepe Jeans spring/summer campaign, which saw her pose around the streets of London's Notting Hill in a more streetwise look. Following in the footsteps of Alexa Chung and Sienna Miller, Cara revealed that she was honoured to be modelling for the brand, which originated as a Portobello Road market stall. 'I'm very happy to be part of the team, considering the line-up before me,' she told *Vogue.co.uk*. 'Alexa and Sienna are also great friends of mine.'

Burberry also chose her to star in their new fragrance campaign, Body Tender, while YSL had her 'act' in their Baby Doll spring 2013 campaign under the headline, 'YSL Baby Doll Mascara. More than a mascara'. While the launch of the cosmetic wasn't until May, Cara kept fans up to date with her antics by tweeting about her new job back in January: 'Just finished my last day shooting YSL cosmetics! Feeling like a baby doll!'

The beginning of the year also saw American *Vogue* feature her in a 'Sweet & Lowdown' campaign, while British *Vogue* featured her in a spread modelling the latest look from Ralph Lauren with the tagline: 'Who better to show off the individuality and charm of this spring's collection than Vogue's Brit pack of star models, English thoroughbreds Rosie Tapner, Sam Rollinson and Cara Delevingne'. The shoot, which took place in Winchester at Avington Park, was a fun fashion day out for the girls; Cara, who was also on set with Edie Campbell, especially loved the live props that accompanied them in the photos – kittens. 'We wanted it to have a really personal feel,' confirmed photographer Angelo Pennetta. 'We also wanted to celebrate the incredible British models who ruled the catwalks during Fashion Week. It's great for us to back home-grown talent, we have so many fantastic models.'

Cara also took part in another shot for *i-D* magazine in the 'alphabetical' issue and was snapped in edgy black-and-white shots with fellow models Louise Parker and Magda Laguinge. Each model was asked what their favourite word was and Cara's response was, well, typically Cara: 'I love the word "mélange". I'd love a mélange of everything… but I have a love-hate relationship with the word "moist". I don't know why, but I kind of really hate it.'

It was a busy start to what was to be a busy year for Cara, but she took her workload on the chin and told one journalist that she doesn't let the pressure of being 'Britain's supermodel of the moment' get her down.

'I have a great support network – my family, my model agency Storm and people I work with in the fashion industry. And of course, there are all my followers on Twitter who stop me from feeling lonely. I love them all, they keep me grounded.'

Justin Bieber has his 'Beliebers', One Direction have their 'Directioners' and Lady Gaga has her 'Little Monsters' – now it was Cara's turn to introduce her 'Delevingners' as she affectionately calls them, and at the beginning of 2013, she had more than 800,000 followers on Twitter. Her profile and the accompanying quote –'Professional human being. I also love eyebrows and playing the drums!' – hasn't changed since she first set it up, but as well as her official Twitter account there are numerous Twitter accounts set up in her honour by her worldwide fans. She remembers the day when the first fan Twitter account to her eyebrows was set up and finds it hysterical that so many pay homage to various parts of her anatomy. But in tribute she follows them all, including: @YouDaOneCara, @Carascupcakes, @Thecaraarmy, @Carasnipples, @Caras_fingers, @Caraonesies, @Cara_tattoos, @carawouldgetit, @delevogue, @Carasmine, @caras_my_queen, to name just a few.

'I remember the day that happened… the day someone made a "Cara's eyebrow account",' she told *Vogue.com*.

'There was just one then all of a sudden there were like 300 accounts: Cara's thigh gap, Cara's eyebrow hair – my virginity is on there too, I think! But it's so funny, it's so sweet they all talk to each other, all my body parts they all tweet! It's like these people have found a family – weird but it makes me laugh.'

Speaking to *Vogue* one year later about Twitter and Instagram – which she describes as being 'a full time job' – she considered the influence she has on some of her fans. 'You never realise you have an impact on other people's life,' she told them. 'I don't anyway when I'm tweeting. I get girls tweeting me things like, "Thank you so much, you've helped me realise that being weird is OK!" I try and take time to speak to as many people I can as I just think if there are people out there who are having an awful time and dealing with so much crap in their lives and then say to me, "I love you as a model", I'm like, "What?" How can I not respond to that? It's weird but it's incredible.'

Cara also explained to *Vogue* the pressures of being in the public eye and the way young girls want to share their worries and anxieties with her as if they know her well: 'They talk to me about anything really, eating disorders, depression, family problems, especially because they know the things that may have gone on in my life, stuff with my mother. It's really sweet. It's horrible the stuff they go through. I try as much as I can to help by saying one little thing like, "hello", and it cheers them up. It's the coolest.'

Cara also went on to speak about how strongly she feels about the downside of social media and how devastating to youngsters it can be: 'Kids should speak to each other. They're horrid to each other online, they bully each other –

they should shut up and stop it. The problem with social media is there is too much freedom, it's too much too young.'

As well as making contact with her fans simply by saying hi, Cara regularly tweets those who ask about her modelling career and gives advice to aspiring models, all wanting to be the next Cara Delevingne. 'Don't let people knock you down,' she has said. 'Keep grounded and be happy, find yourself a great agent and have a good relationship with them. And above all, be confident. Even if you don't have any confidence, pretend you have.'

CHAPTER 11

HIGH HEELS AND HARD WORK

'The physical side of modelling isn't great, the getting ill, the not sleeping, the having to work 78 days consecutively...'

On 4 February 2013, the news that Cara was to grace the front cover of *Vogue* was announced, causing great celebration among her fans, who sent their congratulations via Twitter, not to mention messages of excitement from her celeb pals, too.

'So proud of my little sis @caradelevingne for her first Vogue Brit cover! #prodigies,' tweeted Poppy, while Rita of course also congratulated her wifey. 'So happy for my girl #vogueUK,' she tweeted.

Of course, Cara couldn't contain her excitement and was over the moon at being asked to be the cover star for the publication – not that she could quite believe the news herself. While the success of her career was never in doubt, having a *Vogue* front cover was something that was a long-term career dream for any model and now it was coming true for a girl who treated modelling like she could take or leave it at any time.

'Being asked to do a British *Vogue* cover – I didn't believe it at first,' recalled Cara in an interview with *Vogue.co.uk*. 'I think it's something that as a kid you look up to so much. It's one of the most shocking things that has ever happened to me, I think. I just stood back and had to get someone to pinch me. I was like, "What's going on?" I couldn't believe it.'

The issue, which was to hit the shelves in March during the most prestigious time in the fashion industry (the big four fashion weeks) meant that Cara would be seen everywhere that month – on the catwalks and the magazine covers. And no one was going to buy more copies of the magazine than the supermodel herself.

'It doesn't really sink in until you actually see it, that cover, that actual magazine, *Vogue*, it's so great,' she gushed. 'Especially the March issue, it's the big fashion issue, so it's going to be pretty amazing. I'm going to run out of the shop with 20 copies in my hand, going, "Oh my God, this is me! Oh my God!"'

British *Vogue* editor Alexandra Shulman introduced the issue as 'one of the most relevant of the year', and describes Cara, who was shot by Mario Testino for the cover, as the 'new name on the block'.

'Cara is one of those girls who combines energy, wit, enthusiasm and the kind of edgy beauty that marks her out from the general pool of beautiful models,' she went on to say. 'Emily Sheffield has interviewed her for this issue, and "Chasing Cara" vividly and accurately portrays what it is like to meet the girl who is unquestionably the model of the moment.'

To celebrate, the magazine paid a visit to Storm Model

management HQ to find out more about what it's like being a model-in-demand from the model-in-demand herself and how she felt about being shot by Mario Testino for the iconic cover. Five short videos were released by *Vogue* of Cara being interviewed, chatting away as if she's talking to an old friend at 50 miles an hour in an animated, yet enthusiastic style.

'I was really nervous, even though I've worked with everyone before,' she confessed. 'But this is British *Vogue*! It makes you so proud. I used to look at these models and be like, wow, who are, like, these goddess women? These superwomen? And then people say I'm one of them? You're crazy, that's not me! It's mad. The best thing about modelling is the clothes and the people I get to meet and the places I go. Every time I do a shoot, it's always different. That's the one thing about the industry, no two shoots are the same.'

In the past Cara has spoken about her dislike for wearing high heels for the fashion shows and it comes as no surprise to learn that she rates the towering heels she has to sometimes wear as the worst aspect of the job.

'I hate high heels. The physical side of modelling isn't great, the getting ill, the not sleeping, the having to work 78 days consecutively. That's crazy!'

This was the first time the press got an inkling that Cara wasn't completely happy about the modelling industry. Famed for her wacky, happy, kooky style off camera, and her professionalism in front of it, she had never spoken of her troubles on the catwalk before, but during the following shows in Milan, New York, London and Paris, the press picked up on her tremendous workload and made a point of asking the question, 'Is Cara heading for a breakdown?' Coupled with the fact that over the next few weeks, the supermodel would openly speak about her skin condition, psoriasis, and how she might eventually quit modelling altogether because of it, the press were ready with stories that speculated on her longevity as a supermodel.

But back to *Vogue*… Asked what advice she would give aspiring models, as she had said before, Cara was very clear that working hard and showing confidence, even if you don't have any, is vital.

'The point of being a model is all about confidence. I think of myself as a shy person, I know people won't understand that but I am, and I speak, that's how I get over it. I just keep talking! It's all about being a chameleon, too, trying to be exactly who people want you to be – if it's a day out or on a catwalk.'

And according to her, having too many clothes to choose from is a nightmare: 'I never used to think about what I wear; now it's a different story. Having more clothes makes it harder, though. I don't overthink an outfit – if I like it and it's comfy, I wear it. I love trainers, probably 'cos I don't like heels at all. Shoes and jackets and skinny jeans. The couture shoot. I love to design, I would love it! My own design of onesies. I love T-shirts, nicely-cut tops or T-shirts are so hard to come by. I would design some of those. I love modelling, I really want to be acting and music [sic]. I run around singing and dancing all the time, I bring it into my daily life.'

Asked who she rated as the 'top' supermodel, there was no hesitation – Kate Moss, who she believes has enjoyed an 'unbelieveable' career. But Cara didn't just have supermodels on the brain and of course spoke about her admiration for leading ladies in the movie industry: 'Away from modelling, Meryl Streep's career is incredible. Her and Judi Dench. And Charlize Theron, she's another one. She's incredible and she started off as a model. She's the most beautiful woman – an Amazonian goddess – and then she did *Monster*, where she plays this really ugly person, a thug. I want to do that; I'd love to play a crazy cave woman or a demon-possessed child. I want to be that ugly, that ugly is the most beautiful. Scorsese, Spielberg, Tarantino, Peter Jackson, I'm ready! I can sing, I can dance. Hire me!'

Speaking about the downsides of being a supermodel and having your face plastered everywhere, Cara revealed that she wasn't so keen on the trappings that fame can bring: 'The press attention can get a bit much, not the press as such but the fame. It's so weird when people are shouting your name! I love having photos with fans, I'm always like, "You want your photo with me? Sure!" And I'll put my arm around them. But then it gets different when people are just grabbing you and that's the flipside, when it takes me half an hour to get to my car after a show, that's when it can get a bit much, a bit scary.'

In February Cara also graced the pages of W *Magazine* in a shot entitled 'Heavenly Creatures'. Snapped among the gorgeous backdrop of a crystal-clear ocean, knee-deep in the water, she wears a short bobbed wig beehived up above her forehead, giving her an almost regal look. The magazine ran the photos alongside the tagline, 'Model Cara Delevingne ascends to the pantheon of runway stars', while claiming the 'bushy-browed wild child who cites Charlie Chaplin as her style icon and Milan-based street-wear brand You Need This Shit as a favourite label has a quirky sense of humour that the fashion world has found captivating.'

But it wasn't to be the last of her magazine coverage that month – she also appeared in a glamorous shoot that saw her naked in the bath, using her hands to cover her modesty. Accompanying the photos was a quick-fire Q&A about her personal life that Cara answered in a tongue-in-cheek kind of way when asked if she could name all five members of One Direction...

'Liam, Zayn, Louis, Niall and... who's the other one?'

She also revealed that she loved watching The X Factor and EastEnders, thinks Prince Harry is 'cute', likes to share her bath with 'bubbles and ducks, live ones, two if possible' and does sometimes worry about her weight: 'I wouldn't mind having a bit more junk in my trunk! I wanna be able to twerk it out.'

Tweeting was also a regular part of her everyday 'job' and she continued to post quirky sayings and odd messages every now and again to keep her Delevingners on their toes: 'That's life! Haters gonna hate! Vibrators gonna vibrate!' she posted in February, along with another wacky reference to her brows: 'Don't worry! My eyebrows are like a boomerang, they always come back.'

Fashion month was looming and on 7 February, New York Fashion Week got underway. Over the course of the next month, Cara was to walk in more than 40 catwalk shows (42 to be exact), not to mention finding time to party with her pals in-between. StyleCaster.com labelled her 'the busiest girl at fashion week' and tracked the shows she walked in what was 'her busiest season ever'. In New York alone she would be walking in 11 shows over the course of five days.

However, NYFW wasn't all about Cara's busy workload. That weekend the much-anticipated 'Storm Nemo' was set to blast the city with heavy snow, rain and high winds and had seen many flights to and from the Big Apple grounded. The storm meant that even some of the most hard-core fashion followers wouldn't risk becoming stranded, but freezing temperatures didn't deter the professionals and it wasn't long before websites were instructing fans that even though a Winter Advisory warning of two feet of snow had been published, this was no time to 'slack off' as 'there is fashion to report on, people!'

Tom Cruise's ex-wife Katie Holmes decided to cancel the final presentation of her fashion line Holmes & Yang intended for Friday, 8 February due to the adverse weather conditions and the fact that she didn't want to be late to pick up her daughter, Suri, from school. Meanwhile the biggest upset came from Marc Jacobs when he had to postpone his show. The designer, who was meant to showcase his designs on 11 February was forced to reschedule his collection to the last day of the week, normally the quietest in the calendar to allow people to fly to Britain in anticipation for the start of London Fashion Week, as there had been a delay in the transportation of important essentials – shoes, fabrics and bags.

Robert Duffy, Jacobs' business partner, issued a statement: 'Marc and I are extremely sorry for this inconvenience. We just want to have the best show possible and show all the products that our design team has been working on so hard for the last six months. We completely understand if people have to get on a plane to go to London. We're not expecting people to change their plans or other plans just for us.'

For Cara, it was business as usual and her first appearance on the catwalk was for Jason Wu on Friday 8; she strode down the runway in a short white dress and black gladiator strappy heels cheered on by her greatest supporter, big sister Poppy, and *Girls* actress Allison Williams. Later that afternoon she hit the catwalk for Rag & Bone in a short black shirt-dress and suspenders and unusual eye-make-up – eye-liner inspired by the sixties cat-flick look – and observed by Hollywood actress Drew Barrymore in the front row.

After a day off, she started Sunday, 10 February at the Derek Lam show in a deep-navy fringed dress and sleeveless fur jacket; the designer posted a video online of Cara singing to herself while having her hair and make-up done for the show. She was unaware that she was being recorded and her voice sounded so effortlessly soulful, it prompted the *Telegraph.co.uk* to ask: 'Is there anything this girl can't do?!' An hour later, it was time for Cara to be seen and not heard as she hit the runway for DKNY in a shirt and beige jacket, looking nude and glossy. But that wasn't the end of her schedule that day: there was a frantic race across Manhattan to star in Diane von Furstenberg's show, and she even had time for a cuddle with the celebrated designer (who planted a big smacker on Cara's cheek) backstage. The model Instagrammed herself in a 'Kiss Me' T-shirt before the show and had the chance to chat to *PopSugar* journalist Allison McNamara, who described her as 'one of the most in-demand models right now', about her style of fashion after the show.

'What's my style? I'm a bit of a tomboy. I keep it casual but try and make people laugh with a slogan T-shirt or something. I'm normally in a hat and a bomber jacket, quite low-key. How do I prep for fashion week? I don't have much holiday so I try and take as much as I can beforehand. I'm the most stressed-out person anyway; it's really hard. I don't ever sit still! I find it hard to sit still. The relationships I've made in the fashion industry are probably the best thing about working in the industry. Working as a model is like working with a big unconventional family. All the people are kind of weird and wacky. It's fun!'

She led the way in the DVF show and had the honour of closing the show too, in a slender red-and-white dress. Walking out backstage, the models faced posters that read, 'Life is a party' and 'Smile, be happy, be you' to instruct them to look happy on the catwalk. While the other models were noted as being fairly stony-faced on the runway, Cara took the instructions to heart and sported a carefree smirk throughout the show. Later that evening, she headed to the Park Avenue Armory, where she was the standout model in Tommy Hilfiger's show, rocking a beanie in a sixties-style ensemble. But there was no rest after such a busy day and with a call time of roughly two hours, it was an early start for Cara at Carolina Herrera's show at 10am the next morning, after which she was able to catch up on a few hours' rest before walking in the Marc by Marc Jacobs show.

Backstage she spoke to American journalist and stylist Sally Lyndley about what she likes and doesn't like about

NY Fashion Week: 'I love catching up with my friends and taking part in this crazy, dysfunctional family. I don't like being shouted at, though, or getting pins, you know those big pins you get? And being zipped into things too. Enough! I love Marc by Marc Jacobs though, and I'm in a big blue onesie today, it's so totally me! Marc's designs are always so chic yet young-looking. That's a look that I try and go for in everyday life.'

Taking to the catwalk in blue printed playsuit and big, wavy hair, Cara was the talk of the show. She was pictured backstage with American singing star Miley Cyrus and they shared a face-pulling moment for the cameras. The frolics continued backstage as usual whenever Cara was at a show, goofing around with the other models and designers. This 'takes herself with a pinch of salt' attitude is exactly the reason why she is so popular – she even tried to cheer up Marc Jacobs after the disappointment of his postponed show by offering to take him to a gay bar. Stylist Katie Grand told *Grazia* magazine, 'Of course she'll generate publicity, but for me she's just great fun to be around. When she had her fitting for Marc Jacobs she squeezed him on the shoulder and said, "Shall we go for a drink at the nearest gay bar?" She doesn't do it to get on, she's just naturally sociable and fun.'

The next day, 12 February, Cara was up bright and early at the very serene and elegant Pierre Hotel for Tory Burch's show. Among the sparkling chandeliers and with soft piano music playing in the background, she sashayed down the catwalk in an elegant two-piece ensemble, a cropped nude and white jacket and high-waisted pencil skirt. With a side-swept fringe and barely-there make-up, she oozed aristocratic glamour. Two hours later, heavily made-up this time with thick black eyeliner, she was on the Rodarte runway with Jourdan Dunn, being watched from the front row by the likes of photographer Terry Richardson and fashion editor Anna Dello Russo and wearing a black shift dress with heavy white collar draped across her shoulders and a netted side-split. That evening she took part in the Oscar de la Renta show, one of the most glamorous, talked-about events of the season, in bright red lipstick that matched her heels, a thick fur scarf wrapped across her shoulders, a fitted-cropped jacket, patterned A-line skirt and elbow-length pink gloves.

The next day it was all about monsters and Halloween in the Jeremy Scott show, as she strutted her stuff in a green cropped bra-top, mini-skirt with a cartoon monster across it and bright yellow lace-ups. Her hair was black and piled messily on her head while her make-up was kept pale with contrasting green eyeshadow. Backstage, Cara revealed photos from behind-the-scenes at Scott's show, including a shot of her kissing another model with the caption: 'Jeremy Scott is the 1!'

The feeling was mutual, it seems: Scott had his photo taken with Cara after the final fitting and described her as his 'love of love'.

Next on Cara's schedule was the Michael Kors show, which saw her in bright, bold block colours, her hair scraped back in a tight ponytail and wearing a long blue futuristic jacket and cropped leggings. There was something of a Hollywood get-together in the front row with the likes of Michael Douglas, actress/singer Willow Smith and her mother Jada Pinkett Smith and actor Cheyenne Jackson all watching the action. In the evening, even though Paris Fashion Week was still two weeks away, there was a decidedly French, by way of the sixties, style to proceedings on the Anna Sui catwalk. The show opened to Cara and the other models doing a dance-routine at the top of the catwalk – to Kylie's hit single, 'The Locomotion', in French. With her hair in a tight ponytail, Cara wore a psychedelic green-patterned dress and sparkly green tights. To say that New York Fashion Week was proving to be somewhat demanding was putting it mildly and Cara openly admitted to one journalist backstage at the Anna Sui show that the schedule was crazy: 'This is, I think, the craziest industry. I mean, I love it but the fashion industry is like a big fucked-up dysfunctional family, but everyone's mad and amazing and everyone's so different.'

Poppy was busy visiting all the New York shows so only saw Cara a couple of times, but she nonetheless showed her support when she posted a picture of the pair of them on Instagram declaring how much she was missing her younger sibling: 'Shnuggle bugs Cara Delevingne – missing you.' And of course, there was another person who wasn't entirely happy with Cara's workload: BFF Rita, who wasn't able to support her pal at the shows due to her UK tour. So to show how much she missed her Cara, she posted a picture of the pair of them nearly kissing, taken at the beginning of the year, with the message: 'I miss the wifey... baby come closer Haa!'

The day before Valentine's Day, Rita revealed in an interview with *The Sun* that she had officially taken Cara 'off the market' and she wasn't going to share her with any man: 'She's officially mine. She's like untouchable. I've taken her off the market. We call each other "wifey". You know what a wifey means? It's like your other half, like when you get married. That's your wife!'

She went on to moan about how much she was missing Cara, being across the pond and strutting her stuff on the catwalk: 'Cara's in New York for Fashion Week so she couldn't make this week [to her London show]. I'm a bit sad. Of course, we talk all the time, she was just texting me now. I have no time for the opposite sex at the moment, strictly none. I've only got a wifey!'

Cara's coverage in the American press continued to grow, thanks to her popularity on the catwalk. The *New York Post* dubbed her 'the new Kate Moss' while *The Wall Street Journal* reported that Jason Wu and Carolina Herrera had already booked her for the next season to showcase their spring/summer 2014 range.

Whether or not Rita's threats of Cara being 'officially' hers scared off any potential Romeos, there wasn't much time for romance for Cara on Valentine's Day. She did, however, manage to give Jake Bugg a saucy Valentine's Day treat even though they were on opposite sides of the pond when a video of her in sexy underwear was released on *LOVE* magazine's website. It shows Cara dancing around in a skimpy pair of knickers and a bra to the soundtrack of En Vogue's 'Whatta Man'. She is also seen hugging a heart-shaped box of chocolates, and lying down on a bed strewn with glistening Swarovski crystals before playfully jumping up and down on the mattress. In the final shot, she is seen on the bed with two loveheart sweets over her eyes and mouthing, 'I love you' to the camera. Awww... Jake was a lucky man! The *Mail Online* reported that after that public display of affection, 'they are fast becoming the hottest celebrity couple in the UK'. *Grazia* magazine also noted how the romance was blossoming, despite their busy schedules. 'Cara is really into Jake and though they're both very busy, they are trying to make it work,' a source told the magazine.

But there was to be no romantic candlelit dinner for Cara, as around 1am on Valentine's Day she was spotted ordering a McDonald's by 247@papstv, who questioned why she was in the fast-food outlet and what she would be ordering – it was a Big Mac, large fries and a Coke. While most people would try and ignore the intrusion, especially at such a late hour and when clearly exhausted, Cara, who was wearing bright blue jeans, black jacket and Adidas Originals by Jeremy Scott, smiled and chatted away happily as the reporter wished her a happy Valentine's Day.

There wasn't time for much of a break as the rescheduling of the Marc Jacobs show had been announced and it was to fall on the last day of New York Fashion Week. Storm Nemo had forced most of the British press, fashion commentators and other models to catch their flights back to Blighty sooner rather than later, but Cara strode out on the circular runway without a care in the world, clad in a short sweater dress, a toy fox curled round her neck, and a short cropped black wig. Celebrities also stuck by Jacobs and the likes of Hollywood actress Christina Ricci, film director Sophia Coppola, Blondie's Debbie Harry and US stylist, editor and designer Rachel Zoe were all spotted enjoying the action. Due to the hastily rescheduled show, there was barely time to catch her breath before Cara jumped in a taxi headed for the airport on an overnight flight that was to take her back to the UK in time for London Fashion Week. And what did she wear for her long-haul journey? A trusted, comfy onesie, of course...

CHAPTER 12

THE ENDLESS WALK

'Would I ever want to pack it all in?
Only to run away with the circus.'

Back on home soil, there wasn't much time for Cara to catch her breath as the schedule for autumn/winter 2013 at London Fashion Week was fierce. The press were on to her as soon as she arrived and left the shows, leading her to comment on the intrusion in a interview with *The Times*: 'Fame, do I like it? No. It has brought a lot for me in my career but there are a lot of downsides to it. You give up your privacy. I did it to myself but not to my family and to my friends. You don't ask for it, it just kind of happens, you just have to deal with it and you just live with it.'

On how she dealt with fame, she said, 'People always ask me how you deal with it and you just have to. It's not a nice thing. I'm lucky there are times when I can nip out and find places [away from photographers] but they are lethal in England, they are really bad, the paps. You have to try and be nice to them; that's the worst thing because they are always after you, but if you are rude to them, they will try and get the worst shots of you.'

LFW week kicked off with a very fashionable affair at 10 Downing Street, where Samantha Cameron welcomed designers, models and celebrities to celebrate the start of another week showcasing the best fashion in the capital. Designers Christopher Bailey, Henry Holland and Matthew Williamson rubbed shoulders with L'Wren Scott, Anna Wintour, Salma Hayek, Helena Christensen and Donatella Versace and prompted Natalie Massenet, chairman of the British Fashion Council, to remark that London Fashion Week was now 'unmissable' and with the *Telegraph* speculating one of the reasons for this was because 'We have the new most famous model in the world: Cara Delevingne.'

Despite taking part in eight London shows, Cara was pictured so many times over the course of the next seven days that you might be forgiven for thinking she had walked in all 56. The press were hot on her heels due to her winning the Model of the Year, with photos of her eating, looking tired and out partying filling the pages of magazines and online articles. The *Mail Online* were keen to find out her secrets on looking good throughout the season 'despite her packed schedule and hectic lifestyle' and she revealed that the answer was a Venus Freeze Facial, a non-surgical skin-tightening procedure.

'Dude, it's insane,' admitted Cara. 'My skin gets worse during the shows because of all the travelling so I prepare at the beginning of the season by having Venus Freeze face lift facials, which zap heat onto your skin. You come out with plump skin because it helps to create collagen.'

On Saturday, 16 February, Cara kicked off the week at

the Sister by Sibling show. It was 9.30 in the morning and the star strode out in a giant knitted beret hat, flowery sweater and fur cuffs under a leotard. At 5pm that day, it was time for the Issa show. She was pictured backstage with her hair in rollers, smiling at the cameras and pointing to a 'Cute as f#per centk' T-shirt before she opened the show wearing a fedora hat and floor-length dress covered in Aztec patterns, with waves of fabric billowing out behind her. Issa is one of the Duchess of Cambridge's favourite designers and Cara brought out Daniella Issa Helayel (best known for her middle name) to a round of applause at the end of the show, smiling and clapping alongside her.

Rihanna was also in London showcasing the new collection that she had designed for high street store River Island on the Saturday, and despite having walked in two shows that day Cara made sure she was front row to support her pal. She took snaps on her phone and danced along to the RiRi soundtrack as the models came out, giving the designer a standing ovation when she made an appearance at the end of the show.

'Rihanna is great, I love her,' Cara gushed to one reporter backstage. 'She's amazing! She had such a good collection, her designs are unbelievable, so incredible. Really good clothes. I have half the wardrobe already, I'm so excited!'

Then it was time to celebrate in style and Rihanna decided to snub her own River Island after-party, much to the upset of those who had worked on her show, to party with Cara and they headed to The Box nightclub in Soho. But things got a little scary for the ladies when the *Mail Online* reported that an irate fan of the 'Diamonds' singer threw a Lucozade bottle at her, causing her security staff to chase him down in the street. It was a late night for Cara, who was still out at 2am despite having three shows to walk in the following day...

On Sunday, 17th, Cara took to the catwalk for the Topshop Unique show at the Tate Modern; backstage, she was keen to show off her dancing skills and get her fellow models giggling when she performed her version of the Harlem Shake with partner-in-crime Jourdan Dunn. At 3pm she opened the show for the high-street chain in a black tank top and leather skirt worn under a knee-length black trench coat. The show, despite the collection indulging in nineties nostalgia, was also in collaboration with Google, who had created Model Cam, a camera positioned on the models to show the rest of the world what it was like walking in their shows. Positioned on four of Topshop's famous model faces – Cara, Jourdan, Rosie Tapner and Ashleigh Good – the cameras streamed footage of the models onto the Google website from their first fittings for the show to the moment they hit the catwalk. It also broadcast footage of the 'red carpet hangout', which allowed viewers to be part of the hustle and bustle of the celebrity arrivals. Hollywood actress Kate Bosworth, Olivia Palermo, Pixie Geldof and Daisy Lowe were all in attendance. And there was also a member of One Direction on the front row, but Louis this time, not Harry! This wasn't as suspicious as it first seemed, though. Louis was with his girlfriend, Eleanor Calder, enjoying some quality time together before the band embarked on their epic world tour at the weekend. After the show the paparazzi were waiting for Cara and security were on hand to help her get to her taxi for the next catwalk – which was rather fortunate as the paps were so eager to photograph her from the best angle that they ended up falling over each other and a large bundle on the floor ensued. Cara, of course, from the safety of her car, found it hilarious.

Next stop was the Mulberry catwalk and Alexa Chung, Juno Temple, Lana Del Rey and actor Douglas Booth were among some familiar faces packing the front row as Cara took to the catwalk in a knee-length black coat with lacy sleeves worn over cropped black trousers. She had the honour of closing the show and British *Vogue* editor Alexandra Shulman, who also saw the show, commented, '[Cara] radiates personality. She has a very individual face and stands out.'

Later that evening it was time to head to the Matthew Williamson show and Cara was snapped by Net-A-Porter's Twitter feed fast asleep on the stairs of the Royal Opera House before the show began. It was an indication that the catwalks were taking their toll, but nevertheless she took to the runway in style, sporting a pleated toxic-green skirt and patterned teal shirt as Anna Wintour, Daisy Lowe, Yasmin Le Bon, Atlanta de Cadenet and Olivia Palermo sat transfixed in the front row. Earlier that day she'd made the online-magazine pages, pictured straight after her rehearsal for the Matthew Williamson show wearing a beanie and munching on a sandwich. *New* magazine reported: 'This is our kind of girl. Cara Delevingne proved that models do eat when she sat in the back of her car munching on a huge (white bread) sandwich. So good to see a tiny LFW model eating some real food!'

The following day, Cara wrapped up warmly for the Peter Pilotto show in a fur-trimmed peplum monochrome jacket and black brogues. The same day, the *Mail Online* reported that Cara looked 'in need of a good night's sleep' when she was papped arriving at the Burberry Prorsum autumn/winter 2013 collection show with 'dark rings surrounding her usually perfectly made-up eyes', and speculated on the reason for the unusual dishevelled appearance: 'It would seem a series of late nights of schmoozing with her celebrity pals had finally caught up with her. The "model of the moment" looked a far cry from the usual flawlessly fresh-faced look as she sported considerable bags under her eyes.'

If Cara had seen the feature, she didn't dwell on it as there was work to be done, back home with her Burberry 'family' and she strode out with her girls – Edie Campbell, Jourdan Dunn and Karlie Kloss – inside the giant transparent tent in Kensington Gardens. Before the show she revealed to a journalist how happy she was to still be working with Burberry after all this time.

'This is where I began, you know? I've done this show five or six times and I'm so happy to still be involved with the same people, the same family. The music is great, the atmosphere, it's fantastic. Everyone always asks me how am I coping and I don't know if I am or not. Am I?! I drink a lot of water and try and sleep as much as possible – and I try and be a bit sensible and not have too much alcohol!'

The Burberry show was all about romance and Christopher Bailey went for animal prints, nude colours and semi-transparent fabrics, with Cara wearing a leopard-print bodysuit and high-waist pencil skirt. Brit singer Tom Odell, who features in the spring/summer 2014 campaign, sang live vocals as the models walked out, and the front row was, as per the norm for the Burberry Prorsum show, a who's who of celebrities. From the likes of Tinie Tempah, who revealed he loved the gold belts and heart prints, to actress Freida Pinto, who adored the bodysuits, the audience was packed with famous faces including Topshop supremo Sir Philip Green, Kate Beckinsale and her daughter, Lily Mo Sheen, *Downton Abbey* actress Michelle Dockery, *Les Misérables* director Tom Hooper, TV presenter Donna Air, Douglas Booth, Rosie Huntington-Whiteley, Olympian Victoria Pendleton and Yasmin Le Bon. And, of course, there was also Rita Ora, who proudly showed off her Queen Delevingne T-shirt, which had a sketch of Cara on the front, under her blue suit. The T-shirt was created by designer Simeon Farrar for *Grazia* UK, who had presented it to Cara before Rihanna's River Island show. Cara then gave it to Rita, with strict instructions on when to wear it.

'She told me to wear it to Burberry as she said, "It would be funny for me to be wearing her face!"' Rita explained after the Burberry show. 'I had this nice dress all ready to wear.'

The best friends managed to catch up with each other after the show and celebrated another successful runway for Cara by heading to the O2 for the War Child BRIT Awards concert with Muse as the headliners. It was there that they met up with Harry Styles, The Kills' Jamie Hince, Kate Hudson and Douglas Booth. Cara and Harry caught up with each other over a few drinks in the backstage VIP area of the Muse gig. There had been no tension between the pair after their 'romance' ended and the fact that Cara was now dating Jake Bugg; they looked like a trio of youngsters enjoying themselves according to onlookers.

'As soon as they ran into each other they all started chatting animatedly, laughing and joking away. At one point

Cara had her finger pointed at Harry while Rita giggled along. They were just having fun,' revealed a partygoer.

In fact, the three of them were having so much fun they decided to carry on the party and headed to the *Dazed & Confused* bash at the Café Royal, where they rubbed shoulders with London's fashionable set: Alexa Chung, Daisy Lowe, *The Voice UK* judge Will.i.am, Mary Charteris, Paloma Faith, Mark Ronson, fashion designer Gareth Pugh, Otis Ferry, Edie Campbell and Arizona Muse. The 'wifeys' let their hair down and enjoyed the evening. Not wishing the party to be over, the pair of them ended up at football manager Dave Gardener's house for a nightcap. How Cara managed to keep her eyes open, let alone stay up all night socialising is anyone's guess, but there was little doubt that her hectic schedule and social life would soon take its toll. Indeed, in the early hours, the press photographed her leaving Dave's house looking very unsteady on her feet as she stumbled down the front steps.

As well as being as eager to know how she maintained such a full-on work/ life balance, journalists were keen to find out more about why everyone wanted to be her best friend and how she made the friendships she has. Simple, replied Cara. It's all about making the right connections: 'The friendships I've made... You just find a lot of connections with different people and you're dealing with similar stuff, so in a way you are all going through the same things. You understand each other, naturally move in the same way. I have made some amazing friends who are always there for me and will always understand me, which is really good. And working as much as I do, I see more of them than I do most of my family!'

On 18 February there was time for Cara to take part in the Giles show at The Stationers' Hall in the heart of the city. The theme was otherworldly and ghostly and Cara, alongside Georgia May Jagger and Edie Campbell, wore pale make-up with dishevelled hair and Wednesday Addam's style eyes. Cara rocked in a giant cream beanie and loose white and gold dress adorned with mid-thigh tassels.

At the end of London Fashion Week, Cara played up for the eager paparazzi again when she was snapped leaving The Cockpit pub in West London proudly holding a packet of Haribo in one hand and a copy of the *London Evening Standard* in the other as she was on the front cover. *Mydaily.co.uk* ran a picture of her under the headline: 'Who is the Superstar taking London Fashion Week by storm?' and reported that there is only 'one superstar taking over London Fashion Week right now – not a celebrity, not even a fabulous designer but the all-about-madness model Cara Delevingne.'

While she was in the capital Cara also managed to squeeze in some time to see still-rumoured boyfriend Jake Bugg and although it was to be another two months until their relationship was officially confirmed, they were snapped several times during LFW. With Samantha Cameron's sister Emily Sheffield, deputy editor of *Vogue*, declaring Cara looked like 'the super [model] she is', the stage was set for the next leg of the fashion week tour: next stop, Milan.

Milan Fashion Week, the third instalment of the month, was met with some trepidation as the weather forecasters predicted more chaos for the fashionistas. Snow was forecast and show-goers tweeted about the impending snowdrift but it was business as usual for Cara – although not so for Jourdan Dunn, who stayed in the UK and missed the start of the Milan show because she was presenting a Brit Award. The *Mail Online* reported that Cara was upset at not being able to stay in London for the awards as it would have given her the perfect opportunity to mix with record bosses and to start making contacts in the industry to launch her music career. It was also reported that she had asked her new pal Rihanna to help her get started, but while Cara has made no secret of her love of music and singing, her management wanted her to focus on the upcoming shows before veering off-course with talk of making music.

'Cara is an excellent drummer and we know she can sing too,' confirmed a pal. 'She wants to leave the catwalks behind after Milan and Paris and concentrate on magazine modelling so she has more time for music. But at the moment she has to stick to a tight schedule and continue to walk the catwalk. She found it hard not to be in London for the Brits but she understands that the [catwalk] show must go on.'

With two fashion weeks down and two to go, Cara was still heavily in demand and seen everywhere – and this can be taken quite literally, as the 'aristo-model' as the *Telegraph* liked to call her, was stretched to 20ft in a giant poster for the launch of Katie Grand's second collection for Hogan. The campaign shots were all about zebra stripes, which appeared on clutches, trainers and loafers, modelled by Cara in the promos. And to celebrate *LOVE* magazine's editor-in-chief Katie collaborating with Hogan again, Cara recorded her version of the 1980s hit 'I Want Candy' for a music video. Katie called upon other models she had befriended over the years – including Poppy Delevingne, Edie Campbell, Abbey Clancy, Eliza Cummings, Liberty Ross and Stephanie Seymour – to star in the video to lip-sync and dance along to Cara's vocals and the result was a hit. *Grazia Daily* revealed that 'Cara is firming another skill on her CV: singing. And it clarifies that this girl can really sing.'

On 20 February 2013, the first day of Milan Fashion Week, Cara hit the catwalk in the morning for Fendi, which saw head designer and creative director Karl Lagerfeld take a catwalk bow at the end of the show. He had opted for a 'Last of the Fendi Mohicans' theme, and hair guru Sam McKnight was responsible for giving all the models a tight braid and topping the look off with coloured fox fur Mohawks – Cara sported a fluffy purple Mohican head-piece, plum lipstick and large grey cropped fur jacket. It was to be the first of her three shows that day, which would also include Ports 1961 and DSquared2.

Speaking backstage at the Fendi show, Cara revealed that although the show was fun, she was also in a lot of pain: 'My feet are bleeding, they are bleeding but I'm doing it all for you guys! If I didn't look like I was in pain, that was my acting skills right there. It's been a crazy fashion week but I'm so happy to be in Milan – everything is so crazy here but the energy is so good. I kinda feel I've got a little boost of energy again. How do I manage to post so much on Instagram? My Instagram and Twitter is like a full-time job, it's mad!'

The DSquared2 show featured next in Cara's schedule but this time there was no Jedward in sight on the front row. Designers Dean and Dan Caten went for a 1940s in Paris 'all that jazz' theme and Cara donned a double-breasted suit, giant bowtie and high pink hat for a more masculine look. Backstage it was all girly giggles, however, as she and the other catwalk models and the fun-loving designers took part in a music video for the brand, which saw Dean and Dan pose, sing and dance along as the finishing touches were added to their autumn/winter 2013 show.

Then it was time for the Ports 1961 show, which saw Cara in a mid-calf grey and white long-sleeved dress and elbow-length white gloves. With hair swept to the side in a ponytail, the look was quite schoolgirl preppy and a complete change from Fendi. There was barely time for Cara to enjoy the sights of Milan, although she was snapped taking some time off as she strolled the streets of the Italian capital with a group of friends before appearing in the Iceberg and later, Etro shows. For Iceberg she rocked a sequined rainbow-style smock top and blue-and-black gloves, and at Etro she gave futuristic glares, wearing a high-neck black coat with burnt-orange shoulder and arm detail; the hair this time was swept up into a high-fringe beehive. Later, Cara was snapped fully dressed, sprawled on the floor backstage, giving her overworked tootsies a well-earned rest. Well, those six-inch stiletto-heeled boots were a killer!

Cara was asked how she found each show and about the fact that the looks are so different and she responded in typical blazé fashion about the simplicity of being a supermodel. 'It's important when you open a show you represent what the other women should be: you are the starter, the essence, the vibe of everything. Whatever the designer wants, that is what you should try and portray.'

And on where she gets her energy, she confessed, 'I have no idea where my energy is from... I'm just so happy and so excited to be with everyone and work with all these people that I think, even if I'm in a bad mood or exhausted, it's better to be smiling than grumpy. I like to make everyone laugh and entertain people. It's all about determination and confidence.'

On Saturday evening it was time for the Emilio Pucci show. Designer Peter Dundas described the show as a 'celebration of the Pucci girls... about being happy and looking good, inside and out'. Cara looked effortlessly sexy in a cut-out teal-coloured short dress with a thick designer fringe. Anna Dello Russo, Anna Wintour and Alexandra Shulman were in attendance on the front row, as was Rita Ora, in a sexy white double-breasted suit jacket and shorts. Rita (who wore Pucci exclusively on her tour as Dundas designed her entire show wardrobe) is the designer's very own modern-day Pucci girl and she congratulated him after the show. Of course there was also time for Cara and Rita to catch up with each other backstage and spend some quality wifey time together in between Cara's busy schedule. The pair were spotted – sans fringe – 'partying up a storm', according to *Grazia* magazine, at the Hotel Principe.

But it was during the Versace show on the Friday, in which she wore a red cut-away floor-length gown with thigh-high split, that Cara received the most press coverage – and not for the right reasons, either. Fashion show spectators were shocked to see red marks on her shins and feet, exposed by the designs of Donatella Versace. At first the press and spectators believed that the marks were bruises, with the *Mail Online* warning, 'Take care Cara: Miss Delevingne steps out on the catwalk with bruised pins'.

But it was only when Cara tweeted after the show that it

was confirmed that the marks on her legs and feet were not from injuries sustained during the show but were due to the skin condition psoriasis. Psoriasis causes red, flaky, crusty patches of skin and is found most commonly on the elbows, knees, scalp and lower back, but it can erupt anywhere on the body. Affecting around 2 per cent of the population in the UK, the severity of the condition varies greatly and Cara, being under 35, was in the category at most risk from the disorder. While it might seem surprising that the condition hadn't been spotted earlier, according to NHS Direct sufferers usually have long periods of time when they show no signs or mild symptoms followed by periods when the symptoms are more severe.

'Be gone psoriasis, you're no fun,' Cara tweeted after the Versace show. A few eagle-eyed journalists and medical professionals had spotted the telltale signs of the disease from which American reality TV star Kim Kardashian, Kim's mother Kris Jenner and singer LeAnn Rimes also suffer. Philip Kingsley, an authority on beauty and hair, wrote on one journalist's blog: 'I applaud Miss Delevingne for her candidness and bravery but urge others not to self-diagnose from the pictures they see.'

The show itself was a success in other respects, Lana Del Rey, Grammy award-winning artist and actress Janet Jackson, actress Melissa George and designer Christopher Kane all graced the front row and *Grazia Daily* reported that Cara had put the 'va-va-voom in Versace', but for the first time a chink had appeared in her supermodel armour and later, when she hit Paris for the final leg of the tour, her skin condition would once again make the headlines. But it would be Cara's comments about the condition that would bring it to the attention of the press. When the model of the moment talks about the disease, suddenly the fashion world takes note.

As Milan Fashion Week drew to a close, reports began to emerge that Cara had followed in the footsteps of Victoria Beckham and Kate Moss and had trademarked her name. The businesswoman in her had obviously decided that now would be the ideal time, while her fame was at a peak, to protect her name against misuse and give her sole rights to use it as a marketing tool – an idea that was also encouraged by her management team. *The Sunday Times* reported that she had registered her name with the Intellectual Property Office in December 2012 with Cara & Co the name of her listed company. Her father, Charles, is the co-director and Cara has trademarked her name against numerous product lines, ranging from perfumes, handbags and nail files to umbrellas, key rings and, rather unusually, walking sticks.

The press decided that Cara was 'not just a pretty face' and the *Mail Online* declared she was a 'savvy supermodel' for trademarking her name. Cara was not just impressing the media with her looks but with her brain too, proving that by protecting her name at such a young age, she was in the fame game for the long haul.

CHAPTER 13

PARTYING HARD

'By the end of the year I'm going to look like I'm 45.
All the soul will be sucked out of me.'

An exhausted Cara flew to Paris to complete the final leg of fashion month, but even though this was the concluding week of shows, there was no let-up in her schedule. Kicking off on 26 February 2013, Rita Ora was also in the French capital with her model friend as she was performing in the Etam Lingerie show. Lily Allen, who'd taken a break from the music industry to have two children, was also performing at the show, four years after she'd last picked up the microphone. Cara, who wasn't walking in the show, was able to watch the runway models and her pals perform before heading back to her hotel for a few hours' sleep.

On 28 February Cara walked in the H&M show, a fairly stand-out event as it had been eight years since the high-street brand featured in Fashion Week, the last time being in New York. The show itself was set inside a 'home' within the grounds of the Musée Rodin, to set it apart from the high-fashion drama of the other catwalk shows, and featured a lounge, dining room and kids' room where the likes of Pixie Geldof, French actress Roxane Mesquida, *Home & Away*'s Melissa George, Daisy Lowe, Ashley Olsen and Emma Roberts were watching the action. As Cara featured in the brand's advertising campaign, she was a certainty for the catwalk and strode out in knee-high boots wearing a sexy sheer blue dress that showed off a jewel-encrusted bra and hot pants underneath. Backstage there was time to party with her pals Daisy and Pixie and, rather worryingly, she revealed to *Grazia Daily* that there would be no time to rest once Paris Fashion Week had finished: 'I'm working straightaway after Paris, first up American *Vogue* and then a ton of other shoots, so no rest at all. Nothing at all. I think by the end of the year I'm going to look like I'm 45. All the soul will be sucked out of me!'

In the Vanessa Bruno show, which showcased a more sophisticated, tailored look, Cara looked relaxed when she strode down the catwalk in a black-and-white sparkly shift dress and silver strappy heels. For Stella McCartney, she wore a grey, off-the-shoulder loose-fitting top, and Nicole Richie and Jessica Alba, who sat side by side, Russian supermodel Natalia Vodianova, Mario Testino, Paul McCartney and U2 frontman Bono all watched the action.

In the Chanel show, Cara's make-up stole the limelight when her eyes were adorned with heavy silver sparkling eye shadow. The presentation came from the Grand Palais and featured a large globe spinning in the centre to mark the label's worldwide success. Daft Punk's 'Around The World' blared out as the models strutted, and Cara teamed her bejewelled eyes with a fluffy white shooting hat, thick linked necklace and black thigh-high boots under a royal blue jacket. The front row was packed with celebrities, including supermodel Milla Jovovich and Johnny Depp's former wife, French singer, model and actress Vanessa Paradis, model Alice Dellal, musician Frank Ocean and DJ and model Leigh Lezark, but backstage Cara's relentless schedule was beginning to take its toll and she was pictured snoozing during the show. Lying on the floor with her head under a table to keep out the light, Cara proved she could catch up on 40 winks wherever she was if needed, but it did nothing to ease the concern of those close to her that she was overstretching herself.

With tiredness came bad moods and Cara, who was still the professional on the catwalk, started venting about the pressures of being in the media spotlight on Twitter. 'Have woken up in a terrible mood today,' she wrote on 28 February. 'Why do people take what I say and change it to what they want to hear?! Also, I don't think I have ever appreciated my privacy more than now. Cameras = RUUUUUNN!'

But there was no time to dwell on her annoyance; the Louis Vuitton show was scheduled for the final day of Paris Fashion Week and Cara would soon be hitting the catwalk with her idol, Kate Moss. Before the show she larked about with creative director Marc Jacobs, who sang her praises and ability on the catwalk as well as her effortless ease at having fun in what was often such a po-faced industry.

'She's a silly goose. She has great energy. She turned up to the Vuitton show wearing a zebra outfit from *Madagascar*, a onesie. She'd been traipsing round Paris all evening in it; you've got to love a girl like that. It's rare in life that you meet a person who doesn't care. It sets a good example,' he gushed.

But at the Vuitton show her psoriasis flared up once again and this time it was hard not to notice the marks on her body. 'It's an autoimmune disease and I'm sensitive,' she explained. But help was at hand when Kate Moss, who was backstage getting ready for the show too, saw Cara's skin. It was the start of a mentoring relationship between the pair, as Cara was to reveal to *W Magazine* later that year; Kate became very protective of the youngster.

'Kate saw me before the Louis Vuitton show at 3am when I was being painted by people to cover the scabs. She said, "This is horrible! Why is this happening? I need to help you." And she did, she got me a doctor that afternoon.'

Taking to the catwalk in a short, blunt-cut black wig, a slinky pair of cami-knickers and oversized fur coat, Marc Jacobs brought the romance of the boudoir to Paris with his latest collection for the brand. Jamie Hince and actresses Naomi Watts and Jessica Chastain watched as the models strode out of separate bedroom doors onto the set and sexily strutted their stuff.

The marks on Cara's legs weren't noticed at the time and only on closer inspection of photos from the show can you see the numerous raised bumps on her shins that have been covered in heavy make-up. The confession came to light in an interview that gave hope to thousands of other sufferers (according to totallyliving.co.uk, one in 50 people in the world suffer from the disease). Cordelia Jenkins, who suffered from psoriasis from the age of 16, was a case study in *Women's Health* magazine and she praised Cara's honesty about her situation: 'I am surprised, fascinated and so pleased to see someone with psoriasis on a catwalk. I think it is extremely brave of her and I hope she carries on doing it. If someone who is as intensely scrutinised as Cara can openly display her skin then I think that sends a real message to girls with psoriasis. It's such a mental as well as physical disease – spurred on by depression and stress causing it in turn.'

Kate Moss made sure she caught up with Cara after the show and took her out for lunch at Le Meurice hotel in the French capital on Wednesday for a good natter. No doubt she passed on some top industry tips to the youngster, while warning her not to overdo the catwalks for fear of exhaustion. 'It was great seeing Kate offering advice to the model du jour,' commented one fashion journalist. 'Kate has been through it all and come out as an icon the other side, so she is the best person to advise Cara on life after the catwalk.'

Moss had, in fact, just recently spoken publicly about the pressures she'd faced being a model in high demand in her teens and she was obviously keen for history not to repeat itself with Cara. 'I was really little and it was just really weird – a stretch limo coming to pick you up from work,' she confessed. 'I didn't like it but it was work and I had to do it. Nobody takes care of you mentally. There's a massive pressure to do what you have to do.'

The show itself caused some controversy when the video promoting the Louis Vuitton autumn/winter 2013 collection was aired. Directed by James Lima, with *LOVE* magazine's Katie Grand as creative director, Cara – alongside Edie Campbell and Georgia May Jagger – starred in the film, entitled *Ladies of the Night*, in which they are seen scantily-clad (sometimes topless/bare-bottomed) posing along the rue du Pont Neuf in Paris. But the video came under fire from left-wing French newspaper *Libération* for promoting prostitution. 'It is an extremely shocking representation of women,' confirmed Dominique Attias, a leading lawyer who signed a letter criticising Louis Vuitton.

With all the fashion weeks now firmly behind her, there was other work to be done and Cara headed straight to New York to shoot the new DKNY advertising campaign. Looking relaxed in denim while posing on the streets of the Big Apple once again, Cara also made sure her fans knew how much she loved her cartoon characters by sharing an image of herself on the streets of the city in a Bart Simpson midriff-baring top. It wasn't the first time she had worn the top; proving not all models have an endless wardrobe of clothes, Cara had worn it the previous year to the Osklen after party in September. This time, though, just to get more laughs, she then photoshopped a cartoon of SpongeBob SquarePants onto the picture with the caption: 'Lick me sponge bob! Lick me!' The *Mail Online* praised her good nature and commented that, 'She may be partying with all the top celebrities and have a string of glossy covers under her size four belt, Cara has shown she's still a teenager at heart'.

In March she also starred in a video for International Women's Day 2013, and alongside actress Amanda Seyfried, Karlie Kloss and others, held iPads with inspirational writing in the short film, *Some Words to Make a Change*. Marc Jacobs also collaborated with Cara on the 'Protect The Skin You're In' project, which saw her pose naked on one of the specially designed T-shirts to raise money and awareness for skin cancer research at the New York University Cancer Institute. Cara managed to find time to attend the Karl Lagerfeld and Melissa (a footwear brand) launch party on 26 March in a sexy silver blouse, cropped blazer and maroon skinny jeans.

Keeping Cara in the magazines even when she wasn't working was becoming increasingly easy for the editors, as her Instagram snaps provided enough fodder to fill the pages. As well as her SpongeBob antics, at the end of March she posted snaps of herself and pal Sienna Miller goofing around at Easter. Enjoying a brief respite over the bank holiday period after the previous four weeks' gruelling schedule, Cara was back to her goofball best and dressed up as a bunny, complete with a carrot in her mouth to wish all her Instagram followers a Happy Easter, tweeting: 'Easter takeover!! Happy Easter my love bunnies!! X'. She then shared photos of herself and Sienna in bunny-ear hats, with the caption: 'Happy Easter from me and Sienna!'

On 2 April, the *Daily Mail* reported that 'the world's most sought after model, who seems to have enough energy to work all day and party all night' had finally confirmed her relationship with Jake Bugg. After months of speculation it seemed the press could finally put the rumours to rest when *Grazia* magazine reported the couple's romance to be official. 'They're in constant contact with one another and whenever they are in the same city they try and meet up,' a source told the magazine.

Cara featured in *i-D* magazine again that month, not on the cover this time but dressed as a sexy woodchopper, and she also graced the pages of *W Magazine* in a fashion shoot entitled 'The New Guard: Couture's Outre Attitude'. The magazine described her as 'model, muse, society darling and bearer of the most epic eyebrows since Brooke Shields'. She also appeared in the Victoria's Secret Spring 2013 catalogue after her stint on the catwalk at the end of the previous year and shot a Pepe Jeans advertising campaign on location in London.

But her most exciting appearance in April 2013 came when she appeared in Jourdan Dunn's online cookery show, *Well Done with Jourdan Dunn*. Airing on YouTube channel Life & Times, owned by Jay-Z, Cara appeared in the first episode of the second series with Jourdan teaching her how to make shrimp tempura. She had dressed for the occasion in typical Cara style, a purple onesie, and was happy to play sous chef while Jourdan went through the stages of making the dish. While shelling prawns, the pair reminisced about how they met on a cold day on Brighton beach for the Burberry campaign, what qualities are involved in being a good wifey – Cara admitted she only cooks toast and baked beans, but she maintained that a modern-day wifey doesn't cook. When Jourdan asked what she would do when she had kids, Cara replied that she'd take them to McDonald's. Jourdan continued to question her culinary skills – Cara could crack an egg – which impressed Jourdan and she knew what a 'wok' looked like, which also surprised her pal. She did admit, though, that in the kitchen her cooking was 'crazy!' Cara said she'd never chopped in her life – but that this was 'my wifey training'.

On 13 April, the 3am gossip column in the *Mirror* reported that Cara had dumped Jake, who was said to be devastated. After five months of dating, the article suggested that Cara had called time on their relationship as her career was so hectic and her schedule so busy that it didn't leave a lot of space for romance. A source close to the supermodel told the newspaper, 'Jake is very upset. Cara is a great catch and lots of fun. She definitely won't have any trouble finding a replacement for him but her career is going so well, so perhaps she's erring on the side of caution and concentrating on that. She's weighed things up and with Jake's career taking off too, they didn't get to see a huge amount of each other anyway.'

The speculation surrounding the story continued, as the press wanted to find out whether or not the pair were in a relationship. *Entertainmentwise.com* and *Cosmopolitan* also ran stories about the supposed break-up, the *Sunday People* ran with the headline 'Cara is Over her Bugg', while at the Ivor Novello Awards in May, 19-year-old Jake wasn't happy to talk about it, saying 'no comment' when Absolute Radio tried to get his opinion on what it was like dating the supermodel. However, at the beginning of August, he spoke for the first time about his relationship with Cara and the experience of being a high-profile couple, telling *The Sunday Times* that for a shy boy like him, the situation was very intense. 'It was an interesting experience but I didn't get it,' he said. 'It was quite intense, flashing cameras and all that crap.'

Interestingly, though, he didn't deny or confirm whether or not they were still an item, saying, 'I don't even know [if I'm single],' when asked. Nevertheless, in Cara's eyes, the relationship was over, and if the reports did hold any truth to them, it was the fact that her busy schedule left little time for romance.

At the end of the month, she appeared in the *Vogue*

festival alongside editor Alexandra Shulman, *Vogue* fashion director Lucinda Chambers, hairstylist Sam McKnight and make-up artist Charlotte Tilbury to discuss what happens behind the scenes on a *Vogue* cover shoot. Seated on a stage in front of a packed auditorium, Cara wore a black blazer and skinny jeans and described how she felt being the March 2013 cover girl. 'I didn't anticipate how scared I was going to be,' she admitted. 'It felt like I had just started modelling again. But when I got there I just sat down and I breathed – I have to remember to breathe on the shoot, otherwise I look dead. There is a lot of pressure, but you can't overthink things, you just have to relax and be yourself. Being on a *Vogue* cover is like a badge of honour, a stamp of achievement.'

Vogue might have come with a 'badge of honour' but Cara's next shoot, with *Interview* magazine, wasn't the sort of affair that afforded any clothes to pin her newly acquired badge on – she featured mostly topless and baring her naked body on the floor save a thigh-high pair of stockings. The black-and-white risqué photos accompanied quotes and a full-page interview and marked her out as a sexy, seriously edgy model. The word 'youngster' could no longer be linked with the star, she was all woman although there was still a little childlike innocence to her interview. Quoted as saying, 'I'm aiming for an Oscar, a Grammy and a Nobel Peace Prize. And maybe Prime Minister', Cara showed she hadn't lost her love of acting – or dreaming! 'I don't do that kind of overthinking. I just spiral. I'm a spiraller.' She even mocked the fascination with her busy eyebrows, joking, 'Are my eyebrows real? No, they're not. It's a wig. It's a transplant. I had an eyebrow transplant.'

May was to be a significant month for the model in two very defining ways: she was to learn how the media and the fashion industry could be both a friend and a foe and the 'innocence' that had surrounded her so far in her career and media portrayal would be lost. First up was the launch of *Miss Vogue*, a younger sibling to the grown-up *Vogue* magazine and aimed at teenagers. Cara was to be the first cover girl for the new supplement. Free in the June edition of the main magazine, *Vogue* editor-in-chief Alexandra Shulman says she chose Cara to be the first cover girl – with the headline 'All Star Cara' – because of her maverick sense of style and fun: 'Cara is *Miss Vogue* made physical. The magazine is targeted at younger readers specifically, its remit is the same: to inspire even if you're a bit short on cash.'

On Tuesday, 30 April, Cara and wifey enjoyed some time together at the Beyoncé concert at the 02 in London. 'Beyoncé time!' tweeted Rita Ora that evening, but once the show had finished, they were determined to make a night of it. Cara, who was dressed in an open suit jacket that exposed her toned tummy and mini-crop top and her trademark beanie and dark sunnies, and Rita then carried on the party at Soho nightclub, The Box. The pair let their hair down and enjoyed some champagne with the likes of Kate Moss and Stella McCartney but when that wrapped up, they left at 2am to attend another party in Chelsea. It was a long night and the next morning, Wednesday, 1 May, Cara was photographed outside her home dropping a mysterious packet containing white powder. With paparazzi waiting outside on a regular basis, she was feeling exhausted from her night with Rita and in her partied-out state searching for her front door key on the doorstep, the small sachet tumbled out of her handbag. Instantly the paps saw this as an opportunity for a big story and took a series of photos of Cara, who realised what she had done and covered the packet with her foot before using her bag to help her pick it up out of view of the cameras.

One photographer commented later in an article in the *Mail Online* that Cara seemed 'energetic' when she first arrived back at her house with her friend and 'hyper' when she began searching for her front door keys. 'She was really giggly,' he said. 'She found it hilarious but her friend was really edgy about it. Suddenly Cara dropped something and very discreetly put her foot on it and then rolled her handbag across it so it looked like she was just kind of bending over. The friend realised they were in trouble once that little packet had dropped on the ground and kept saying, "Can you stop taking pictures?"'

Cara, who could not find her front door keys, had then sought help from her modelling agency and headed for the Storm offices, returning later with two official-looking guys in suits, who let her into the house. The incident sparked a chain of worry over Cara's partying habits and when the pictures were published, stories about her partying taking its toll were rife. *The Sun* had the picture exclusives and were first to publish the photos, while Perez Hilton, celebrity website journalist, ran the story of the model with the headline: 'Cara Delevingne Using Drugs?!'

To show that she wasn't troubled by the incident – or perhaps because her management wanted the press to see that she wasn't feeling ashamed of anything, that she was young, free and carefree – Cara put on a good display of 'having fun' with Rita in Hyde Park the next day. The newspapers picked up on the pair, frolicking in the sunshine and larking about, carefree. Whether it was a PR stunt or a well-timed fun day out, Cara was all smiles for the cameras who 'papped' them. The pair, both dressed down in casual gear for the day – Rita in an all-white outfit and Cara in her now trademark boots, stripy leggings and baseball cap – had a kick-around with a football, something tomboy Cara loves to do, and she was eager to show Rita her keepie-up skills with the bright black-and-red ball. Rita wasn't quite so coordinated but laughed and giggled along as she watched Cara show off some seriously impressive moves. There was also time for a bike ride across the park, with Cara hitching a ride on the back of Rita's stylist, Kyle Devolle's, wheels. The whole day was a fun-filled experience for the girls, a chance for both to let their hair down before they flew to New York to attend the Met Gala Ball. And if there was any suggestion that Cara might be suffering a fallout after Wednesday's incident, going by these snaps there was no evidence to support the theory.

So Cara jetted off from Heathrow on Friday to attend the Gala and to see her friend Rihanna perform in concert in Brooklyn. Forming part of RiRi's mammoth 'Diamonds' world tour entourage, Cara had a backstage pass, along with her housemate, Georgia May Jagger, and Rihanna tweeted a picture of herself, Cara and Georgia backstage with the caption: 'Yup! We definitely have more fun! #blondelife #backstagebehaviour @caradelevingne @georgiaiamjagger'. Cara also shared the love with her Twitter followers by tweeting: 'last night was amazing @georgiaiamjagger @badgirlriri thank you boo!!'

Cara confided in Rihanna what had happened a few days

before but her pal told her to try and forget about it and not to comment on the situation. 'Rihanna knew Cara had spent the previous 24 hours nervous as hell but she told her to chill and enjoy the Met Ball the following night,' revealed a friend of the model. 'RiRi knows the importance of not letting the press see you affected by anything and to go out and enjoy herself.'

Timing-wise, it was a bonus that Cara was across the pond and at one of the biggest celebrity extravaganzas of the year. Away from the hounding of the British press and lost in a sea of A-list celebrities, she was able to put the white-powder incident behind her and enjoy the event, this time in the company of her other BFF, Rita Ora. Perez Hilton's speculation that Cara's reported drug-dropping faux pas would be what the celebrities in attendance would be whispering about proved unfounded and pictures of the supermodel smiling and larking around dominated the press and fashion mags the next day. This was Cara's third attendance at the event and the 2013 Met Ball held at the Metropolitan Museum of Modern Art on Monday proved to be one of the glitziest in history. The *Mail Online* was quick to run with the angle that this year, it was all about Brit glamour: 'British punk chic: Cara Delevinge takes the plunge in studded gown while Rita Ora shows off some side boob as the lead UK stars at Met Ball.'

Hitting the red carpet in a dazzling plunging black gown by Burberry, which had heavy studded embellishment, there was a real 'punk' feel to the fashion this particular year. Cara epitomised the dress code to a T, sporting heavy, smoky eye make-up and a LeiVanKash dagger necklace around her neck. She added to these other fierce accessories

– a knuckleduster-style ring and series of cuffs at the top of her ear. 'Queen Delevingne!' announced *Elle* online, who put Cara in their best dressed category, as did the *Guardian*, who placed her in their 'Punk Princesses' category, commenting: 'Minxish Cara attitude, piled on earrings, rings, necklace and bad-girl plait are all working here. They don't call her the new Kate Moss for nothing.'

With her hair plaited down one side, Cara larked about with her long-term friend Sienna Miller, who was also wearing a Burberry floor-length gown and studded jacket in the same style as Cara's and wore her tresses in a similar side-up style. The pair were captured having a giggle on the red carpet, and pulled silly 'punk' poses at each other before they entered the Met. The Gala was, as usual, packed with the crème de la crème of A-listers: Madonna, Anne Hathaway, Sarah Jessica Parker, Kim Kardashian, Kanye West, Gwyneth Paltrow, Emma Watson, Nicole Richie, Blake Lively, Miranda Kerr, Kelly Osbourne, Gwen Stefani, Katy Perry, Stella McCartney, Kristen Stewart, Jessica Alba, Cameron Diaz, Heidi Klum and Beyoncé Knowles were all in attendance and posed and pouted their way along the red carpet.

Cara's wifey, Rita, was also at the event, dressed in a side-gaping white Thakoon dress, which had a sexy thigh-split and beaded detail. The pair arrived separately for the event but caught up with each other once inside, posting various pictures of themselves on Twitter and Instagram with other celeb pals. Kelly Osbourne Instagrammed a picture of herself with Rita, Cara – who was photographed giving her a peck on the cheek – and Jourdan Dunn, while Pixie Geldof tweeted a photo of herself, Cara and Rita all showing off their best lippy looks in an OTT pout. But the most talked-about backstage snap of the night award went to Cara and Sienna, who puckered up for a picture and snogged for the cameras. Cara tweeted it with the caption 'Studded love x' and the British press went mad for the smooch, with headlines varying from: 'Cara kisses Sienna – What would Rita say?!' to 'Cara snogs away her recent troubles'. Coverage of the supermodel at the party also varied in its seriousness, with the *Mail Online* reporting that Cara didn't let her 'recent slip-up, when she was caught on camera dropping a bag of suspicious white powder, get in the way of having a good time', while the *Mirror* wrote: 'Cara isn't going to let any alleged drug controversy get in the way of having a good time.'

And that is exactly what she did. But if Cara wanted to keep her party girl image in check for a while, it wasn't working as the following day, pictures emerged of her and Rita looking worse for wear after the Costume Institute Gala after party at the Standard Hotel in Manhattan. After changing from her Burberry gown into a blue jacquard suit which revealed a matching blue bra underneath, back-to-front baseball cap and Doc Martens boots, Cara and Rita, who also ditched her first outfit in favour of a silk jumpsuit, looked a little dishevelled as they were greeted by fans and the paparazzi outside the hotel.

By now the press were taking Cara's partying at the event to be a sign that she wasn't letting the controversy back home get her down. The general consensus at the time was that she wasn't hiding away; therefore the speculation as to the degree of severity of what they'd seen was limited. Had she been in real trouble, she'd be back home and would have issued an apology by now, surely, not be out partying all hours, snogging other girls and looking drunk? But that wasn't to say parallels between Cara and Kate Moss didn't begin to surface again; they did, and this time not in a positive way.

The two models' careers might have started with the same agent 'spotting' them and Cara's recent 'drug' incident was looking eerily similar to Kate's fall from grace when footage of her snorting cocaine had emerged in 2005. The *Daily Mirror* ran the photos on the front page, which seemed to show Kate snorting several lines of a white powder that was presumed to be cocaine at a Babyshambles recording session. Five days later, H&M, which had intended to feature Moss wearing their autumn clothes range designed by Stella McCartney, announced they were dropping her from the campaign, and a day later, Chanel revealed it wouldn't be renewing its contract with Kate. The possible effect Cara's 'incident' could have on her career and advertising campaigns was not lost on the media and they ran speculative stories about whether H&M, with whom Cara had worked on their 2011 Authentic Collection, would renew its contract with the youngster. No official comment had been made about the incident and a spokesman for H&M, which has a zero-tolerance drugs policy, initially released a statement that revealed they would look into the allegations before they took action: 'Our team will evaluate the evidence over the next few days. If the story is true then we will take action. We have a zero tolerance policy towards drugs and this also forms part of our advertising campaign.'

Nevertheless, two months later, on 4 August, the retail brand revealed that they would no longer be working with the model and had axed her from future advertising campaigns. 'She is not a model with us and I think there was a misunderstanding that she was the face of H&M,' a spokeswoman told the Sunday edition of *The Sun*. 'We just used her for one catwalk show.'

The press reported the story in varying degrees: The *International Design Times* ran with the headline: 'H&M fired Cara!', while most other reports suggested that Cara had been 'dumped', 'dropped', 'ditched' and disowned by the chain. Cara was told by her management to keep her head down and continue to work hard. Sarah Doukas had given similar instructions to Kate Moss back in 2005 and had managed to convince a lot of the supermodel's big clients at the time that they shouldn't believe everything they read in the newspapers. 'Unfortunately all press actually is good press in this world we live in, so keep calm and don't have a knee-jerk reaction,' was Sarah's official comment to the press.

Those who had worked with Cara in the past also believed that the incident wouldn't have a lasting effect. 'It is almost certain that the incident will be nothing more than a blip,' confirmed PR expert Mark Borkowski, adding, 'From Twiggy onwards the modelling world has always needed characters who are able to transcend fashion alone. She works hard and judging by how often she is seen leaving parties, she clearly plays hard. I don't believe the white powder incident will cause any lasting damage.'

CHAPTER 14

RITA AND RIRI

'Cara hijacking my video and my life and just
basically hijacking me – it's pretty awesome.'

May 2013 was going to be a month when Cara drew all sorts of attention from the media – that month there had been the drugs scandal, the A-list snogging (even pal Sienna counts on that score) and the general worry about her non-stop partying from those closest to her. But May was also the month that Cara decided to do something she had been keen to do for a while – get her first tattoo!

Cara had first revealed she wanted to get inked when journalists asked her at the Met Ball if she would be going to the after party. She'd said at the time that she wouldn't because she wanted an early night as she was getting a tattoo the next day. Ha! As we know, her plans changed somewhat and she ended up partying late into the night with Rita, but that didn't mean getting her first tat wasn't going to happen – and lo and behold, on 14 May, Cara got inked! And who better to get a tattoo with than your best pal, Rihanna, who asked her favourite tattoo artist, Bang Bang, to perform the inking on the supermodel at the Gansevoort Park Hotel, NYC, where she was staying.

Cara knew she had to be careful not to jeopardise future modelling contracts with any large or grotesque markings that might offend designers or their labels and was given a tough talking to by Sarah at Storm about the importance of being a 'blank canvas' for designers. But the headstrong 20-year-old wasn't going to let the models handbook stand in the way of something she wanted, after all, her success so far meant she was in demand, not just starting out with the need to be 'perfect'.

'I think people prefer models without tattoos but then, they don't mind so much,' Bang Bang theorised. 'Make-up artists can take that straight off if it doesn't work for the shoot. In my opinion, when you reach the level Cara's at, it's cool. People will want to use it. She's a famous model, they don't want a plain piece of paper.'

After speaking to Bang Bang about what she wanted – a tattoo of the word 'lion' on her finger – he didn't think it was sexy enough and persuaded her that an actual lion's face would be the best idea. Cara loved it and agreed that a small, detailed lion's face on her index finger would be perfect. A little bit nervous about the pain as it was her first tat, she sat like a professional for the half-hour it took. 'Getting a tattoo on your finger is one of the most painful places to get inked,' admitted tattoo artist Tom, from Red Dragon in Sussex. 'For her first one, it would have stung – plus the fact that it was a very intricate, detailed design.'

Whether or not it hurt, Cara was so happy with the result that she tweeted a picture of her hand in a fist with a lion's face on her forefinger, along with the caption: 'My first tattoo!! Lions rule! Thank you so much @bangbangnyc @badgirlriri'. Rihanna was also proud of her pal and took to Instagram to share the picture with her followers, along with the message: 'My lover @caradelevingne just came over and got tagged for the first time!! Only by the best @bangbangnyc #zodiackilla'.

The image of the lion's face may not have been too much of a mystery to those who knew Cara best – she's pulled many a 'roarrrr!' face at the paparazzi in her face-pulling moods, after all, but, most obviously, her star sign is Leo. Tattoo artist Keith (Bang Bang) McCurdy first inked Rihanna in 2007 when she asked him to etch a Sanskrit phrase onto her hip. The nickname 'Bang Bang' comes from a pair of revolvers he has inked on his neck, and as well as Rihanna and Cara, he has worked with other big names stars like Justin Bieber, Rita Ora and Katy Perry. In fact, it was wifey Rita who first told him about her 'model friend' who wanted to get her first tattoo, but Cara had been busy the last time she'd been in New York.

In an exclusive interview with *Heat* magazine after he had done the inking, Keith explained what had happened the night the singer asked him to come over. 'Rihanna left me a hilarious message because my phone was dead and said something about doing a tattoo. I got all my equipment together and went over to the hotel, headed up to Rihanna's room and it turned out I was there to tattoo Cara,' he recalled. 'It was her first tattoo but she was perfect! She was really good in the chair, real good. First tattoo and she was an absolute pro. She is ready for another one already! There was no diva supermodel behaviour, not at all; she's the coolest, most down-to-earth girl. I see why they all [Rita, Rihanna and Cara] get along. All three of those girls are cool as shit. You know it can be easy for people to lose track of themselves and become a fuck head. But these girls are cool and it's fun to watch. Afterwards Rihanna and me watched the basketball. Cara didn't seem to care quite so much!'

In fact, it was only a week later that Cara got inked for the second time, this time around opting for her initials on the side of her hand. It has often been said that having tattoos is addictive and this seemed the case for Cara, for whom it was a straightforward decision what to have done next. Bang Bang again performed the inking of a scripted CJD on her right hand, the same one as her lion. She again put the new inking on Instagram, writing: 'My new CJD [Cara Jocelyn Delevingne] tattoo by @bangbangnyc'. Keith kept to his tradition of getting his A-list clients to tattoo him after he has inked them, to form a kind of 'autograph' book on his leg. Justin Bieber inked him a mouse, RiRi did an umbrella with the initial R inside, and he let Cara take to the needle to perform her own signatory tat. 'Me tattooing a tattoo legend!! You must be crazy!' she tweeted afterwards, alongside a picture of her performing the inking – a heart with her initials inside. Was this to be the last of the tattoos for the model? Nope. Just a few weeks later she revealed she wanted more. 'I want them all over my body, I want loads more!' she told *Glamour* magazine. 'But I wouldn't go anywhere but Bang Bang in New York,' she admitted. 'Rihanna recommended me and I'll definitely be going back.'

May was turning into a busy month for the model: as well as getting her new permanent accessories, it was once again time to walk the red carpet, this time in Cannes. The

Cannes International Film Festival is an annual event that previews new films of all genres from around the world. The invite-only festival is a prestigious, heavily publicised event held at the Palais des Festivals et des Congrès. It usually lasts about 10 days and the opening ceremony, which in 2013 was hosted by French actress Audrey Tautou, premiered *The Great Gatsby* starring Leonardo DiCaprio. The film, which was directed by Baz Luhrmann and along with DiCaprio also stars Tobey Maguire, Isla Fisher and Carey Mulligan, tells the story of the life and times of millionaire Jay Gatsby and his neighbour, Nick Carraway, who recalls his encounter with Gatsby at the height of the Roaring Twenties.

On 15 May it was time for the opening ceremony and Cara treated the red carpet as her new catwalk, oozing glamour and sophistication in a plunging black lace Burberry gown. Dripping in diamonds – she wore glittering Chopard chandelier earrings, necklace and ring – and wearing a lot more make-up than usual, with striking red lipstick and heavy smoky eyes, Cara wowed the crowds with her elegant yet sexy look and pouted to perfection in front of the scores of photographers lining the red carpet. It was a windy occasion and drops of rain had started to seep through the carpet, but Cara and pal Georgia May Jagger, who also wowed the crowds in a Roberto Cavalli floor-length red satin dress, didn't care. Nicole Kidman, Cindy Crawford, Kylie Minogue, Freida Pinto and Beyoncé's sister Solange Knowles were all there for the event, and the cast of *The Great Gatsby*, which was to be previewed in 3D later that evening, received a warm welcome – DiCaprio getting the biggest cheer, of course, with some of his fans having camped out since the weekend! Cara's glamorous look was praised by the British press, causing many of them to comment on her ability to outshine other A-list actresses, including the leading lady of *The Great Gatsby*, Carey Mulligan. 'Cara smoulders at Cannes,' screamed the *Huffington Post*. 'Doesn't she look utterly ravishing?' asked *Grazia Daily*, before answering, 'That's a big fat yes!' Although there was the underlying question on some journalists' lips too, which was why was Cara at the film festival, having only had a bit part in the *Anna Karenina* movie the previous year? The *Independent* newspaper asked, 'And why exactly are vous here?' over a picture of Cara at the event.

But it wasn't just Cara's sexy look that was getting the attention in the press. Earlier that week, rumours had begun to circulate that Leo himself had wanted her to accompany him to the festival. Whether or not those rumours were true, the press were full of stories the next day about how Cara essentially 'snubbed' the Hollywood actor because he was too old! The *Metro* reported that she had refused an invite for a private party with the star and wasn't keen, and a source told *The Sun*, 'He spent the night chasing after her and essentially she blew him out. They spoke and he was pretty forward, inviting her to a party back at his suite. They swapped numbers but that was about it.' The source continued, 'He tried every trick in the book and apparently kept lunging for her but she kept dodging them. Normally all Leo has to do is to look at a girl and they fall at his feet, though Cara was having none of it. Everyone is howling at the fact she actually knocked back the biggest actor in the world. She thought he was too forward and too old.'

The press all picked up on the fact that Cara had reportedly turned down on of the world's sexiest men with headlines ranging from: 'Cara says no to Leo because he's too old!' to 'Cara knocks back Leo' and 'Leonardo rejected by Cara at Cannes'. But keen to dampen the rumours that made Hollywood's leading man look desperate, Leonardo's spokespeople reported: 'He has never talked to her, they never met. The story is all lies.'

The evening didn't end there for Cara: after the screening she headed for Roberto Cavalli's luxury yacht. The rainy weather hadn't got any better and to protect her gown from getting too ruined, she hitched up her dress to reveal some chunky, wedge-heel biker boots. She and Georgia May Jagger enjoyed partying into the early hours. The next morning, Cara emerged having ditched her glamorous gown and opting for a more masculine suit and back to her trademark flat biker boots. Reports suggested that a hostess from the designer's boat was worried about her leaving in the early hours as she was so drunk and managed to persuade the model to stay on board for the night. In the morning, with the paps waiting, she emerged in dark sunglasses and wearing a smart blue suit. There was no larking about for the paps; this was a far more serious exit from the yacht in order to get back to her hotel as soon as possible to catch up on some sleep and prepare for another evening of parties.

Even if the press were disappointed that Cara didn't make any romantic connections during the festival, she was making another A-list female pal in the shape of Hilton heiress, Paris Hilton. The following evening, Cara and Paris were papped leaving The Gotha Party at 5am, Cara looking a little bleary eyed as the flashbulbs went off around her. She wore a Roberto Cavalli suit blazer with nothing underneath and a long see-through skirt with a mini skirt beneath it while Paris wore a short red dress and sensibly opted for dark glasses to hide her tiredness. Both looked a little unsteady on their feet after the party, arms around each other's waists as they walked out of the club.

Earlier in the evening, Cara had attended the Calvin Klein Celebration Of Women in Film party, where she'd rubbed shoulders with Nicole Kidman and Carey Mulligan. She posed happily with actor Jeremy Irvine, who was dating singer-songwriter Ellie Goulding, Naomie Harries and DJ Bip Ling. At the party she told *Glamour* magazine that she was looking for an end to modelling soon and had ambitions beyond the catwalk. Of course, this wasn't a secret but it was the first time Cara had opened up to a national magazine about her desire to quit modelling in the near future. 'I want to act and I want to sing. That's what I'm going to do next,' she revealed. She also told the journalist what it was like to be constantly photographed, by fans and by the paparazzi: 'It's kind of my job but it might not be forever.'

She then hooked up with Paris, whose other BFFs include Nicole Richie and Britney Spears, for the evening, even though Paris spent most of the evening snogging her boyfriend, River Viiperi. Awkward? We doubt it, not with Cara's social skills! Besides, there was another A-lister keen to make Cara's acquaintance: pop legend Kylie Minogue. Kylie got chatting to Cara when she discussed her ambition to make it as an actress with the legendary Aussie singer. It was later reported that Kylie had told the supermodel that having a career in the music industry and the film world would be tough so she ought to stick to one or the other. 'Kylie has taken her career into her own hands and talked her out of being an actress,' revealed a source close to Cara when later that year it was revealed that the superstars had exchanged phone numbers to keep in contact. 'She knows both jobs mean spreading yourself thin, but Kylie has made it her mission to take Cara under her wing and make sure she doesn't get herself into the trouble many models have got themselves into. She knows the pitfalls of the industry but sees so much potential in Cara. Kylie quit *Neighbours* for pop, but when she did *The Delinquents* film, it didn't really work.'

After a busy few weeks partying and owning the red carpet, there was still work to be done, and Cara's YSL Baby Doll mascara campaign was launched. She was also chosen to be the new face of Saint Laurent for their autumn/winter 2013–14 advertising campaign, alongside musician Cole Smith from the band DIIV. It was a significant job for Cara, as the creative director of the fashion label Hedi Slimane has made a point of making the brand synonymous with the music industry by using a series of established as well as emerging artists in his campaigns. In the past, Courtney Love and Marilyn Manson have featured, making the choice of Cara even more poignant given her publicised desire to work in the music industry.

In May, Cara also took part in an original photo shoot for American *Vogue* magazine that played on her acting abilities as well as modelling prowess. In a spread that was entitled 'It Takes Two', Cara and Tom Hiddleston, a British stage and screen star, took part in a *Vogue*-scripted romance that pretends the pair are on set in a Hollywood location, learning their lines together. Cara, who is described in the feature as 'the most desired model to come out of the UK in years', smoulders her way through the shoot and is likened to Audrey Hepburn in one shot of her 'learning her lines' with Tom. 'Not since *Adam's Rib* with Hepburn and Tracy has there been a screen match so electric,' concluded the magazine. While the feature was a make-believe set-up of the glamorous film industry of yesteryear, it was still a nod to Cara's acting ambition and referenced her desire to perform in more films.

Her next assignment took her back to the music industry and had a personal touch as it involved working alongside her bezzie Rita Ora. On 16 May they both starred in a new version of 'Facemelt', a video for renowned photographer Rankin's new *Hunger TV* website. Following a series of many teasers – Rita had revealed earlier in the month that the remix video for her latest single 'Facemelt' would feature her wifey – *Hunger TV* finally released the video. Rita released a second snap of the two of them, which showed Rita attempting to lick Cara's face in another photo that was taken back in January by Rankin. The accompanying comment, 'Live. Love. Laugh A Teaser for what's about to come! @rankin @hungerTV #face melt remix vide with a little special guest @caradelevingne', gave away clues that the new music video would be a quirky, sexy instalment with both Rita and Cara. In the video, directed by Rankin, who has also directed videos for Cheryl Cole and Iggy Azalea, Cara dresses up and mouths along to the track from Rita's album, *Ora*. Cara even sings a few solo lines from Carly Simon's track, 'Nobody Does It Better', at the very end of the video.

'Cara hijacking my video and my life and just basically hijacking me – it's pretty awesome,' Rita said. 'She's crazy like me. So it makes sense. Having the most beautiful girl in the world in your video can't be bad.' And it's not, in fact – this video is nothing if not two pals having fun while working. The speculation of the two of them working together on a music video prompted some publications to surmise that Rita was helping Cara kick-start a music career with the possibility of the pair working on a pop song together. And a music career was something that Cara's model pal, Karlie Kloss, thought she should definitely aim for when she was asked in an interview in June what she thought of her fellow catwalk buddy's singing cred. 'I've heard her play the guitar before and sing, and she has an incredible voice. I would come to her concert any day!' the model gushed.

But it was back to the industry Cara knew best in June when she graced the covers of both China and Portugal's *Vogue* as well as featuring in a spread in the UK's *Miss Vogue* magazine under the headline: 'Miss V loves Miss D'.

Then there were the prestigious *Glamour* Women of the Year awards to attend on 4 June and that evening Cara had the honour of presenting a very special award. Arriving at the event, held at Berkeley Square Gardens in Mayfair, she posed for the press in a low-key Burberry outfit – black trousers and T-shirt top (emblazoned with a picture of a woman grabbing her bottom, along with the comment, 'squeeze this').

It was noted by several publications in their fashion round-ups the next day that Cara was a little underdressed for the glitzy event with so many other A-listers wearing their finest frocks (although *OK! Magazine* put her at the top of their 'best-dressed list' as she personified 'low-key glamour and supermodel-off-work chic'), but there was a reason Cara had opted for something a little less formal: she didn't have time to change! Pictured in the same T-shirt earlier that day as she arrived in Paris at the Gare du Nord, Cara was on a whirlwind visit to the French capital before heading back to London for the awards. Earlier in the day she had teamed the T-shirt with a pair of denim hot pants and beanie hat but for this evening she managed to spice up the eye-catching top with a spot of bright red lippy and red wedge satin heels. It was later revealed that the image on the T-shirt was that of Rihanna's bottom, taken when she performed at V Festival, back in 2010. It was a present from RiRi to Cara, which might suggest why she was so keen to wear it!

During the arrivals outside the event she was able to meet and greet her godmother, Joan Collins, who was also attending the bash to present an award, and once on the red carpet, Cara posed with fellow model Jourdan Dunn, who looked elegant in a slinky black dress. But it was her wifey Rita, who took along her mother as her 'plus one', who oozed the most glamour that evening, wearing a beautiful floor-length grey and silver gown.

The awards, which were presented by Graham Norton, were attended by some of the most A-list celebrities in showbiz, including Victoria Beckham – who took her eldest son Brooklyn as her 'date' for the evening – Kylie Minogue, Amanda Holden, Emma Willis, The Saturdays, Lisa Snowdon, Pixie Geldof, Jessie J and Miranda Hart. For Cara, the night was extra-special as she would be presenting one of the awards of the evening, the Glamour Award for Solo Artists. It perhaps wasn't going to be a big surprise as to who the winner of this category would be, but Cara left the audience in no doubt as to the victorious lady before she revealed it officially. 'Thank you so much for having me here to present this award. I am so happy that I will be presenting it to a very good friend of mine. I genuinely don't know anyone who deserves this more, she's my best friend,' Cara told the guests before the announcement. She later tweeted her excitement at her pal winning the award: 'So proud @ritaora Well done!!'

After the official ceremony there was time for Cara and Rita to pose on the red carpet, with Rita proudly showing off her gong to the official photographers while Cara stood proudly by her side making silly faces. There was also time for the pals to let their hair down and they were snapped sipping champagne and enjoying giggles with singer Ellie Goulding and Joan Collins. Cara tweeted her amazement at being linked to such a glamorous acting legend: 'So proud of my Godmother!! Joan Collins! Legend!'– and the pair, along with Rita, posed happily for snaps.

But Rita didn't stick around for the after party; she opted to head home and see her new boyfriend, DJ Calvin Harris, instead. There were the usual reports that Calvin was coming between the two wifeys and that Cara was upset that Rita wanted to spend more time with him than with her but nothing was confirmed. And while Cara probably asked her pal to stay on at the showbiz after party and have a giggle with her, it was doubtful that she felt rejected when Rita decided to ditch the event and jump into a waiting taxi for her boyfriend's London pad. And the fact that she was without her wifey for the evening didn't mean Cara didn't let her hair down!

'Cara was having a great time at the party, dancing away with Ellie [Goulding] and chatting and posing for Twitter pictures,' confirmed a fellow partygoer. In fact, she had such a good time at the bash she was pictured the next morning heading back to her home in her favourite high-tops while carrying the same red shoes she had worn at the event. Looking altogether less glamorous than she had done the night before, she opted for dark glasses to try and disguise her hungover state and a suit jacket with nothing but a bra underneath – although wearing the same T-shirt for two days running was a bit much, even for Cara! She had carried on the party with other famous faces at a hotel until the early hours and so even though Rita wasn't by her side, the model didn't seem to have any problem finding some new drinking pals to spend the night with.

Seven days later, on 11 June, Cara was back to her usual preened self when she Instagrammed photos of her latest campaign for Bo.Bô Bourgeois Bohême. Cara was chosen as the face of the Brazilian brand's latest campaign and shared pictures of herself behind the wheel of a truck in a pair of blue snake-print trousers and black top on the shoot for the label.

Just a couple of days later, on 13 June, the previous predictions that Cara wanted to collaborate on a song with Rita rang a little truer when Cara performed on stage with her wifey at the DKNYArtworks party in South London. The model, dressed in a sexy black jumpsuit with a white strip down the side, tweeted to her fans that there was plenty of fun to be had that evening: 'It's @dkny time tonight!!

Can't wait for later!' To make things more fun, she was hosting the event at the converted firehouse in Lambeth and joined Rita on stage while she performed hits including 'Party' and 'BS (How We Do)'.

At first, Cara was happy just dancing manically around the stage while Rita strutted her stuff to the excited crowd, but the pair couldn't resist a little public display of friendship and Rita went in for a hug with her best buddy. After that, Cara couldn't resist the temptation to grab the microphone and she started singing along while Rita danced next to her. Several times Rita tried to take the mic back but Cara was having none of it, and stood in the centre of the stage wailing out the lyrics. There was a mixed reception from the crowd as to the standard of her vocals, though: one partygoer described her singing as 'rocking!' while others weren't quite so impressed. 'It was a bit of an embarrassing spectacle, she was singing massively out of key,' complained one partygoer. 'Lots of people looked uncomfortable, it was like watching a car crash. Rita tried taking the microphone back a couple of times before succeeding, only for Cara to snatch it off her again.'

While the opinions on her singing were mixed, there was no doubt that the crowd loved watching the girls bump'n'grind on stage together, gyrating and putting on a dirty dancing display that delighted the onlookers. Professor Green, who was at the event with his fiancée *Made in Chelsea*'s Millie Mackintosh, was a little annoyed that Millie didn't let him enjoy any of the girl-on-girl action! 'So @RitaOra is dancing with Cara, the birds enjoying it but I'm not allowed to look. #doublestandards,' he tweeted.

And quite a display of friendship it was. At another

moment in the act Cara got down on her knees to pretend to strum a guitar and later stood behind her pal while she was twerking. The fact that Cara was enjoying an evening of music and partying with her BFF was in stark contrast to earlier in the day when she'd taken to Twitter to announce her anger at being continually hounded by the paparazzi. After leaving the St Martins Lane hotel where she'd been getting ready for her night out with a number of friends, she looked visibly annoyed at the awaiting photographers and showed them her middle finger once inside the safety of a taxi. She tweeted that the extent of being papped daily was beginning to get her down and sometimes even frightened her. 'The paparazzi actually scare me!!! Seriously guys, it's horrible,' she tweeted.

CHAPTER 15

NEVER WORK WITH ANIMALS

'The owls kept pooing on me, there was a real
problem with poo on this shoot.'

There was a bit of light-hearted press for Cara in the
middle of June when it was announced that she was to
feature in her own colouring book. It wasn't such a bizarre
concept: Hollywood actor Ryan Gosling had had his own
Colour Me Good Ryan book released and now it was the
model's turn with *Colour Me Cara*, a 16-page ode to the
model in colouring-book form. Aimed at her 850,000+ and
rising Twitter followers, the devout #Delevingners, the book
features pictures of Cara pulling wacky faces, posing
backstage and on the red carpet with the idea that keen
artists can then colour. Published by I Love Mel, the book
pitched itself as: 'The cool colouring book for good
colourer-inners as well as beginners.' Indeed it has been
snapped up by her loyal Delevingners.

Cara also took part in the Chanel pre-collection
autumn/winter 2013 film in June, entitled *Women Only*. It

wasn't much of an acting gig, more of a walk-on part as herself. She and other models, all dressed in the latest Chanel clothes and accessories, assembled in a theatre audience waiting for a film to start. The camera panned around the room as the girls chatted, played with their cuff bracelets and waited for the movie to begin, all the while showcasing Karl Lagerfeld's latest collection.

Meanwhile as the press continued to speculate over the possibility that all might not be well in the Rita-Cara camp after Cara's supposed 'upstaging' of Rita at the DKNY event and the idea that her boyfriend, Calvin Harris, wasn't keen on the singer spending so much time with the model. Cara's love life was once again also causing a bit of a stir. This time, the fella rumoured to be getting close to the supermodel was Gary 'Gaz' Beadle from fly-on-the-wall reality show, *Geordie Shore*. The programme, a spin-off to the American show, *Jersey Shore*, launched in January 2011 and was based on the antics of a group of girls and guys from Newcastle upon Tyne, with Gaz, a self-confessed ladies' man, often snogging or sleeping with a different woman each episode after a night on the town with his co-stars. As expected, the press went a little crazy for the unexpected pairing of socialite Cara and drunken 'man-slut' Gaz, but it was Cara who started the rumours first by tweeting to the star about taking part in a drinking challenge with him. Flirting on Twitter by suggesting that she could drink him under the table, Cara wrote: '@GazGShore the battle is yet to begin but the war is already won! Are you ready for a challenge?' to which Gary replied: '@Caradelevingne next Sunday your ass is mine hope ya not a bad loser #bluewkdlightweight haha!! #goingtogetmessy'.

Cara wasn't deterred by this though, and flirted back: 'We'll see about that', to which Gary responded: 'My victory dance is already planned don't worry ill hold ya hair back.' A friend of the supermodel reportedly told *The Sun on Sunday* that Cara has been a fan of *Geordie Shore* since the beginning and had developed quite a big crush on Gary. 'He's lapping it up, he can't believe his luck,' a source revealed. But a couple of weeks later, Gary told MTV News that at first he'd had no idea who Cara was when his friends told him she was following him on Twitter.

'She must just watch the show and follow us on Twitter and someone was like, "You do realise that she's following you" and I was like, "I dunno who it is." I didn't know who the girl was... I think she's just an absolute party animal,' Gary explained. He also revealed that it was Cara who sent the first tweet, which implied she wanted to spend a night partying with him the next time he was in the capital. 'She messaged me and was like "Next when you're in London, we need a night out, I will show you how to party." I was like, you are definitely barking up the wrong tree there and she was loving it. We had a bit of banter and she just wants a night out, really. Next time she's around we'll have a night out and see who wins. I might crack on at the same time.'

A few weeks later, on 21 June, 25-year-old Gary told the *Daily Mirror*'s 3am column that his friendship with Cara was developing well and they had been enjoying daily flirty phone calls – and that it was hard to actually meet up with the supermodel as she was always out partying with Rihanna!

'We speak every day. She's the most down-to-earth, wicked bird ever. We're total opposites, but we get on really well. We always send each other pictures and videos of where we are. During our first conversation she had to correct me on her surname 'cos I couldn't pronounce it. She thinks my accent is really funny.' And it seems that Cara was enjoying a daily flirt with the man who claims he has a degree in 'pulling women' so much so that she had already invited him to help celebrate her 21st birthday a few months later in August.

'Cara's having this massive Ibiza party in August, which I'll be going to. But hopefully I'll see her before then,' he continued, before revealing that she recently 'trumped' him on a night out by name-dropping a certain A-list pal she was out drinking with. 'The other night I sent her a picture of a bottle of vodka saying, "I'm in preparation for our night out". She was clubbing with Rihanna and hit back at me, saying, "If anyone can prepare me for a night out with you, it's Rihanna".'

Despite Cara staying pretty quiet on the subject of Gaz, possibly after another nod from her model agency that he wasn't quite the right influence on her career, the *Geordie Shore* star was adamant that she could possibly be the one to tame his wild ways.

'Next time we're both in London we'll def meet up. She is so fit, but she's cool too. She could brag about her amazing lifestyle 'cos she's always off to New York and Paris, but she doesn't. She's like, "I'm in the airport scoffing my face with McDonald's." That's what I like so much about her. And she likes me 'cos I'm a bit of a bad boy. She's not interested in expensive bars and clubs.'

Gaz also revealed to 3am that he had a foolproof way of impressing Cara when they eventually hook up. 'When we finally do meet I'm going to impress Cara by meeting her in

Maccy D's, getting her a quarter pounder cheeseburger meal, then take her to the nearest bar to get smashed.'

While that romance was playing out – and it must be said, playing out from Gary's point of view in the press – it was business as usual for Cara, who had the chance for the first time at the end of the month to showcase her drumming talent. Performing at the closing of make-up artist Charlotte Tilbury's House of Rock 'n' Kohl pop-up in London's Selfridges – part of a week-long beauty festival in the department store – Cara impressed the audience with her percussion skills. Charlotte, who originally met the model when she starred in her first big campaign for Burberry, invited Cara for a chat to close the pop-up and then gave her the chance to show-off, with a drum kit having been already set up for the star to perform.

'I'm so nervous, my hands are shaking,' squealed Cara before the energetic performance. 'I hope I'm good.' As drumming had been a passion of hers from such a young age, it was understandable that the pressure of now performing something she'd been working on for years got to the otherwise cool and collected model. But she needn't have worried. The *Telegraph* revealed that she could now count drumming as one of her many skills, commenting, 'It wouldn't surprise us if she popped up on stage at Glastonbury this weekend banging a drum for The Rolling Stones', while *E! online* said they were 'seriously impressed by the multi-talented gal's jam session' and *Entertainment Wise* wrote, 'Cara is taking over the world and her mad crazy skills seem to have no limits! Not just a pretty face, that girl can rock hard. And with drumming skills like this, we think she might just make it.'

The praise of her drumming ability must have come as a huge relief to Cara, who had made a big deal of her desire to work in the music industry. But it was back to the world of fashion at the end of June when Mulberry announced they had asked Cara to be the face of their autumn/winter 2013 campaign. The *Mirror* commented that it wasn't surprising that she was in demand by the big fashion houses who were eager to snap her up, Mulberry being the latest. 'After closing our London Fashion Week show, Cara was the first name in my mind for this season,' confirmed Mulberry's creative director, Emma Hill. 'She's beautiful, bold and British.'

In the pictures that were released to the media, the campaign shots, taken inside the grandiose setting of Shotover House in Oxfordshire on the theme of a wild and romantic woodland, see Cara co-starring with a series of owls. Photographed by British fashion photographer Tim Walker, she poses in the fashion label's winter season coats, shoes and signature tote bags while surrounded by a parliament of the birds – holding a tawny owl in one shot and in another, halfway up a tree while the owls perch on the branches around her.

So why did she choose to be the face of the new Mulberry campaign? It was an easy decision, she revealed to *Grazia Daily* when asked about the new adverts: 'Mulberry is such an iconic brand – it's British and I love the bags and clothes. The products are sexy and cool and it's one of those brands that everyone needs a little bit of in their wardrobe. It's not just the handbags, the luggage is gorgeous and I especially love the trainers. I walked in my first Mulberry show last season and it was beautifully produced with a magical period vibe. It was also a lot of fun. And so was this shoot, it was amazing. I got to shoot with owls! I love working with animals, especially owls. The best moments were when all the owls kept pooing on me – there was a real problem with poo on this shoot!'

As well as praising the 'spectacular sets' Cara also decided that it was time she launched her very own Mulberry handbag, following in the footsteps of Alexa Chung's 'Alexa' bag. 'My favourite Mulberry bag would be the Cara bag… actually, that hasn't been made yet! I want to design a Mulberry bag; there needs to be a Cara bag. I have so many ideas, Mulberry need to call me. And they have to let me design some trainers too!'

At the end of June it was time for one of the biggest musical festivals in the calendar, Glastonbury, and eager to fit in a couple of days of partying, Cara found time in her busy schedule to let her hair down and enjoy some family time with big sis, Poppy. The pair arrived at Worthy Farm in Somerset on the Friday, the third day of the festival, and headed for the backstage area, where they promptly bumped into Alexa Chung, who had also just arrived, and Pixie Geldof, who was trying to go incognito by wearing a long black wig; she was joined by her sister, Peaches, and Nick Grimshaw and Miquita Oliver completed the fashionable group. With the weather predicted to be wet, Cara had dressed for comfort, opting for skinny Hudson jeans, a bright Helen Steele reversible jacket, a grey beanie hat and black biker boots, and was excited to be at the music festival with a big group of friends. However, she wasn't going to 'slum' it like the masses, in a tent in a muddy field. Poppy and Cara opted for the more celebrity-friendly Winnebago, as did Rita Ora – but the wifeys found it more convenient to be neighbours! As they're not the biggest modes of accommodation, Rita's Winnebago was practically next-door.

The fun kicked off for the sisters as they enjoyed a performance from Rita, who made her Glastonbury debut by performing on the Pyramid stage. Pulling out all the stops to make sure her first performance would be a memorable one, she excited fans by tweeting about her upcoming set on Friday morning: 'Glastonbury we're on our way!!! Here we go! Arrgghhhh! Who's ready for a little pop and mud?!!!...'

Watching from the side of the stage and cheering her on was Cara, of course, and when Rita took to the stage in a red dress that was completely tasselled from the waist down, revealing black pants and black biker boots, the 'Ritabots' – as her fans are termed – went wild! She performed hits including 'R.I.P.', 'How We Do (Party)' and 'Hot Right Now' and afterwards tweeted that she'd had an amazing time on stage: 'We did it!!! Glastonbury my life has changed forever!!! Thank you!! Pyramid stage, main stage!! Thank you!!' With her performance over on the Friday night, the singer was able to chill on Saturday and enjoy watching some of the acts herself and catch up with BFF Cara.

Other celebrities at the festival included Kate Moss and Sienna Miller, who were spotted enjoying performances from The Rolling Stones, Professor Green, Primal Scream and Mumford & Sons. Cara made sure she had a good view of The Rolling Stones performance too when they took to the stage on the Saturday by climbing halfway up a pylon to get a birds-eye view of the action. Dressed in a Stones T-shirt, she ignored her friends' warnings to be careful and shouted down, 'I can see now', while the band belted out classics like 'Honky Tonk Woman'.

Earlier in the week there had been reports that Cara was going to 'gatecrash' the Rolling Stones' headline performance after taking to the stage at the DKNY party with Rita. A source told the *Daily Star* that she 'wanted to rock out with her idols on the main stage mid-set. She thinks Sir Mick and co would see the funny side if she managed to pull it off.' But nothing of the sort happened and Cara was happy to watch – albeit from a unique position – as the band performed.

Wanting to experience the 'real' action of the festival, Cara persuaded Poppy to leave the VIP section and venture into the more risqué areas of Worthy Farm. She was spotted wandering around the Shangri-La area with Poppy, a place that includes fake sex clubs, underground clubs and an area called Hell, but one festival- goer commented that she didn't seemed phased by anything happening around her: 'There were so many double-takes as Cara strolled through, she'd clearly had a few drinks and fancied sampling some of the lesser-known parts of Glastonbury. There were no airs or graces about her, she just wanted to blend in.'

Known for enjoying an all-night party, Cara lived up to her reputation by visiting Glastonbury's trendy Rabbit Hole, a dance club located in The Park area of the site. Dancing and drinking with Poppy and fellow model Suki Waterhouse, Cara looked the worse for wear the following morning when she emerged make-up free and visibly hungover as she left the music event on the Monday. In a baggy floral tracksuit, she made sure she got more attention from the paps and onlookers when she teamed her bright outfit with a cat mask. She pulled down the half-face feline disguise as she strode through the VIP section towards the exit, but had to lift the mask off her face because she wanted to text while walking. It wasn't the only wacky fancy-dress accessory she sported that weekend either. Before she arrived at Worthy Farm, she tweeted a photo of herself in a gorilla mask, ski goggles, sequinned cape and 'security' T-shirt and the only clue as to who she was, was the lion tattoo on her finger.

On her final day of the festival, being the supermodel that she is, Cara used the event as a fashion parade. Spending the day in the sunshine with her pals, the 20-year-old showcased her fashion sense in two outfits: first in a pair of navy leggings, black biker boots, camouflage T-shirt, Matchless leather jacket and Le Specs sunglasses. She also wore a grey baseball cap and then later that day changed into a black-and-white geometric-print T-shirt – and turned her baseball cap back to front! – singing along as she strolled in the sun. Previously she had credited her pals Sienna Miller and Alexa Chung for inspiring her chilled look: 'My style is a mixture of both Sienna and Alexa, although I'm more tomboyish than either of them. They dress very casually, but still look very chic all the time,' she said. 'I love T-shirts and I wear them all the time. I can never find really plain ones. The devil is in the detail.'

But the music festival wouldn't just provide a weekend of fun and frolics for the supermodel: there was trouble brewing between herself and wifey Rita and things came to a head one night over the weekend. After a heavy drinking and dancing session in the sunshine watching the bands perform, Cara was stumbling back to her Winnebago with the help of Poppy when Rita walked past them. According to onlookers, Rita, who thought her pal was deliberately ignoring her, shouted over to her, 'Sort yourself out, you're a mess!' Her outburst came as a rude shock to Cara, who couldn't understand why her supposed 'wifey' had been so rude. 'It was really feisty and nasty. Poppy was livid,' said a festivalgoer.

The next day, Cara continued with the festival as if nothing had happened but those who witnessed the incident had already made up their minds that there was trouble ahead for the pair. Rita posted a particularly poignant dig at Cara on Twitter when she commented about how much fun she had had at Glastonbury with her new 'wifey', Stella McCartney. After posting a picture of her cuddling the designer, Rita wrote: 'Till next year Glastonbury! We had so much fun with my new wife @StellaMcCartney in Stella McCartney of course! #uwishuwurhur #boooom'.

Cara didn't respond to the tweets and the silence between the pair on Twitter and Instagram was enough to encourage the press to speculate that there was a real problem between the friends: 'For two girls who had spent their whole friendship tweeting their love for one another and Instagramming photos of themselves having fun, snogging or just hanging out, the radio silence on the social networks speaks for itself,' commented one journalist.

Keen to keep up appearances after Glasto, and show that she can party with or without her best friend by her side, Cara decided to attend The Rolling Stones Hyde Park gig the following weekend. Even though she had only seen them perform a mere week ago, the Delevingnes are big fans of the ageing rockers – Poppy had told Cara that she was looking forward to seeing the band at Glastonbury – 'I can't wait for the Stones, I'm going to go absolutely ape shit,' she was overheard gushing. So it came as no surprise that Cara, who had earlier tweeted a picture of herself in her garden in a Bob Marley T-shirt enjoying the summer sunshine, was ready to watch Mick and co perform at the Barclaycard British Summer Time Concert. And mingling backstage with other famous faces as The Stones belted out a collection of their hits was just what she needed, tweeting: 'So ready for @Rollingstones at Hyde Park tonight'.

Presenters Tess Daly and her hubby Vernon Kay, Caroline Flack and comedian David Walliams and his wife, supermodel Lara Stone, who had given birth only a few months before, were all hanging out in the VIP area, as was Holly Willoughby, Gemma Arterton, Bradley Cooper, Jameela Jamil and Chris O'Dowd and his wife, Dawn Porter. Cara, who was wearing a chic black headscarf, T-shirt, leggings and her trusty white high-top trainers, spent a lot of the evening chatting to Lara Stone and swapping modelling advice while listening to the music and soaking up the festival atmosphere.

The parties continued for Cara that month but it was not always a stress-free affair for her family and friends. Known for her wild house parties, she had invited friends around for a party but it had got out of hand. It was up to big sister Chloe, who had previously told a journalist how she quite often has to play chaperone to party-loving Cara to eject dozens of Cara's friends from her parents' house in Belgravia.

'Chloe threw everyone out – it looked as if there were almost 100 kids there,' a source told the *Mail Online*. 'There were no celebrities, just all of her friends from her Bedales days and lots of trendy public school types. At 5am, Chloe emerged and was running around the house in a panic. She said that her parents, who had been on holiday, would be back in three hours and everyone had to leave. She chucked them all out into the street.'

Chloe accompanied Cara to Roberto Cavalli's 40th anniversary party at Les Beaux-Arts in Paris. It was a decadent affair; the likes of Kylie Minogue, Naomi Campbell, Tyra Banks, Bar Refaeli and Heidi Klum were all dressed up to the nines to celebrate Cavalli's fashion anniversary.

Chloe and Poppy made sure they were there for Cara if she ever needed them and for friendly big sister advice about staying out of trouble. 'Cara listens to her sisters, she doesn't want to disappoint them or her parents,' confirmed a family friend. In an interview a couple of months later for *W Magazine*, Cara did admit that her family were worried about her but she was adamant that she didn't want a 'good girl' reputation, knowing there is nothing cool about sticking to the rules all of the time: 'Everyone worries about me. It's hard for my family and I know I have to be careful but people have to realise that I can take care of myself. I've done a great job so far.'

Just two days after the Cavalli party there was another event for which Cara would be putting on her glad rags, but this time it was to be a family affair. Cara, Poppy, and parents, Charles and Pandora, attended the Animal Ball at Lancaster House, St James's Palace. Hosted by the Elephant Family, a charity dedicated to protecting the Asian elephant, the lavish event enlisted the help of fashion designers, stars and models to raise money and enjoy a star-studded affair.

All guests were invited to wear animal masks and Cara and Poppy jumped at the chance of playing dress-up. Cara wore a floor-length black Burberry dress with an owl mask, designed by Leonora Ferguson, and carried a whip – she also tried on an iguana fascinator during the evening – while Poppy opted for a gold feather mask and a sequined Dolce & Gabbana shift dress.

As well as being attended by the likes of Jerry Hall, Nancy Dell'Olio, James Caan, Rupert Everett and Mario Testino, HRH Prince Charles and Camilla, Duchess of Cornwall were also at the party and mingled with guests. Cara, Pandora and Poppy were introduced to Prince Charles while other guests mingled around them outside and Cara made Charles giggle when she apologised for the lion tattoo on her finger and initials CJD on her hand when she went to shake his hand. Cara, feeling a little cheeky, asked if the Prince had any tattoos himself. The pictures were all over the press the next day with Cara photographed joking with the Prince, who was seen chuckling away at the model. It was reported that she also let slip that she had a Made In England tattoo on another part of her body, which had amused Charles greatly.

Poppy Instagrammed a snap of herself and Cara posing – Cara in full dress-up while sticking her tongue out for the camera – and commented: 'Babes in the wood'. The fun night ended with the whole family piling into the back of a taxi before Poppy helped walk Cara, who was feeling a little worse for wear, back home.

The Made In England tattoo was Cara's third inking and something she'd kept quiet from her fans until 14 July when she Instagrammed a picture of the sole of her foot with the tattoo running down the centre and the caption: 'Made in England! Finally… @bang bang'.

The summery month of July brought about more heat for Cara and the speculation over her friendship with Rita. In an interview with *GQ* magazine at the beginning of July, Rita had added more fuel to the fire when she suggested that Cara wasn't even a real friend.

'To me, I have friends who I've known my whole life, and I can count them on one hand. They're people I went to school with. Everyone else I meet from that point on, if they happen to become a friend that's incredible – come and join the family. But if not…'

Her comments might have come on the back of reports that Cara's friendship with Rihanna was causing some friction between herself and Rita. The *Daily Star* revealed that Cara's friendship with Rita was put under pressure from the 'Diamonds' singer when she told the supermodel that if she wanted to further her career in music, she would have to choose which singer to hang out with. 'Rihanna loves her friendship with Cara and is even helping her with her budding music career,' a source told the newspaper. 'But she has now told Cara she can't record with her right now if she's recording with her music rivals. So RiRi's message is, it's me or her.'

The press continued to speculate that things had been going wrong for the pair ever since Cara had taken the mic off Rita at the DKNY party and the *Daily Mirror* ran a story that claimed Rita was forced to end her friendship with Cara for fear of it affecting her career: 'There's a lot of hurt on both sides but Rita's been working towards her singing career and carefully crafting her image for four years and it was all in danger of being a joke after that shabby performance. Rita's been advised to distance herself from the model.'

Perhaps the most telling evidence that there was a problem came about when on 13 July it was time for the 2013 Wireless Festival at the Queen Elizabeth Olympic Park in Stratford, East London. Although her official performance wasn't until Saturday afternoon, ahead of mentor Jay-Z's show, Rita took to the stage on Friday to duet with hip-hop artist Snoop Lion. They performed their dancehall collaboration 'Torn Apart' before a crowd of about 50,000 and Rita, who wore a gorgeous green Vionnet dress, tweeted later: 'Jumped on with snoop torn apart!! @snoopdogg love uuuuu!'

On Saturday, Rita took to the main stage in the blistering heat to perform an impressive set-list, and wowed the crowds in her black Lycra shorts (her bottom was trending on Twitter), an embellished top and bright red lippy. She changed her outfit halfway through to a red PVC raincoat and then rocked a floor-length red hooded cape. Speaking backstage afterwards, Rita said she was thrilled with her performance but had felt slightly nervous singing in front of Jay-Z – whose performance at Wireless was the only European gig he was doing in 2013 as part of his Magna Carter world tour. 'It's Jay-Z, you know what I'm saying,' she said. 'But for me it's like my older brother and he's got nothing but professional support and things like that. It's so nice and it's great when you can perform in front of him and you know your team are here. You feel more like at home but there's always that nervous part as well.'

It was an extra-special day for Rita, who watched her boyfriend, Calvin Harris, take to the stage with Jay-Z in a special collaboration. But there was one person missing from the festival – Cara. The papers picked up on her deliberate 'snubbing' of the event at which her 'former wifey' was performing and decided it was the final nail in their friendship coffin. To make matters supposedly more fraught, Cara wasn't just sitting at home deliberately missing the music festival, she was in fact in the South of France and had been for the past few days, having a fantastic time on a girly holiday –with Rihanna.

CHAPTER 16

HANDLING THE PRESS

'The press will say whatever they want but they will never really know. They should start writing science fiction novels.'

According to *The Sun*, Cara and RiRi's summer holiday had been planned for weeks, and both needed to let their hair down because they like to 'work hard and party hard'. Certainly the timing of the girly holiday had had to be carefully planned as it was to take place when Rihanna had a two-week break from her tour and so it happened that Cara and her showbiz bestie got their holiday groove on together in Monaco.

Since getting together on RiRi's yacht in the Côte d'Azur, Cara and Rihanna looked like any other girlfriends enjoying themselves in the sun and the pair were thoroughly at ease on board the luxury vessel, with Cara of course posting plenty of snaps of their bikini-clad selves posing for her Twitter and Instagram feeds. The Mediterranean jaunt was causing great speculation in the press due to the amount of money spent on the holiday in the sun. 'Cara and Rihanna blow £300,000 on super-yacht,' cried the *Daily Mail*, while the *Metro* decided most money had gone to waste on partying: 'Cara and Rihanna splash the cash on £300,000 yacht cruise in France with £200,000 left over for clubbing.'

The money wasn't an issue for Cara; she wanted to spend a couple of days chilling in the sunshine and did just that, smoking and drinking with her pal in her bikini and having fun in the sea. As well as knocking back shots of tequila – with Rihanna showing Cara the correct technique of having the lemon right after the shot – the pair drank champers, beer and a range of cocktails. There wasn't a shortage of alcohol on board the yacht but then it was a luxury liner designed for partying; the friends drank, chatted and soaked up the sun, occasionally going for a dip in the sea to cool off. 'It was non-stop booze, they haven't had much sleep, maybe a couple of hours a night,' a source told one of the paparazzi. The paps, of course, were having a field day, taking snaps of megastar Rihanna and Cara relaxing in just their swimwear. The papers and magazines were full of the shots, including one of Rihanna putting her hand on Cara's bottom.

But the girls didn't let the fact that their holiday was being shared with the world's media stop them from having a good time. Daredevil Cara also enjoyed some watersports and held on tight to a giant rubber-ring that was pulled across the sea by a speedboat, before jumping on board a jet ski with another friend from RiRi's yacht. As a model, her choice of swimwear was obviously very important to the fashionistas in the media and Cara didn't disappoint, opting for a quirky black-and-white eye-print bikini, sales of which fashion editors claimed would go through the roof with girls wanting to emulate the super-model's summer look.

The holiday came to an end after a few days as Rihanna jetted back to England to make a surprise appearance at the Wireless Festival. Wanting her bestie to know how much she had enjoyed her girly mini-break, Cara tweeted a cheeky message to her pal, in reference to her grabbing her bottom for the paps: 'Thank you my boo @badgirlriri for always making me smile and of course for keeping my bum cheek warm'.

Even though Rihanna's performance with her mentor Jay-Z and Justin Timberlake wasn't publicised, she had given her Twitter followers a sneaky clue as to where she was headed by posting a picture of herself outside Jay-Z's dressing room. But the screaming crowds were unaware who was waiting in the wings – initially there were shouts for Beyoncé – as Jay-Z and Justin, aptly billed as 'The Legends Of The Summer', performed more than 35 tracks for the final day of the festival. When she joined the boys on stage, Rihanna and Jay-Z performed 'Run This Town' to rapturous applause and she tweeted afterwards: 'London you were on one tonight!! One Love!!'

But the crowd-thrilling performance was just the first of her UK performances that week as she continued her 'Diamonds' World Tour, heading to Manchester and Birmingham the following week. Cara hooked up with her at the end of the week, Friday, 19 July, before RiRi had to fly to Paris to continue the French leg of her tour. The party-loving pair visited Cirque Le Soir in London, for which Cara kept her look casual for the evening with some

Aztec leggings, black high-tops and black T-shirt, while Rihanna opted for a Roberto Cavalli jacket, white skin-tight trousers and crop-top. Cirque Le Soir, which is billed as a 'Temple of Decadence', is a favourite for A-listers wanting to experience a crazy, champagne-filled night (there is only champagne on the wine list). Kanye West, Bradley Cooper, Miley Cyrus, Benedict Cumberbatch, QI presenter Stephen Fry and Brit hard-man actor Jason Statham are just some of the guests who have visited the nightclub (Justin Bieber also famously paid the Soho club a visit but was furious when he was told to leave by security staff after they discovered he was partying with Will Smith's son, Jaden, who was just 14 at the time), which features circus acts performing on small podiums, dancing dwarves, magicians, clowns, sword-swallowers and burlesque dancers. Cara, who bagged herself a white top-hat for the evening, and Rihanna posted snaps of themselves on Twitter cuddling up with the club's host, or 'Ringmaster', Tom Berg, and then later with a bald masked dwarf and burlesque dancer.

After leaving the club the pair headed back to Rihanna's hotel to continue the party before Cara headed home to her flat with Georgia May Jagger. Clearly having a blast with her model pal at their flat, the very next morning Cara and Georgia tweeted a picture of themselves dressed up in life-size bacon and egg costumes, tweeting, 'Wakey wakey with egg and bakey'. Cara pulled a pout in her giant fried-egg get-up, while Georgia giggled in her streaky bacon costume. They decided to ditch the cossies later in the day for a spot of shopping before hitting the town again in the evening, with Cara opting for a hip-hop T-shirt and Chanel sneakers and whitewash jeans. Georgia had spoken to *Grazia Daily* about how she and Cara had bonded over their love of music and were hoping to start up their own duo band. 'We haven't come up with a name yet,' she said. 'My friend suggested "the blondes" but obviously Blondie has taken that already. Dance routines included, we should make a music video. But I think Cara will be doing music before me.'

Out partying with Rihanna and goofing around with Georgia showed that Cara wasn't short on friends, but the supposed fallout between herself and Rita Ora was still an issue in the press. It came to a head when Rita decided to take to Twitter to rubbish such claims. On 21 July, she tweeted: 'I don't know what all these stupid stories are about but I'm always going to have my best friend @caradelevingne I love you!' The press took the message loud and clear, with online magazines revealing that the former wifeys seemed to be getting their friendship back on track. However, Cara didn't respond immediately to the singer's tweet, prompting some to speculate that this might have been a bit of a PR exercise on Rita's behalf, with Cara's popularity soaring. But Cara didn't leave her best mate hanging for ever and she took to Twitter a few hours later: 'It's mad @RitaOra the press will say whatever they want but they will never really know. They should start writing science fiction novels! X'.

It was the first public acknowledgement of the fallout and the girls were happy to set the record straight using their Twitter accounts. But it wasn't the end of the story: DKNY released a press release saying they were making Rita, not Cara, the face of their DKNY Resort 2014 campaign. Only days earlier the brand had released pictures of Cara fronting their DKNY autumn/winter 2013 campaign, posing on the streets of New York in their new season clothes. The new series of photos featuring Rita, also posing out and about in Times Square, were a heavily publicised event and the singer even tweeted her American fans to come and join her as shooting began: 'Good morning. Hitting the gym then we do a HUGE photo shoot in the middle of Times Square! Come and say hi! 12pm! It's going down!' And her fans did; she Instagrammed photos of the crowd that had gathered around the scene as the shoot took place. 'Thank you bots for coming out!! Today was awesome you always crack me up! Didn't even feel like work I love you! More than you'll ever know…#DKNY #NYCNights #TimesSquare,' she later tweeted.

Meanwhile *The Sun* reported that the friendship was still not on track at the end of the month as Rita was supposedly now going to supermodel Kate Moss for advice in a deliberate snub to Cara. 'Rita sees Kate as an upgrade from Cara. She started to see Cara as a liability after she interrupted her set at a DKNY fashion show last month and things have deteriorated since then. She knows Kate can give her advice about making her career last decades,' a source told the newspaper.

Being compared to Kate Moss was a long-running theme in Cara's career and personal life. With their heights in common and their sparkling personalities, Cara was also likened to the Croydon supermodel when it was reported she was getting friendly with Pete Doherty from The Libertines (Kate's ex-boyfriend), had dropped a suspicious packet of white powder outside her home (Kate was photographed snorting cocaine on the front cover of a national newspaper), and in wanting a career in music (Kate has taken to the microphone on several occasions and in September 2013 her voice featured on a single, 'Day and Night', by DJ Brendan Fallis).

But there is one person who doesn't believe that Cara should be compared to Kate – fellow supermodel, Naomi Campbell. Speaking in an interview in October 2013, Campbell revealed that Cara hadn't quite yet reached the iconic status enjoyed by Kate Moss: 'Cara is Cara Delevingne, Kate is Kate Moss. People are just saying they are alike because she is the same height as Kate. But there is only going to be one Kate Moss. Kate is an icon. Cara may become an icon: who knows how long she wants to do it for? It has just begun for her and she is doing amazingly well... I was actually asked to speak to Cara, but I don't know her very well. I've met her a few times and she's been very pleasant. I haven't spoken to her properly yet. For me, the timing has to be right.'

Karl Lagerfeld also shared the view by admitting in an interview how much he hated the comparisons that the two ladies draw: 'I hate when people say she's the new Kate Moss; Kate is unique, no one wants to be second anything.'

While the press might have been pitting the two women against each other in the modelling stakes, there was one area where Cara reigned: bagging herself the top spot in *Grazia*'s Best Dressed of the Summer 2013. Voted for by the readers of the magazine, the Delevingnes were out in force to support Cara, making sure she had enough votes to hit number one (Rihanna was number three, Alexa Chung number two). 'Everyone wants a piece of her,' revealed the fashion editor of the magazine, 'She's everywhere, every campaign going, every catwalk. In particular it's her T-shirts that have caught our eye. She always has a wacky T-shirt with a slogan or a message or a motif. She has a very distinct look. And she wears her T-shirts on the red carpet, prompting a flurry of designers to create "novel-tees" that feature her pulling her goofy faces.'

But it wasn't all goofing around. At the beginning of August, there was time for Cara to take a more subdued break with her sister, Poppy, to Greece for a few days. Without the paparazzi around it was meant to be a low-key, relaxation holiday for the supermodel before the stresses of Fashion Week descended just over a month ahead, but she later revealed in an interview that it wasn't the idyllic break she had hoped for: 'I thought it would make me happy and relaxed, but when I stop everything, it's really bad. I go crazy.'

Later in August, Cara was back in the spotlight after appearing in September's UK *Vogue* magazine with hip-hop star and music producer, Pharrell Williams. She starred in a feature entitled 'Born Lucky', in reference to Pharrell's collaboration with music duo Daft Punk, which was called 'Get Lucky'. Photographed by David Bailey, Pharrell had personally asked to be pictured with Cara after meeting her at the Met Ball earlier in the year and having instantly picked up on her good energy. Backstage at the shoot, Cara decided to take the opportunity to sing as much as she could to show that she had the vocals, talent and drive to pursue a career in music – if only Pharrell would give her a chance. *Vogue*'s journalist, who was backstage at the fashion shoot, noted that Cara was singing non-stop and commented in the article: 'You'd be forgiven in thinking she [Cara] was at an audition rather than a photo shoot – and quite a few Pharrell songs are in the mix. Pharrell says he'd like to hear her material and they swapped numbers.'

Cara was as excitable as ever about working with the American star and gushed about singing his songs with her pal Rihanna: 'I was so excited about working with him, he inspires me so much,' she said. 'I went on tour with Rihanna recently and "Blurred Lines" was blasted from the bus to get everyone singing.'

Cara giggled away as the 'Get Lucky' singer complimented her on her spirit and her depth before the pals shared a burger for lunch. They continued with the shoot and the final pictures for the feature revealed a series of playful poses, including the rapper cuddling Cara from behind, Cara on the floor cuddling his leg in another shot, and in one particularly intimate pose, her bending backwards in a short black dress holding on to the collar of his shirt while he leaned in towards her.

While appearing in *Vogue* in such a prestigious feature was another major credential in her portfolio, it was making the front cover of her first major America magazine, *W*, in their 'no-holds-barred, full-on, totally major, unapologetic' autumn fashion issue, that caused the biggest stir and got her the most media coverage. Looking straight into the camera with her hair pulled back, in glowing minimal make-up, and with her arms folded across her body, Cara featured alongside the tag 'Style Rebels' and was billed as 'Cara Delevingne: The Anti-Role

Model'. In the accompanying photos – Cara caused a bit of a stir by posing topless in one – and interview she was very frank about her skin condition, psoriasis, and how she was longing for a future career that wouldn't upset her delicate skin. 'I want to make music, I want to act, I want to sing,' she said, 'I want to do something that doesn't make my skin erupt.'

While many fans have congratulated her in the past about being so open about the angst she suffers with her skin, she still faces some nasty comments online from certain individuals who want to focus on her weaknesses. She took to Twitter at the beginning of October to defend herself once again: 'Just to reiterate, I have psoriasis and it's [sic] leaves scares [sic] and I will have for the rest of my life. I can handle the negative comments but just remember that no one is perfect. EMBRACE YOUR INDIVIDUALITY! It makes you who you are x'.

The *W* interview was one that also showed a very vulnerable side to Cara, who openly admitted that she struggles to switch off when she has some free time – and no one to share it with. With no boyfriend on the horizon, she was feeling a little lost and a little tearful and as there was time to 'stop everything', she said, it made her yearn for a little companionship. 'In Greece, it was a lot of couples, and I felt alone, which made me sad,' she confessed, talking about her holiday with her sister.

Nevertheless, there was one person she could turn to if she needed a little cheering up – the same lady she'd recently shared more of a rowdy, non-stop party holiday with: Rihanna. And she did just that.

'I called Rihanna. She said, "It's easy to drown yourself in work. That's a form of escapism. So if you're alone and you want to cry, cry." And I did. But by then, it was time to leave and get back to my life.'

CHAPTER 17

TURNING 21

'Happy birthday to me...'

With her 21st birthday looming on 12 August 2013, Cara had a big party to plan – and like any youngster about to celebrate a landmark birthday, she wanted the party to be a big event!

'She's planning on a week-long celebration in Ibiza,' a source told *The Sun* newspaper. 'She's going for a massive blow-out bash!' The rumours about Cara's wild party had been in the press for a few weeks and were escalating as her birthday drew nearer, with reports suggesting that after she had flown out over 100 guests to Ibiza, she was going to get her tattoo artists to treat all her guests to a special tat. *Sugarscape.com* even hinted that she was going to make the party a 'festival theme' to honour her love of music festivals.

'Cara couldn't decide between a muddy UK field and guaranteed sunshine for the celebration, so she decided to make her own festival in Ibiza,' a source told the *Daily Star*.

And then there was the guest list speculation too, with the likes of Kate Moss, Pixie Geldof, Nick Grimshaw and Rita and Rihanna all thrown into the mix of the 'definitely invited'. Harry Styles didn't go without a mention as it was reported that he had got in contact with Cara after hearing about her party plans through mutual friends and had cheekily requested an invite.

'Harry kept hearing about the party through their mutual pals so he texted Cara to ask why he wasn't invited. Cara quickly apologised and told him she'd only left him out because she thought he'd be too busy on his tour to come anyway.'

But the 'planned week-long party' wasn't ever going to materialise, as her family and friends and the bosses at her modelling agency, Storm, were none too keen on her extreme partying ways and were worried about her health.

'Cara has, by her own admission, been burning the candle at both ends over the past year or so. Partying has taken its toll and she is absolutely knackered,' a friend told the *Daily Mirror*. 'Her family especially were worried she was taking the partying to extremes and sat her down for a talk. She agreed to ease up, and take herself away to totally chill out, detox and unwind.'

The press were full of stories about Cara 'cancelling' her planned week-long Ibiza bash, with *Heatworld* suggesting she cancelled to 'get some rest', while the *London Evening Standard* reported: 'stressed out Cara cancels 21st to go into detox'.

In reality, in the week leading up to her birthday, Cara had been enjoying some quiet rest and relaxation time in Mustique with her friend Georgia May Jagger at her dad's villa in the Caribbean. The pair had spent the past 10 days swimming in the sea, drinking fruit smoothies and eating healthily, and a friend revealed that Cara had never felt better – 'She's totally recharged. But she feels there is only so much eating, sleeping and vitamin inhaling one can do.'

True to her energetic form, Cara didn't stay off the radar for long and on Monday, 12 August, her actual birthday, she enjoyed a big fancy dress party with an intimate group of pals and two days later shared the photos with her Twitter and Instagram followers. Deciding to stay in Mustique to host the party, she had flown a small group of close friends, including Lizzie Jagger, to whom she had become close through her friendship with Georgia, out to Mick Jagger's villa to help her celebrate with an evening of cross-dressing craziness. She opted for a party outfit of sparkly American-flag leggings and black cropped top while her guests wore a range of circus-inspired costumes, including a floor-length black-and-white striped dress, a guy in a pink satin dressing gown and pink wig, another in a flowery dress and a girl in a gold sequined top and floral headdress. Earlier that day her Delevingners had uploaded a collage picture of their fingers (with various home-drawn lion inkings) and the message: 'Delevingners Love You Cara, Happy Birthday Queen Delevingne!' Touched, Cara replied: 'Thank you to everyone especially my Delevingners for making my birthday so special!! Stay weird and wonderful forever and always x.'

As an extra treat, she also shared with her two million Instagram followers some snapshots from her cross-dressing themed birthday bash, including one of herself sprawled out on a big double bed behind a message written in flower petals that spelt out 'Happy birthday Cara'. In another shot, she is grinning at the camera while wearing a multicoloured party hat as a large rectangular birthday cake is brought out, featuring a big lion's face in the top left-hand corner. Rihanna made sure she posted a comment online as she couldn't be there partying with her pal: 'Awwww happy birthdaaaaay,' she tweeted. In another one of the fun snaps, there is a photo of a table laden with wrapped-up presents, captioned: 'Best birthday ever #sparkles #cameo #crossdressing', and in another shot, she poses on the beach with eight of her costume-clad pals and tweets: 'Thank you to all my friends for all their love and support and for making my birthday so special. I would be nothing without you! #crossdressing #sparkles #camo #itsbeenemotional'.

Wifey Rita was noticeably absent from the celebrations, but Cara focused on the few close friends that she had asked to share her special day. In another snapshot posted with her sticking her tongue out and posing with Lizzie Jagger and another friend, she comments: 'Thank you again to wolf mother and cat/dog whisperer! You sisters keep me sane! LOVE YOU!!'

But celebrating your 21st birthday isn't always a one-day affair. Back home in London, it seemed only right that Cara should share her special day, albeit two days later, with her family. So she did just that! For round two of her celebrations the birthday girl enjoyed a civilised evening with her family that included a big meal, cake and more presents. The relaxed evening was made all the more special as the whole family went to visit Cara's grandmother, Margo, in hospital for a get-together. For what would normally have been a private occasion, Cara, who wore a smart Vivienne Westwood trouser suit, proudly shared an Instagram snap of the whole family crowding around Margo's bedside, with Cara sharing a joke with her mum, while her dad, Poppy and Chloe posed around Margo, who was sitting up in bed smiling broadly for the camera. Cara captioned the intimate pic: 'Family Birthday dinner time!' and continued to share the rest of the evening's civilised antics with her Twitter and Instagram followers by uploading snaps. As well as seeing her blowing out the candles on her big birthday cake, she tweeted another snap of herself cutting the large white cake with her dad, or 'Dada Delevingne' as she likes to call him, in the background looking on proudly.

'It was a lovely, intimate evening for Cara,' a family friend revealed. 'Her family are very close-knit clan and the fact that they were able to visit Margo before enjoying a big family meal together was extra special.'

And when it came to presents, her family didn't disappoint either, with her sister Chloe topping the best pressie ever list with a personalised guitar case. As well as a sketch of Cara on the front cover above the name 'Queen Delevingne', there was a coat of arms and 'Bow to the Brow' on the other side. It was a cheeky reference to the youngster's trademark bushy eyebrows and she was over the moon with it. Eager to show what a fabulous pressie she had received from her eldest sister, she Instagrammed the guitar and case with the caption: 'What an amazing present. Thank you so much.'

While she has been known to stay up and party into the early hours on other occasions, and look bleary-eyed and tired the next day, that evening there would be no drunken nocturnal goings-on. Instead, in a bizarre selfie of herself and Poppy, she Instagrammed a cute black-and-white photo of the pair of them with their eyes closed tucked up in bed at 11pm. But then, she had had a busy day. As well as her family birthday dinner, earlier she'd decided to make a trip to Vivienne Westwood's store in Conduit Street, London for a little retail therapy. Hitting the shops in a tight pair of grey skinny jeans, round sunnies, a black jacket and a loose white T-shirt, Cara treated herself to a series of outfits from the designer and brought home a number of bags which hid her morning's purchases – including the green-and-navy check suit she wore for her birthday meal.

Cara was no stranger to Vivienne Westwood or her famous family as she had featured in that month's *LOVE* magazine, the fifth anniversary issue, with Vivienne's granddaughter, Cora Corre. The August edition, entitled 'The Sweetie Issue', had Cara on the front cover sporting loose ringlet curls and a pair of red mouse ears, proudly pointing her lion tattoo finger towards the camera. While she hogged the front cover limelight, inside the magazine she posed alongside Georgia May Jagger and Cora and the trio modelled the new Marc Jacobs cosmetics line.

The range, Marc Jacobs Beauty, was inspired by the rite of passage teenage girls go through in putting on make-up and was the main reason why editor-in-chief Katie Grand had chosen Cora, who had just turned 16, for the shoot alongside Cara, who had just turned 21. Even though this was her first foray into modelling, Grand observed that Cora, whose parents are the founders of Agent Provocateur, was 'well placed' to be a hot new face, while the *Evening*

Standard took it one step further and proclaimed that she was going to be 'the new Cara Delevingne'.

The 'old' Cara was still very much in demand, however, and featured in September *Vogue*'s 'pink lady' story in which *Vogue* fashion editor Francesca Burns revealed that pink was set to be the colour trend of the season. 'For most women, pink resonates with them,' she commented in a behind-the-scenes interview on the shoot. 'It's a lovely way to bring colour into a winter wardrobe. Pink isn't Cara's favourite colour but it's a playful trend so Cara was the perfect choice to model.'

Now that Cara had turned 21 she had decided it was time to let the world know that she really did mean business in the music industry and so she hooked up with family friend and singer-songwriter Will Heard, and together they hit the recording studio. The pair had been friends since their early teens, and knowing of her enthusiasm for music, Heard had decided to invite her into his recording studio in London to record an acoustic version of 'Sonnentanz' ('Sun Don't Shine'). This was a dance version of the song by Austrian producers Klangkarussell that was currently in the UK iTunes chart, and when Cara took to the microphone, with Will sitting on a stool and strumming on his guitar behind her, it would also prove to those who'd criticised her performance at the DKNY Artworks party with Rita that she could actually sing.

'She's quite angry about the way she was portrayed,' a source told *Look* magazine. 'The criticism of her going on stage with Rita and being a liability really stung. Cara is actually an experienced musician, there's definitely a sense of wanting to hold two fingers up to the doubters.'

While the four-minute track actually consists of her 'ooohing' along to the track, she looked thoroughly at ease in the studio and sounded equally soulful. And Will, for one, was very impressed with the outcome: 'I've known Cara since we were both 14 or 15 years old, through mutual friends. Her vocal is really understated and what she does with it is unique, not what you would typically expect,' he explained. 'Also, her guitar skills are ridiculously good and she's great fun to jam with.'

Heard has been gaining recognition in the music industry for his collaboration with other music artists' writers, including Justin Parker, who writes for Lana Del Rey, Rihanna and Ellie Goulding, and Baby Daddy, who writes for Scissor Sisters and Kylie Minogue.

The recording was well received by the media and it suddenly seemed that the girl who had always spoken of her desire to perform – and, more recently, to 'sing, act or do something that doesn't make my skin erupt' – might just be able to turn her hand to anything. 'Not just a pretty face,' remarked the *Telegraph*. But Cara wasn't quite so thrilled when she learnt that the video had gone public so quickly.

'Standing next to him, I sound like a goddam backing singer!' she said of their duet. 'We did it twice, his guitar string broke and the next day it was out. I was like, "Oh my god! Jeez." I wasn't prepared. Wherever we go, we're making music. Whether we're sitting in the bath or wherever... We just jam out.'

Her comments about making music wherever they go were later confirmed by Will, who spoke to the *Daily Mirror* about his friend's love of busking on the streets. It seems that both Cara and Will like to perform whenever they get the chance – even if that means singing to each other while on the Tube!

'We don't want to be recognised but we love freestyling in the street and on trains, and no one knows it's her,' said Will. 'Cara's good at remembering songs and we freestyle in the street, sing harmonies, stand in a circle with mates and have a jam. Whoever wants to join in, can. We move around, do it on the train, down little streets, wherever, and it's just natural.'

There was more musicality in store for Cara when she continued her festival-loving year with a trip to the V Festival. The event, sponsored by Virgin Media, is held on the penultimate weekend in August every year at two parks simultaneously – one in Hylands Park in Chelmsford, Essex, and the other at Weston Park in South Staffordshire – which share the same bill. The line-up for the 2013 festival was impressive: Beyoncé made her second and third European festival appearances of the year as the main headline act, with Kings of Leon as the other featured headliner. Over the sunny weekend there were performances from Jessie J, Paloma Faith, The Saturdays, Mark Owen, Olly Murs and McFly.

Cara, who hit the Essex site, was in the thick of the action from the beginning, making her way into the Virgin Media Louder Lounge in a back-to-front baseball cap, flowery Minkpink sweat pants, black high-tops and a black jacket. She got chatting to pop group McFly in the Mahiki Coconut Backstage Bar and happily posed for several pictures with the boys as the temperatures warmed up and the drinks started flowing. She also spent time with Ben Foden, whose wife, Una Healy, is a member of The

Saturdays and got chatting to Marvin Humes from JLS. But she got tongues wagging when she started chatting away to Niall Horan backstage before spending the rest of the day partying with him. 'This time last year she was supposedly seeing Harry from One Direction; now it looks like she's found herself another band member to get close to,' revealed a V reveller.

But it was her on/off friendship with Rita Ora that was still setting the gossip columnists tongues wagging. Earlier that week Cara had posted a cryptic message on her Twitter page that many assumed to be about her 'wifey': 'If someone wants to be part of your life they'll make an effort to be in it. So don't bother reserving a space in your heart for some-one who doesn't make the effort to stay'.

If it was a dig at Rita, it worked, as it was very noticeable that the pair didn't spend any time at all together during the festival. Rita, who performed at the Stafford site on the Saturday and then came to Essex on the Sunday, spent most of her time backstage with fellow singer Ellie Goulding, while Cara spent the majority of it chatting away to model pals, Clara Paget and Suki Waterhouse, and playing ping pong with Jourdan Dunn.

'For two people supposed to be best friends, they spent no time together at all,' confirmed a spy in the Mahiki Coconut Lounge. 'Cara would walk into the VIP backstage area and Rita would walk out, then when Cara came back, Rita was gone.'

If her Twitter jibe wasn't cryptic enough, Cara also took to Instagram at the weekend to proclaim: 'Don't waste your words on people who deserve your silence. Sometimes the most powerful thing you can say is nothing at all'.

But there was one person who was determined to get the friendship back on track and that was singer Ellie Goulding. She had been friendly with both for a while and they'd hung out at the *Glamour* Women of the Year awards. Her cool new image was credited to Cara and Rita as she spent lots of time asking their advice on what to wear without taking too many risks. 'Ellie, Cara and Rita hang out, swap clothes and talk about boys all the time, so when they fell out, she had to step in,' a pal of Ellie's admitted. 'She seems to be a fairly grounding influence on everybody: they call her Auntie Ellie because she's so good at giving advice. And she's really grateful to Cara for giving her the confidence to just do and wear what she wants. Cara showed her you don't have to be cool to be accepted, it's far more important just to have fun.'

Being a good pal to both girls, Ellie decided to step in and remind Cara and Rita what good fun they have together when a couple of weeks after V Festival, she invited them both out for a night on the town after the GQ Men of the Year awards... and then left them to it! Rita was performing at the swanky event, held at the Royal Opera House in London, with the likes of Hollywood superstar Michael Douglas – who won Legend of the Year – Justin Timberlake, Samuel L. Jackson, Emma Watson – who won Woman of the Year – Jeremy Piven, Douglas Booth, Dan Stevens – who won the Hugo Boss Most Stylish Man award – Jessie J, Daisy Lowe, Pixie Lott and Pharrell Williams – who won Performer of the Year – all in attendance.

After the ceremony, Ellie took Rita and Cara to China Tang restaurant in Mayfair to enjoy some food before they headed to The Groucho Club in Soho. She then subtly left the girls to continue their evening together, which worked a treat as after leaving the club, they decided to carry on the party into the early hours at Cara's house. But not before the wifeys were snapped hand in hand, getting a big bag of takeaway McDonald's to bring home! Chloe also joined them on the night out, staying in the background for the paparazzi photos but keeping an eye on her little sister all the same. She also got cross with the paps when they crowded around her sister and pal in the early hours, telling the overeager photographers that it was 'time to leave the girls alone, enough!'

Ellie's plan of bringing the pals back together had worked, however, and the next morning, Rita was seen leaving Cara's flat at 11am in a red hoodie, purple beanie and black leather trousers.

With her friendship back on track, Cara had various work commitments to fulfill before the onslaught of Fashion Week commenced, including starring alongside hot model Jeremy Young and a cute-looking bulldog in the Pepe Jeans London autumn/winter 2013 campaign. She also starred in a spooky Karl Lagerfeld short for Fendi's autumn/winter 2013 campaign that saw her walk around a dark, spooky house at night with another model. The dramatic background music added to the suspense of the seven-minute film, with Cara, whose hair had been styled in big curls, playing a 'frightened model' to perfection. Her acting included crying in one scene and playing up to the suspense – 'How do we know the food isn't poisoned?!' – before telling her friend that they needed to escape the haunted house. 'I'm scared,' she uttered quite believably, before the pair were rescued and left the house in their Fendi furs.

Her acting skills were set to get even more practice as reports at the beginning of August suggested Cara was to star in a British film, *Kids in Love*. Directed by Chris Foggin, the film, which is based on a group of affluent young Londoners whose lives centre round drugs and parties, was due to start filming at the beginning of September. Cara kept the press guessing as to her role in the flick but it was confirmed that she had a major part when on 24 August she used her Instagram account to show pictures of herself and the cast backstage.

"She's really excited about it and eager to do a good job,' a friend of the model told *Sugarscape.com*. The photos offer a glimpse of the fun Cara is having filming: one shows Cara, wearing a flowery headband, and co-star Gala Gordon lying on a bed, strumming a toy guitar. In another pic she poses with the whole cast, including former *Skins* actor, Sebastian De Souza, and Will Poulter, who starred as Eustace Scrubb in *The Chronicles of Narnia* and alongside Jennifer Aniston in the comedy, *We're the Millers*. In another of Cara's photos, she is seen larking around with the cast wearing Celebration choccies as moustaches and she also posts a pic of the clapperboard, which reveals the filming took place at Ealing Studios.

But the action wasn't just confined to the studios and during the Notting Hill Carnival in London on 26 August, she joined the rest of the cast for a day out on location. Cara, who plays Viola in the film, made sure she channelled her inner party-loving spirit by going all out and dancing crazily on the street. Sticking her tongue out, smiling and singing along, she looked like she was being paid to have the time of her life and along with the rest of the cast, boogied away as the carnival parade passed by. She even hitched a piggyback ride on Will's back and whooped with glee as the party continued. There was a little bit of upset though when fans tried to have their picture taken with the model and a huge bodyguard made sure that filming wasn't interrupted.

Cara later hit the Redbull Music Academy with her new friends and Jourdan Dunn later in the day, and showed no sign of slowing down. Fans also managed to glimpse her filming out on location a week later when she and glamorous Gala Gordon had to evacuate The Box nightclub in the capital after a fire alarm disrupted filming. Waiting for the all-clear to head back inside, Cara showed off a gorgeous gold sparkling halter-neck top and black hot pants. The film, due for release in 2014, also sparked speculation of a possible romance between her and her co-star, Aki Omoshaybi, at the end of September, with the *Mail Online* asking whether they were: 'Kids in Love?'

Whether they were or not, Cara was certainly head over heels in love with the movie industry and had well and truly caught the acting bug. 'It was mad! All of those guys are literally my best friends,' she revealed of her co-stars. 'It's like family. It's one of the most amazing things to do when you work with people you love so much. It's such an amazing, creative energy. It's so nice. It's really wonderful.'

Katie Grand, her long-time supporter, also spoke out about Cara's potential in the film industry. 'She's so animated, happy and excited to be doing something different. I'm really pleased for her that it's all happening so fast,' she confirmed. 'She started modelling and became successful very quickly. I think her kind of true path is probably acting. I'm really pleased that all these opportunities have arisen for her so immediately and I'm happy that she doesn't get tired or cynical – you know, that level of fame could get you down.'

CHAPTER 18

MOVING ON?

'I eat a lot, I have to eat all the time to keep my energy up. Stress keeps me thin.'

Before her role in *Kids in Love* became official, there were rumours that Cara was to star in the upcoming film version of the multi-million selling book, *Fifty Shades of Grey*. But she herself was keen to put that rumour to bed at the end of August, as well as revealing to *The Times on Saturday* that she was looking seriously at other venues to explore apart from modelling.

'Me in *Fifty Shades of Grey*? I don't know where that came from, it's complete bull-crap! I was like, "Really am I in the running for that? I don't think so." That would be funny,' she admitted. 'I'd say acting [is what I really want to do]... actually, that's probably not true. I don't think I've had enough time yet to explore music in the way I want to. I'm not saying I'm leaving modelling, I'm just exploring other things which I've always wanted to do. It's only a matter of time. I will still carry on modelling but hopefully I will be doing other things more.'

With the filming of *Kids in Love* underway and fashion month looming, she barely had a chance to enjoy her ritual chill-out time before the catwalks beckoned and at the end of August she flew to Shanghai for a whirlwind 48 hours to promote Burberry's Shanghai store and the brand's trench-coat campaign. A relative unknown in China, there were hoards of fans pressed up against the windows of the new store as Cara posed in a sexy white suit while the crowds took snaps on their smartphones. But the increasing level of fame was taking its toll on the youngster and she revealed it was stress rather than a tailor-made diet that kept her thin: 'I don't exercise, it's stress that keeps me thin. I went to the gym twice in the last six months and it was too much. I'm rather unfit. It is just stress because I do eat a lot. I have to eat all the time to keep my energy up.'

The quick trip to Shanghai came as it was revealed that Cara would be immortalised as a video character DJ in the new *Grand Theft Auto* game. The *GTA V* game, which was released on 17 September, sees fictional characters engage in high-risk motor thefts and kill people with explosives and firearms in the fictional city of Los Santos. Taking to Twitter to tell her fans the good news, Cara tweeted: 'I am so happy to announce that I will be a radio DJ in @rockstargames new GTA V coming soon! Tune in! woop woop.' She also uploaded a photo of herself in a rock-star pose, wearing a 'Los Santos' baseball cap but she wasn't the only radio DJ in the game: she would be competing for virtual air time alongside the likes of DJ Soulwax, DJ Gilles Peterson, DJ Jesco White and DJ Pooh, with Cara's virtual DJ playlist featuring more pop music than rock.

At the beginning of September, Cara was pictured on the

front cover of *Industrie* magazine, which offers an independent, in-depth look at the fashion industry, with an accompanying interview inside. With the fashion weeks starting in New York on 4 September, it was a well-timed feature that would ensure all eyes would once again be on the 'model of the moment'. But Cara has never been one to hold back on her thoughts on the 'crazy, dysfunctional family' that is the fashion business and raised a few (thickset) eyebrows when asked what she thought about Fashion Week.

'It's horrible,' she responded. 'I mean, it isn't horrible, really – it's amazing. But having to work that much every day is. What I find hard is having to deal with all the people and all the crap. It is when the press and the fans are following me most and it's when I work the hardest, so it's kind of like, fuck.'

The press immediately picked up on the quote, with the *Mail Online* speculating that Cara's 'love-affair with the catwalk is coming to an end'. There were certainly question marks over her loyalty to the fashion industry, and even though she had never made any secret of the fact that her passion lies in acting and making music, there were some who felt that the 21-year-old had deliberately tried to insult the modelling world on the eve of the second-biggest four weeks of the year.

'Doesn't she realise that Fashion Week has catapulted her from just a catwalk model to her "model of the moment" accolade?' asked one fashion journalist.

With New York Fashion Week underway, all eyes were on the model as to how many shows she would be appearing in during the first week. In the autumn/winter 2013 season earlier in the year she'd taken to the catwalk in more than 15 shows in New York alone, but in spring/summer 2014, there was to be just one show and one designer for whom she would be strutting her stuff: Marc Jacobs.

The Marc Jacobs show, held at 8pm on 12 September inside the Lexington Avenue Armoury, had an apocalyptic feel to proceedings. The runway was strewn with cigarette stubs, empty beer cans and piles of black sand, and all the models, Cara included, wore boyish blonde wigs cut into choppy short bobs. She was hitting the catwalk with her pal, Georgia May Jagger, who had not featured in NY Fashion Week before, and they goofed around backstage – pulling silly faces for the backstage photographers and chatting about the upcoming show.

'I love the theatrical-ness behind Marc's show,' Cara told one journalist backstage. 'We're all playing a role, it's always so well thought out and an amazing, beautiful show. It's really, really cool. And the biggest one in fashion week.'

While she took to the runway in an embellished blue sweatshirt with heavy neck detail and black embossed leather trousers, the American press came up with various reasons why Cara was only appearing in the one show that season, with the conclusions varied.

Stylecaster.com argued that there were five reasons why she was MIA (missing in action) during the week and only appeared at the closing show:

'Our five guesses include: 1) she's too good for it and over New York's second-tier designers, preferring to walk in the more prestigious international shows. 2) She'd rather party with Rihanna, who was celebrating the launch of her collection with River Island. 3) She hates fashion week, plain and simple, after describing it as "horrible". 4) She's over modelling as she's currently filming for British comedy: *Kids in Love*. 5) She wanted to make a statement and only walk in the Marc Jacobs show, as after being labelled a "dwarf" she has walked in all the Jacobs and Louis Vuitton runways ever since.'

It was an impressive list of ideas and certainly not unfounded, causing the British press to speculate whether she would be taking part in any of the catwalk shows when fashion week hit London on 15 September.

But Cara hit back at the media: 'It was a conscious decision. For New York Fashion Week I was filming [*Kids in Love*] so I couldn't actually do it. I chose to only do one show exclusively [Marc Jacobs] but I was very happy to do it.'

There was also truth to the rumour that during the action in the Big Apple, Cara was busy supporting her pal Rihanna, who launched her latest River Island collection on 10 September. To show her support for the singer, whom she publicly revealed had helped and given her advice when she was feeling low, Cara arrived at the launch proudly wearing togs from RiRi's latest collection. In a canary yellow, oversized baseball jersey, which she wore as a dress, Cara kept her belongings in a black bag with RiRi and G4Life printed across the handles, plus a beanie hat also bearing those tags, which form part of the high street collection. The new style was called 'Ghetto Goth', and Cara made sure her look showed she was influenced by that tag, with laddered stockings and high lace-up wedges.

Rihanna, who was also in London to promote her newest fragrance, Rogue, described her new 80-piece collection as having something for everyone – and she couldn't wait to wear it! 'I didn't want to wait until it's in stores, I wanted to wear it now,' explained the singer. 'I designed it for myself as well. I wanted it to be things that I really would wear, things that I love, things that I want to see in stores and pick up for myself and that's why I could wear it. I could rock it every day – I wanted to make staples. I wanted to make things that people can have in their closet forever, things that they can use and wear in many, many, many different ways because that's how I like to wear my clothes.'

The River Island flagship store was turned into a nightclub, 'Club RiRi', for the evening (even the bouncers wore G4Life beanies), with Rihanna herself hitting the DJ decks to get the mood just right.

Cara ditched the beanie once she was inside the store and made a beeline for her popstar pal, who was sporting bright blue lippy and a black-and-white varsity jacket. The pals chatted as the white wine flowed, giggling away as they caught up with each other while fans and fashionistas mulled around them, eager to pose for snaps with the pair. Cara posted various Instagram pics of herself and RiRi during the evening, pulling rock-star poses. They were having such fun, neither of them wanted to end the night early after watching Rihanna's second collection being paraded in front of them, so they headed to Nozomi restaurant in Kensington for a spot of food.

But there was one person noticeably absent from this cosy night. Where was Rita Ora? Well, she happened to be in New York, strutting herself on the DKNY catwalk! Yep, Cara's on/off wifey was making her debut stateside in NY's Fashion Week and closed the brand's 2014 show. With Kelly

Osbourne, Bella Thorne and actress Alexandra Daddario in the front row but no Cara to cheer her on, Rita walked out to Beastie Boys' 'Fight for Your Right' after Karlie Kloss had seemingly closed the show 30 seconds before. As the new face of the brand, taking over from Cara, Rita was so chuffed with her appearance on the catwalk that she tweeted a picture of herself seriously rocking on the runway to celebrate the brand's 25th anniversary.

'Conquering America is a big, big plan for me. I'm happy to be working double time and plan on conquering America. It's so fun,' admitted the 'Hot Right Now' singer, who wore a DKNY-logo white top, black skirt and black mesh knee-length leggings.

But that's not to say the pals didn't meet up during NYFW; in fact they got together on Wednesday, 11 September to get new tattoos! Heading to see their pal Bang Bang, Cara, who had previously tweeted her Delevingners asking if she 'should get a tattoo of bacon or cheese??' opted instead for her mother's name in script on the inside of her left arm.

'The tattoo is for my mother, Pandora,' Cara later confirmed to *Grazia Daily*. 'It's a sweet one. Do I want more tattoos? Hell, yeah! Shhh, don't tell anyone. I can't stop!'

Bang Bang Instagrammed a photo of the giggling model lying on the couch after having it done, with a sore-looking arm and the caption: '@caradelevingne your so wonderful to tattoo'.

Rita meanwhile showcased her new inking on her Instagram page, featuring an Alberto Vargas pin-up topless woman holding a rose on the side of her body down her right ribcage. The tat, which took five hours to complete, was one of 'the most detailed' tattoos Bang Bang has ever done for a celebrity. 'Say hello to my new little friend Rosetta... thank you @bangbangnyc she's beautiful,' Rita captioned the photo.

And while getting her tat, for Cara there was of course time for a little silliness: she posed in a giant burger costume, with Bang Bang and Rita jokingly trying to get their chops round the bun and Cara pulling a face in the middle. 'Myself and @ritaora think @caradelevingne is delicious mmmm,' tweeted Bang Bang, who also revealed that Cara is his most favourite ever celebrity client. 'She just pulled it [the hamburger costume] out of her bag, put it on and was like, "just me and my hamburger, what, what!" She's hilarious. She's genuinely fun, one of my favourite people,' he gushed.

Cara flew back to Blighty before the madness of London Fashion Week commenced. With a photo of London at sunrise and the caption 'Goodbye NY! Heeellloooo London!!' on her Instagram page, she let everyone know she was back in town and ready to strut her stuff. She managed to fit in a bit of fun and naughtiness before all that and hooked up with her pal Georgia May Jagger for a night on the town at The Box nightclub in Soho. It wasn't the fact that the two were out enjoying themselves that got the paps excited, though: it was their weird choice of headgear that caused great speculation – both wore black balaclavas with the initials BS in white on the top. Covering up with their wacky headgear, Cara and Georgia posed on Instagram in their white T-shirts pulling goofy poses before hitting the club. Had this just been a crazy stunt for one night, it might have been put down to Cara's usual goofy antics but the balaclava made several appearances during LFW, which caused great delight among her fans and, more importantly, the brand Black Score, who had given her their headgear.

Simeon Farrar, creative director of the brand, had wanted to create a band of 'rogue models' for the season: 'The general idea was to create a band of Rogue Models, like superheroes or supermodels. So I picked some of the most iconic models of the moment. We've had such support from girls like Cara and Jourdan [Dunn] that I wanted to turn them rogue. And they were more than happy. I think they like the anonymity of it too.'

The idea of being a superhero totally appealed to Cara's sense of fun and she made sure that throughout London Fashion Week she took out the balaclava as often as possible – and got her celebrity pals to don the headgear, too!

Along with all the oddball antics, Cara had some serious work to do. She had to be the hostess with the mostest when she played the part of host at *W Magazine*'s dinner on Saturday, 14 September, thrown to celebrate the September issue of the magazine, which featured her on the front cover. For the event Cara went for a sexy lace blouse and metallic trousers and blazer and despite only flying in from the States the previous day, there was no sign of jetlag as she partied with Jourdan Dunn, Ellie Goulding, Alexa Chung, Georgia May Jagger, Douglas Booth and Kelly Osbourne, with Kate Moss turning up later, along with James Corden and his wife Julia Carey, Paloma Faith and Pixie Lott.

Guest of honour Cara certainly enjoyed being in charge and led the celeb guests downstairs to the secret basement nightclub of The London Edition hotel, where vodka shots were doing the rounds and Chelsea Leyland took control of the decks. There was also one other noticeable guest that evening that had everyone in the room buzzing on his arrival – Harry Styles, who was dressed casually in a white T-shirt. The rumours started circulating that Harry had tried to secretly attend the party to see Cara but had had his cover blown when every single lady in the room wanted to have her picture taken with him. 'If Harry had wanted to stay under the radar he failed miserably,' a fellow partygoer told the *London Evening Standard*. 'All eyes were on him when he reached the club, his arrival wasn't exactly low-key.'

It wasn't the fact that Styles was at the fashion party that set the gossip tongues wagging; it was that he was at the same venue as Cara again after the pair had been spotted the night before on what looked like a date. The twosome had been photographed trying to remain inconspicuous in the audience of theatre production *The Book of Mormon* in the West End. Speculation grew that they had rekindled their romance and according to *Look* magazine, when the lights dimmed, the pair had giggled and whispered in each other's ears and put on a 'cosy display'. With Cara remaining tight-lipped, a friend of Harry's told the magazine that the date wasn't a one-off: 'They have great chemistry. They've always agreed to keep things super-casual and private because of their crazy worlds but Harry genuinely likes Cara a lot. He has done ever since they met.'

The British press were having a field day about the two stars who had a history of a relationship and yet were trying to do everything they could to avoid being officially linked. In an interview with *Fabulous* magazine, before the date Harry had hinted there was someone special in his life but he had stopped short of naming his crush. 'I haven't been mingling that much... Touring is so hard and it's hard to get to know someone in a day. You don't get enough time to meet someone, we're rarely anywhere for even two days at the moment. There is… I've got someone that I like, yeah.'

Cara's first show for London Fashion Week was for Mulberry on 15 September at midday. Held in the ballroom of Claridge's hotel, which was decked out like an English garden, the show opened to the soundtrack of former Prime Minister Winston Churchill's voice booming from the speaker: 'This house we have built together, brick by brick, stone by stone, the house we call home…' and then came the song 'Our House' by Madness and out walked Cara, opening the show in a silvery jacquard coat. She took to the catwalk once more to close the show in a loose, white shift dress that showed off her newly acquired 'Pandora' tattoo and was watched from the front row by Alexa Chung, Douglas Booth and Anna Wintour.

At 3pm it was time for the Topshop Unique show at Regent's University and the much-loved high street fashion label once again drew the crowds. Philip Green and his son Brandon sat either side of Kate Moss, while Anna Wintour, Daisy Lowe, Ellie Goulding, Pixie Geldof and Suki Waterhouse all attended to watch as Cara strutted down the fake-grass catwalk in front of them. It was a good show for Cara as none of the models wore heels – plimsolls in metallic tones or white were the order of the day. Appearing first in a short pair of silk shorts and green peplum vest and then closing in a floaty white sleeveless dress, Cara looked as if she was thoroughly enjoying the show on home soil and even gave Ellie a cheeky wink as she drew it to a close. Backstage, she caught up with Kate Moss, who came to see her and congratulate her on the show. And Cara, who was still in her clothes from the runway, couldn't resist planting a big smacker on Kate's cheek and then uploading the snap to Instagram for all to see.

'After Topshop with the one and only Kate Moss! #legend #icon #what babe,' she commented, as Kate put an affectionate arm around her.

The following day Cara would be walking in three shows, kicking off with her Burberry 'family'. In the transparent tent in Kensington Gardens, there were almost as many paparazzi as celebrity guests for the Christopher Bailey show, with the likes of *TOWIE*'s Tom Kilbey, Donna Air, Paloma Faith, Bond girl Naomie Harris, Anna Wintour and Jefferson Hack all taking up the front row. But it was Sienna Miller, the new 'face' of the brand, and her sidekick, Harry Styles, who set tongues wagging. Arriving at the show, the 1D heart-throb was asked by an MTV journalist whether he was looking forward to seeing his Cara walking down the runway, to which he replied, 'She's not my girl! I know what you're doing.' But despite his protestations, all eyes were on him, as he couldn't keep his eyes off Cara when she took to the catwalk twice in the show. Even sitting among a row of gorgeous women – Sienna on one side of him and Suki Waterhouse on the other – Harry only had eyes for Cara as she strode past, first in a pink pastel lace blouse and skirt, and then at the end in a white lace top and transparent cape with silver detailing while rose petals fluttered down over the models. He was also the first to head backstage to be by her side and tell her how well she had done; Cara took the opportunity to tease her fans by posing alongside him in her trusty balaclava.

She was certainly having fun in her Rogue Model

headgear and continued to goof around backstage as Christopher Bailey was being interviewed about his latest collection – although he couldn't help but notice and comment on Cara. 'She's part of the Burberry family, we love her,' he smiled, as she went around giving bear hugs. 'We have worked with her for many, many years. She's someone I'm very close to. We have a wonderful relationship and I adore her, she's beautiful.'

If Cara had suffered with the press at London Fashion Week the previous season, she was ready to play them at their own game this time around, though. Hot on her heels throughout the week, with rumours of a romance with Harry rekindled, the paps were relentless but she was happy to pose and goof around with the press as she took her balaclava everywhere with her. Backstage at Burberry she used it to full effect, even wearing it in a post-show interview with Jourdan Dunn, who looked at her pal in complete bemusement.

'This is called fashion anarchy – fashion anarchy, my friends,' Cara proclaimed as she pulled out the balaclava. 'This show is always the best, it's always cool to be with our Burberry family. The collection is so pretty, the florals and the pastels. And the rose petals? Come on, that is so romantic! Christopher is so romantic, that is what I love about him.'

And when asked about her latest movie venture, *Kids in Love*, she hinted that there might be more film roles in the pipeline, too. '*Kids in Love* has gone great, gone really well, and I've got a couple more movies lined up too, which is really great,' she revealed.

Even Harry didn't escape the balaclava treatment. In the

photo that Cara uploaded to her Instagram profile, she is pointing her fingers in the shape of a gun at the head of a guy wearing the BS balaclava and pulling a funny face. It was of course Harry, with his leopard-print T-shirt a giveaway as to his identity. Cara posted the photo with the comment: 'Got another one @blackscore @bsroguemodels.'

The post-show area at Burberry was buzzing and it wasn't exactly an intimate setting for the pair. Journalists clocked Harry and he was surrounded by the press who wanted to know what he thought about the show. 'It was great,' he told the gaggle of assembled journos. 'I think that show was exactly what Burberry is: iconic and British.' But when asked what he thought about Cara's stint on the catwalk, he was a little more coy: 'Cara's really good at walking, she's got it, she's good at what she does. London Fashion Week is always fun, London has a certain charm about it. Who do I think is most beautiful on the catwalk? All of them, they are all equally as beautiful.'

And he was still coy when pressed on the subject of himself and Cara being an item: 'People talk about anything really, but we're just friends and stuff. She is a lovely girl.'

Sienna Miller also caught up with her pal backstage but wasn't so shy about her feelings for Cara as she planted a big smacker on her lips. Cara Instagrammed the photo with the caption: 'look who I found @Burberry'.

But there wasn't much time to catch up with her pals. Cara had the Peter Pilotto show to walk in at 2.30pm, so she headed across town to open for the designer wearing a floaty pastel green and blue dress with layered top and stiff white collar. And it didn't stop there: the last runway to complete for the day was for Giles Deacon at 6.30pm and

Cara made sure she got there in plenty of time for a quick bite to eat... a McDonald's. Making sure she kept her fans up to date with the challenges of being a model-in-demand, she posted a cheeky photo on Twitter of herself and Jourdan Dunn with two big McDonald's bags between their teeth and the caption: 'My food is faster than yours!!! #fashionweekdietplan'.

The press were pretty impressed that Cara and Jourdan weren't afraid to show that they ate, let alone from fast-food restaurant Maccy D's. 'Cara scoffing McDonalds's... how do models stay thin?' questioned the *Mail Online*, while *Complexstyle.com* adored that the girls were being very open about their love of junk food: 'With London Fashion Week in full swing, collective societal expectations have trained us to think we'd only see models daintily chewing on pieces of raw kale, but Dunn and Delevingne don't give a fuck.'

Feeling better now she had had something to eat – after all, she herself has admitted that she 'gets in the worst moods if I don't eat' – it was time for Cara to get ready for Giles show that was being held at The Stationers' Hall. It was a heavily celebrity-populated front row for the intimate affair, which included Lily Allen, model Abbey Crouch (Clancy), Nick Grimshaw and singer Nina Nesbitt. Georgia May Jagger was also walking for the Brit designer, who revealed before the launch of his spring/summer 2014 collection why he loves working with Cara so much: 'Cara is loved by the fashion industry, but she works with it very healthily. She's very adaptable which makes her supremely exciting to work with; she can be a woman or a fun kid. Her popularity is interesting because she's one of the finest British models to reach a huge number of people proportionately through Twitter. She's fresh and people don't like things being given a veneer.'

Taking to the typically crowded catwalk she wore a short black evening gown and black Adidas trainers, with a giant bat dangling in front of her face. The large black headpiece might have been a hindrance for some but Cara took it all in her stride, causing one fashion editor to observe, 'Only some girls could pull off having a bat across their right eye and not bat an eyelid as it were, but nothing seems to phase Cara. She's a total pro.'

Backstage, Cara was enjoying not running from catwalk to catwalk as for the previous season, but rather enjoying every show as it happened. 'It's been very relaxing. I mean, compared to last time... it's been really good, actually,' she told *Grazia* magazine. She even had time to cuddle up to her mum and post a picture of the pair of them on Instagram – complete with the feathery headgear, too.

Professional as she is on the catwalk, off it as we know, Cara is not adverse to a little tomfoolery and left the Giles show in her trusty BS balaclava and it wasn't the last time her crazy headgear got an outing at LFW. As the capital's fashion-filled five days came to an end, Cara attended the closing-week parties, including the 25th birthday party for *Marie Claire* magazine. Held at the Café Royal hotel, Cara turned up to the red-carpet event in black leggings, a loose white T-shirt and her trusty balaclava. Actresses Jaime Winstone and Gillian Anderson, presenter Laura Whitmore, Jared Leto, Lulu Güinness, Jo Wood, Jo Whiley and Paloma Faith were also in attendance. While Cara let down her hair inside the bash to celebrate the end of London Fashion Week, it was the presence of a mystery man by her side that set tongues wagging. With Harry out and about with his pal Nick Grimshaw, she attended the party with her *Kids in Love* co-star, Aki Omoshaybi.

The *Daily Mail* insisted she was enjoying 'the company of a handsome friend' for the evening and speculation grew when Omoshaybi was asked about Cara dating the One Direction star. 'Cara is definitely not dating Harry,' he told one journalist. 'People always assume she is dating the guy she's seen out with because she's so friendly.' This of course prompted the media to conclude that Cara was in fact in a relationship with her co-star. 'Is Cara's new movie – *Kids in Love* – prophetic?' they questioned.

CHAPTER 19

ONE OF THE STARS

'Only with Kate would I find myself being serenaded by Tom Jones.'

With London Fashion Week over, in October 2013 it was time to jet to Milan for the start of the city's fashion week. And it was straight to work for Cara, who hit the catwalk on the first day for Fendi.

All the models – including Cara and Georgia May Jagger – were disguised in short, roughly-chopped black wigs, which *Vogue* described as making 'the clothes all the more distracting'. Cara wasn't immediately recognisable in her thick black barnet although *Look* magazine decided that she 'worked the beatnik look like a true pro, proof that she really can make anything look good'. Appearing twice on the catwalk, once in dark sunglasses and then in a sixties-style orange shift dress, she didn't let it show that she might have been tired after her five days in London. Compared with last season, it was a relatively easy ride and she even took time to pose with some of her Delevingner fans outside of the show.

FashionTV were backstage and caught up with Cara being made up to chat about the upcoming show. They were surprised to hear that she was feeling apprehensive. 'I am very nervous, very, very scared,' she told the fashion channel. 'Yeah, it's scary! Karl is my favourite [designer]. The collection... it's incredible, it's amazing; everything he does turns to gold. He's a genius.'

Cara posed with the designer backstage before she opened the show and strutted on the catwalk as Anna Wintour and *Vogue* Japan's Anna Dello Russo took their places on the front row to watch as she strode down the pristine white catwalk, cool as always. That evening she looked as if she could still be part of the Fendi catwalk in wearing a dress that her pal Georgia had worn in the show only hours earlier: a Fendi spring/summer 14 black mini-dress. She wore the same transparent heels she had sported on the catwalk and teamed her look with a canary yellow handbag. Enjoying an evening out with friends in the Italian capital, Cara attended the Fendi Exhibition Launch and drew attention from local fans who all wanted to pose with the star. Even a trio of paramedics asked for a photo and posed alongside Cara in their bright orange emergency jumpsuits.

It had emerged in the British press that Cara had been named in the *Evening Standard*'s annual Power 1000 list. Although she didn't make the top spot, which went to Prince George of Cambridge, the two-month-old son of Prince William and Catherine, Duchess of Cambridge, Cara came 20th, while it was noted that Harry Styles came in at number 17. Making the top 20 was an amazing achievement for the 21-year-old, the third youngest on the list, coming in behind the likes of David Cameron (4), Andy Murray (8) and HM the Queen (16).

But Milan wasn't to be as much of a slog for the model as in previous seasons. Fendi was the only catwalk that Cara would be walking, preferring this time around to conserve her energy and listen to the advice from her family and friends who all wanted her to have a more low-key appearance this season after the last when her schedule was beyond hectic. But that didn't mean Cara would be turning into a recluse either. Making sure she was still out and about on the social scene, she flew back from her one appearance in Milan to enjoy a night out in London at a party with Kate Moss and Welsh singing legend Tom Jones. Cara couldn't believe what a night she was having – meeting up with Kate for a few drinks and then being introduced to Tom was unreal for the youngster, who could only dream about having a singing career as iconic as that of Jones.

'Cara was in awe of Tom – who wouldn't be?' confirmed a fellow partygoer. 'She loved the fact that Kate introduced them and made sure all her Delevingners knew what she had been up to that night!' Despite being her usual dressed-down self for the evening in a T-shirt, jeans, leather jacket and trainers, Cara couldn't help but take the mickey out of Kate's micro mini-dress, which had ripped during the course of the evening, exposing more leg than Moss wanted. Cara playfully held the ripped blue fabric in her hand as she posed for a snap, with Kate grinning as if it was the most natural thing in the world. Cuddling Tom on one side and Kate on the other, Cara posted the snap on Instagram with the caption: 'Only with Kate would I find myself being serenaded by Tom Jones #iwouldhaverippedmydresstoo #epic #legends.'

The 24 September heralded the start of Paris Fashion Week and Cara headed over to the French capital by Eurostar to take part in the Stella McCartney show on day five. 'Cara is my London girl, I've got to have her,' explained Stella when asked why she had particularly wanted the model for her show, which was being held beneath the decadent gold-gilded rooftops of L'Opera Garnier. The show was a much-anticipated part of the PFW and the front row was proof indeed. Not only was dad Sir Paul McCartney and his new wife, Nancy Shevell, in the front row – the show ran later than scheduled due to McCartney's lateness (an embarrassing dad moment if ever there was one) – actress Salma Hayek, Mario Testino and Russian model and philanthropist Natalia Vodianova were also in attendance.

Australian model and fellow Victoria's Secret Angel Miranda Kerr opened in a gorgeous black lace dress, with Cara hot on her heels in a similarly romantic yet effortlessly sexy black-lace design. Cara later appeared on the runway in a gold loose-fitting suit with a black boob-tube top and gold-gun pendant necklace. Both girls were quick to praise the designer after the show and took part in various photo calls for the waiting press.

'No matter what you wear from Stella – whether it's a dress or a tracksuit – you feel a sense of elegance without having to try,' Cara revealed to *Vogue*. 'Being a Stella girl is all about being fresh, sophisticated, effortless. And Stella is an amazing woman, an amazing friend and an amazing designer.'

It wasn't all work and no play for Cara, however; there was still opportunity to muck around, even with the world's fashion press in attendance and she photo-bombed

Kerr while she was being interviewed. But the Aussie model, who has a child with actor Orlando Bloom, found it hilarious that Cara had pulled one of her wacky faces behind her back and decided to upload the snap to her Instagram profile to show what really happens backstage at a fashion show. 'Having fun with Cara backstage – love you!' she commented.

Cara made sure that Stella's name was still on everyone's lips when the show had finished too, as she left in the same gold suit she had paraded on the catwalk just moments earlier. She added her own Cara twist to the outfit though, teaming it with trainers and a beanie hat rather than the heels worn for the show, but it was unmistakably the same outfit showcased earlier. It wasn't the first time this had happened – in Milan she'd worn a Fendi dress for a night out and later during PFW she would be snapped out and about in the French capital in a Chanel dress that she had earlier modelled on the catwalk – but fashion commentators reasoned there was a good explanation for this. 'Even though there are generally only one or two versions of each outfit made for the catwalk, few models, no matter how famous, are given the new season's clothes to keep,' confirmed a fashion editor. 'But Cara's staggering popularity, and the certainty of her being photographed wherever she goes means that even top designers are willing to bend the rules for her.'

Cara made sure her Instagram followers were left in no doubt as to her feelings for Stella McCartney after the show and tweeted a picture of the designer planting a big kiss on her cheek, with the comment: 'What an amazing show yesterday @Stellamccartney love you! X'.

On Tuesday, 1 October, the penultimate day of the fashion week season, it was time for the big houses, Chanel and Valentino, to showcase their spring/summer 2014 designs and Cara would be walking in both: Chanel in the morning and Valentino later that afternoon.

Despite being out on the town with her sister Poppy and pal Georgia May Jagger the evening before, Cara was looking fresh-faced and ready for the opulent Chanel show, which was being held at the Grand Palais. While it might have been frowned upon in the past for the model to be partying all night during the most hectic time of the year for fashion, the trio enjoyed a relatively sedate evening at Le Meurice hotel, with Cara in a tartan shirt, leather leggings, white-rimmed sunglasses and beanie hat and Georgia sporting in a gold gun pendant necklace similar to the one Cara had worn for the Stella show. Cara had recently spoken about how spending time with Georgia helped her relax and that she is a calming influence in her life. 'Georgia helps me de-stress so much because I've known her for so long,' she told the *Metro*. 'It's the same with Jourdan [Dunn]. It's just lovely to have those girls around you because they're like family.'

But back to the Chanel show and it was, as ever, an exquisite piece of theatre, featuring around 75 arty installations scattered alongside the catwalk and designed by Karl Lagerfeld himself. Cara made an entrance even before she set foot inside the fashion label's exhibition when she walked to the Grand Palais hand in hand with her BFF, Rita Ora. The press spotted the pals walking into the show looking as if they had never had a falling out in their lives and a number of celebrity magazines speculated on the happy reunion: 'BFFs Back Together: Rita and Cara's Friendship Back On Track,' said the *Mail Online*, while *The Huffington Post* agreed that the 'womance' was definitely back on again.

Cara was still in tartan mode from the night before and had this time opted for red tartan trousers, a Vivienne Westwood tartan backpack, white tee and black trainers, while Rita channelled a more sophisticated look in a black feathery mini-dress and silver Chanel clutch bag. The supermodel then left her pal and headed backstage to get ready for the show – one that she would be opening. While getting ready for the catwalk, she couldn't help but gush over Karl Lagerfeld's talents to a backstage journalist.

'I could sit and talk to Karl for hours. He has so many amazing stories and he just knows so much, and he's a real artist. He's so creative in everything he does, like the clothes we are wearing for this one [the Chanel spring/summer 2014 show] especially make you feel like a piece of art.'

There was definitely an element of art to the make-up and wigs used for the models in the show. Cara was among those who wore blunt-cut blonde wigs with heavy fringes, with the make-up a colourful ode to a painter's palette. 'It's so cool being a Chanel girl!' she gushed. 'Paris is the last one [of the fashion week shows] so everyone's very tired, but it's amazing because everyone's keeping each other going, keep smiling, keep happy.'

Cara opened the Chanel show and sauntered down the runway that had the appearance of an art gallery to the sound of Jay-Z's 'Picasso Baby' in the background, wearing a multicoloured one-shouldered dress topped with mid-calf socks and heels. She followed that later with a second turn in an elegant denim tweed skirt suit, oversized pearls – the size of tennis balls – with Miranda Kerr in a similar futuristic black wig hot on her heels. The front row oozed A-listers, with the likes of Kristin Scott Thomas, Katy Perry, Kate Upton, Vanessa Paradis, Anna Wintour, Clémence Poésy, big sister Poppy and wifey Rita Ora all coming to see Lagerfeld's latest collection.

After the show Rita and Katy had a chance to have a congratulatory cuddle with the designer, who cites Cara as his muse du jour. It's perhaps quite fitting that she views him in a similarly affectionate way: 'He's my fashion dad. He's so lovely and he's such an interesting man,' she gushed, before revealing how she'd like to do more mini-films with him. 'When you're doing his films he has the whole idea in his mind. I've done a few Chanel films but I think he should [direct] more. He's got such a talent for that.'

After the Chanel show, Cara was snapped leaving the Grand Palais in the same colourful outfit and wig that she'd just been showcasing – minus the heels, of course – as she headed to her last show of PFW: Valentino. There was time for a quick spot of lunch with Rita and the pair ate at the L'Avenue restaurant before Cara once again headed for the catwalk.

Taking place at the Espace Ephémère at the Jardin des Tuileries in the French capital, Valentino had created a gothic-romantic style for his models. Cara looked very sultry, wearing a full-length lace Tudor gown and gold headband in complete contrast to the colourful futuristic garments of Chanel.

On the front row sat Olivia Palermo and US actor and talk-show presenter Steve Harvey – plus, of course, sister

Poppy, who cheered on her little sister as the show came to a close to signal the end of yet another season of fashion weeks.

Hoards of fans were waiting for her as she left the show and Cara lived up to her wacky reputation by pulling faces and posing for them. What started off as quite a sedate stand-and-pose photo call for the model, who wore a white 'high-brow' beanie hat, white-rimmed sunnies, swallow print sweater and tartan trousers – the same outfit she'd sported when heading to the Chanel show hours earlier – became a little manic when the over-eager fans kept following her as she walked through the gardens. She took it all in her stride as her excited fans jostled to get close to her and shoved endless camera phones in front of her to get a pic with their idol. But it was a little daunting for the supermodel and she clung close to her PA as they made their way back to the waiting car.

Later that evening, to celebrate the end of Paris Fashion Week and a busy day, Cara hit the town with Rita for the 'Mademoiselle C' cocktail party. Both were dressed to impress. Rita took her look from Cara's daywear by wearing a red tartan jacket, white blouse and black peek-a-boo bra, plus a thick sparkling choker and black veil over the top part of her face, while Cara opted for a black-tuxedo jumpsuit and gold choker. Eagle-eyed fashion journalists were quick to spot that it was the same sleek black bodysuit that had been seen on the Saint Laurent catwalk earlier that day, proof again that designers not only wanted Cara to model their clothes on the catwalk but off it as well.

The glamorous cocktail party, which was held at Pavillon Ledoyen, followed the showing of a documentary about former French *Vogue* editor, Carine Roitfeld. It was filled with A-listers wanting to let their hair down in fashionable style before PFW came to a close: Miranda Kerr, Karl Lagerfeld, Kim Kardashian, Katy Perry, Lara Stone, Kate Upton, Anna Dello Russo, Lenny Kravitz, Lily Donaldson and Joan Smalls all attended the premiere and party. As the evening wore on, Cara and Rita made sure they had plenty of fun on the dance floor, and then when they left the venue in the early hours, Cara happily signed autographs for some of her die-hard fans who were waiting to get a glimpse of her.

The red tartan jacket would get another airing from Rita when she left Paris to catch the train home on the Wednesday morning, opting this time to pair it with the tartan trousers that Cara had been seen sporting the day before. Well, if you can't share your wardrobe with your best mate... Only a week later the singer took her Scottish-style garb for one more outing when she wore a red-tartan Moschino trouser suit to the '180 Years of Cool' anniversary party to celebrate 18 years since the Regent Street launch of cosmetics giant Rimmel in 1834.

Cara appeared in American *Vogue* again in October 2013, but it was her appearance on the front cover of Australia's version of the fashion bible that landed her most attention Down Under. 'Cara Delevingne, Crowned Miss Cool', ran the magazine's cover line, alongside a photo of Cara with a crown half-perched on her head. The issue was dedicated to fashion royalty, hence Cara taking centre stage, and in a series of beautiful shots, she posed in a distinctive Elizabethan-style lace dress with a high ruff collar and gold crown. Queen Delevingne indeed!

However, those publications had been shot well in

advance, and while Rita travelled back to Blighty, Cara flew straight from Paris to Rio de Janeiro to take part in an edgy shoot for *Vogue* Brazil. Just 24 hours after the close of Paris Fashion Week, she had an action-packed agenda in Brazil and teased followers about her next modelling assignment with the following tweet: 'Cause I'm leaving on a jet plane, don't know when I'll be back again.'

After a day of rest, she took to the streets of Rio for the shoot, and showcased a very colourful mixture of street-wear, including a number of pieces by designer and good pal Jeremy Scott for Adidas as well as Chanel. Posing in multicoloured Adidas trainers, slogan baseball caps and colourful, loose jackets, the shoot looked as if it had been inspired by Cara's own tomboy-meets-urban-chic wardrobe, which might explain why she was the only model that *Vogue* Brazil wanted for their funky shoot for the next edition.

Though ever the professional when the camera starts snapping, Cara had obviously been walking in too many serious catwalk shows at that time and wanted to have a bit of fun with the locals too, pulling her trademark goofy faces with fans brave enough to make it past the heavy-set security guard that accompanied her. And ever keen to please her loyal army of followers, she happily posed for pictures with some eager young girls who got the chance to cuddle up to Cara after the shoot. There was also a little time for some sightseeing when she took to the streets of the Dona Marta favela in the Brazilian city and snapped away on her mobile phone. But it wasn't long before the transatlantic flight caught up with her and she tweeted a picture from her hotel of a moonlit beach as she struggled to doze off. 'How am I meant to sleep!!! #RIO #Brazil.'

Later she was to appear at the Bo.Bo (Bourgeois Bohême) after party organised by the brand and *Vogue* magazine in her honour. Tweeting: 'Happy to be in Brazil for Bo. Can't wait for my party tonight', she first appeared at the event in a gorgeous silver cami-top and white Capri pants before changing into a hot pink fringed mini-dress for the after party later that night. It was an evening to celebrate the opening of the new BO.BO store as well as Cara being in Brazil and alongside the scrum of photographers and fans waiting to see her was a particularly keen Delevingner wanting to get the model's attention. Armed with a giant poster of her, the young man couldn't believe his luck when Cara stopped to pose with him, taking a picture on his phone while he kissed her on the cheek and then giving him a big hug too. He wasn't the only one to get star treatment from the model either, who took time to sign autographs, pose with fans and have endless pictures taken with those outside the store. Inside the party, Cara proved to be the life and soul of the evening and made sure she strutted herself with the live singers who had been asked to play, as well as spending the majority of her time in the DJ booth.

The following evening there was another glitzy party to attend: the amfAR – a cause dedicated to ending the global AIDS epidemic through innovative research – charity dinner. Held after a screening of *The Battle of amfAR* documentary film, it marked the first time that The Inspiration Gala had been held in Rio. Cara glammed it up again for the event, held at the Hotel Copacabana Palace, and wore an all-in-one black trouser suit with a neckline that plunged to her naval. She teamed it with smoky eye make-up, her hair styled completely to one side and stiletto heels. Turning heads as she made her entrance, she was once again happy to pose with fans as they snapped away. Once inside she spent most of the evening chatting to fellow model Alice Dellal, who was also in black – a short black leather dress. Supermodel Linda Evangelista was also in attendance, as was Hollywood starlet Goldie Hawn, who hosted the charity auction after dinner.

With her time in Brazil limited now that she had completed the *Vogue* shoot in just 48 hours, and had managed to fit in some parties and sightseeing too, there was one more thing Cara was adamant she wanted to do before flying home: satisfy her tattoo craving. So she visited a local tattoo artist to add to her collection.

Daniel Tucci revealed that Cara wanted roman numerals for number 12 just under her armpit, while also having a southern cross behind her ear. He told *Yahoo.com* what inkings he had provided for the model: 'I drew a number 12 in black Roman numerals about five centimetres big on her. She told me that 12 is her lucky number and that's her lucky place, below her breast. The second tattoo is the Southern Cross, a constellation made of five stars, which is one of the symbols of Brazil. It's a cross made with stars around her ear: one star on the top of the ear, one behind, one on the back, one below and one on the tragus, like a circle around the ear.'

But for once Cara didn't take to Instagram to showcase her inkings – and instructed Tucci not to do so either. 'I have a photo of it but she has asked me not to post it on Instagram before she posts it, she wants to make a surprise of it. She loves tattoos and says she isn't going to stop, she wants to be covered,' he explained. 'She's coming back for another one in a couple of days.' In fact, Cara didn't post the pics on Instagram at all, prompting the press to question whether there had been a backlash against them in the fashion industry.

Sarah Doukas had reportedly received complaints that Cara's tattoo addiction was spiralling out of control, especially since they were becoming bigger and more obvious when she took to the catwalk, and because of what she'd revealed to the press in previous interviews – 'I want to be covered in tattoos.'

'Chanel have already expressed alarm at the quick succession of Cara's tattoos and Sarah has told her to call a halt to it. As far as they're aware, she has six but no one is sure how many there really are. And with some of them in very visible positions, Chanel and Burberry have both expressed concern,' reported a Storm Model Agency insider.

It was at another DKNY spring/summer 2014 shoot in the Big Apple that fans first got a glimpse of the XII tattoo when Cara posed in an orange sleeveless dress. Flying to New York to complete her next modelling assignment, her new inkings were on display on the first day on set, as she posed for the brand.

She was later snapped munching down on a bag of chips from McDonald's, having earlier tweeted to fans that she heads to the golden arches as soon as she lands in the States: 'First thing I do when I get to America… get a McDonald's.'

The new DKNY campaign put paid to the rumours that Rita Ora was the sole face of the brand as Cara took to the streets for this latest spring/summer 2014 collection with fellow model Jourdan Dunn and rapper A$AP Rocky. Posing on top of yellow taxis, Cara had her fans cheering when she dressed in an American footballer's shirt and protective helmet and even held the ball in her hands in a fake sporting gesture.

As well as posing for the new collection, Cara decided that she wanted to visit her favourite tattoo artist, Bang Bang, and get another inking – her third in the space of three weeks. Posting a picture of an empty glass of whisky on her Instagram page, she later revealed her new tattoo to followers at 4am after a night's drinking with Bang Bang. It was the word 'silence' written in script across her wrist and she posted it with the comment: 'silence speaks when words can't @bangbangnyc.'

Considering she had only got her first tattoo, the lion on her finger, in May 2013, this was to be her seventh inking in just five months, although Bang Bang, who also posted the picture of Cara's new inking on his Instagram website, revealed that she might have had three more secret ones that she's not yet ready to share.

'My girl @caradelevingne newest addition… Met her 6 months ago, now she has 10 tattoos! #hooked'.

But it wasn't just tattoos that were coming thick and fast: film opportunities were also coming Cara's way after she signed with the Los Angeles-based acting agency William Morris in September 2013. On 11 October it was announced that she had been offered a role in the film *The Face of an Angel*, initially reported to be a biopic based on the 2009 murder trail of Amanda Knox and her boyfriend Raffaele Sollecito, who were found guilty of killing British student Meredith Kercher. But the director, Michael Winterbottom, was keen to deny reports that the movie is about the murder of Meredith and that Cara would be taking on the role of Amanda: '[Cara] is not playing Amanda Knox. There is no Amanda Knox in this film,' he told the *Daily Mail*.

'Getting Cara is a real coup for the film but is also brilliant for her career. It proves she is an in-demand actress and will help boost her career in the US. With the big film offers coming in, it's looking likely movies will soon be Cara's main focus,' a film industry insider told the *Mail Online*.

Filming of the project, which also stars Brit actress Kate Beckinsale and German actor Daniel Brühl, began in Italy in early November 2013. Cara was interviewed for *iD* magazine and spoke about what life was like for her on set in Siena and Rome and still being a relative novice in the film industry.

'Michael is an incredible director and I'm working with an incredible cast. I do get anxious but with acting I can use that anxiousness. Michael told me that you can't teach natural talent and natural ability. He's never seen a bad actor go to lessons and become good, only a good actor become an even better one.'

Winterbottom was equally generous in his praise and revealed to the *Evening Standard* that the youngster's role would be that of the character of Melanie.

'She's playing a young British student. The character is someone who has their whole life ahead of them; young, enthusiastic, relaxed, with a real sense of energy and fun – and that's Cara.' He also heaped praise on his latest signing and described her as a 'screen natural'.

Meanwhile Cara told the *Daily Mail* in November how

she had tried to use her own experience to find inspiration for the role: 'The idea that I had of her [Melanie] is that she's like me and a lot of my friends who are 21 and travelling around Europe. I'd love to learn Italian and this part is a perfect excuse to learn it. I've picked up very little but I'd like to learn more. It's an opportunity to learn, I wouldn't turn anything down. It's all good experience.'

In fact the model was so keen to show her enthusiasm for acting that she revealed to *iD* magazine that she'd do pretty much anything to land a part: 'I would do anything for the right role. I'd shave all my hair off and my eyebrows, I'd gain weight, skydive, jump off buildings, do my own stunts... I want to learn all there is to learn.'

She also revealed for the first time her insecurities about her body shape, admitting she would like to be 'curvier'. For a world-class supermodel constantly in demand this surprised many of her Delevingners and, of course, her family, not least of all her godmother, who doesn't think she needs to change a thing.

'She's the most natural and down-to-earth girl you could ever meet,' Joan Collins told the *Daily Express*. 'You would never believe she is a top model. She doesn't need any advice. I am very proud and I think it is wonderful what she has done.'

With the wheels in motion for Cara's next movie role, there was still time in her schedule for her second Victoria Secret's Fashion Show. In 2012 she took part in her first runway for the US lingerie brand and spoke of the accolade of hitting the catwalk. A year later her enthusiasm hadn't waned. She Instagramed photos of herself, Karlie Kloss and Jourdan Dunn larking about on the glitter-strewn catwalk before the show, giggling as they lay sprawled across the sparkly runway. It had been reported that Cara was too busy to appear in the show and she admitted to *Grazia* magazine backstage that her hectic schedule did mean she didn't have the chance to fully prepare for walking down the catwalk in a skimpy lingerie outfit.

'I actually found out quite late that I was doing the show because of my filming schedule. I haven't done much to prepare,' she told the press.

And when asked what sort of diet or beauty regime she undertook to prep for the event, in true Cara style she admitted it wasn't typical model behaviour – video games and pizza: 'The new *Call of Duty* came out so I've been playing that like crazy and eating Dominos pizza. And Dominos chicken strippers, all 21 of them.'

The 18th annual show, which was held at Lexington Avenue Armory, was split into six themed sections: British Invasion, Birds of Paradise, PINK Network, Parisian Nights, Shipwrecked and Snow Angels, and 26 models took to the stage in costume. Cara, Jourdan and Lily Donaldson took part in the British Invasion section and headlining the show was American singer-songwriter Taylor Swift, dressed in a Union Jack mini-dress, Union Jack hat and shoes with a flowing Union Jack cape. Cara wore a football-inspired silk playsuit, which was split down the front to reveal a bright blue sparkly bra underneath. Strutting down in red heels and slouched footie socks, she posed with a football emblazoned with the VS logo. And Swift couldn't resist a cheeky tap of Cara's backside as she performed during the British Invasion section, while Cara waved to the singer as she walked off stage. And like the previous year when Cara and headliner

Rihanna first became friends, Taylor Swift and Cara's friendship blossomed with the singer posting a picture of herself, Cara, Erin Heatherton and Lily Aldridge on her Twitter page with the caption: 'Best friends forever VS2013.'

And talking of Rihanna, there was time in Cara's modelling and filming schedules to show support to her BFF as the Diamonds World Tour came to an end. The singer, who had been on the tour since March, celebrated with her pal in style after her New Orleans show, partying until 6am according to the *Mail Online*. Rihanna and Cara flew back to New York and tried to disguise their heavy night's drinking with dark sunglasses as they made their way to their hotel rooms in the Big Apple only a few hours after they had finished partying. Rumours had circulated the previous month that the pals were reportedly looking into sharing an apartment in New York as a base convenient for both their careers. A source told *Now* magazine that Cara and RiRi had decided that being roomies would be fun – and practical, too.

'Rihanna's promised Cara she'll introduce her to all her friends and take her to her fave bars and restaurants. The two have decided that since they have such similar lifestyles – up all night raving at nightclubs – they'd make perfect roommates.'

New York seemed to be Cara's favourite haunt towards the end of 2013. She decided to stay in town after her VS show and made some more musical connections by heading to Kanye West's gig the following week. Posing backstage with the rapper and his fiancée Kim Kardashian, Cara tweeted her excitement at being at the show, part of Kanye's Yeezue tour. Dressed down in baggy sweat-pants, a green beanie and white sweatshirt, the model boasted to her Twitter followers about her 'awesome' night.

At the end of November, Cara announced on Twitter that her big sister Chloe was expecting a baby with her partner Eddie Grant and so she and Poppy would be aunties in 2014. Chloe's marriage to Louis Buckworth ended in divorce in 2010 and she began seeing Eddie, who was best man at their wedding, later that year. With Chloe and Eddie acting as chaperones to Cara while in New York – Eddie tweeted throughout the Victoria's Secret show how proud he was of Cara 'rocking the catwalk' – Cara had grown increasingly close to Chloe and relished the opportunity to become an auntie.

'She's so excited about it,' confirmed a friend. 'She's planning on being the coolest auntie on the planet!'

With 2013 a whirlwind of modelling contracts, music potential, tattoos and the shooting of her debut film – with her second movie following not far behind – 2014 is set to hold even more opportunities for the 21-year-old. Cara's enthusiasm for acting and the premiere of *Kids in Love*, not to mention the publicity surrounding *Face of an Angel* suggest that she could be Hollywood's next starlet before the year is out. Or with her connections in the music industry and best pals Rihanna and Rita by her side, it could be the music industry that she sets alight – going from supermodel to superstar singer – 'C-Diddy' – in just a few years. And with her newest role set to challenge her too, that of being a cool auntie, 2014 is set to catapult Cara Delevingne from catwalk model to global superstar, showcasing her talents in all fields of entertainment. And if there is one person who can meet an increasing level of stardom and fame with her high-top trainers planted firmly on the ground, it's Miss D.

BIBLIOGRAPHY

WEBSITES

www.buzzfeed.com
www.contactmusic.com
www.dailymail.co.uk
www.graziadaily.co.uk
www.harpersbazaar.co.uk
www.heatworld.com
www.herworldplus.com
www.independent.ie
www.metro.co.uk
www.mirror.co.uk
www.models.com
www.neverunderdressed.com
www.nowmagazine.co.uk
www.russhmagazine.com
www.society.com
www.standard.co.uk

www.stormmodels.com
www.telegraph.co.uk
www.vogue.co.uk
www.wmagazine.com
www.yahoo.com

PUBLICATIONS
Daily Mail
Daily Telegraph
Evening Standard
Event magazine
Grazia magazine
Hello! magazine
Independent
Look magazine
Mail on Sunday
Observer
Reveal magazine
The Sun
The Times
You magazine